Re-Emergence

Re-Emergence

Locating Conscious Properties in a Material World

Gerald Vision

The MIT Press
Cambridge, Massachusetts
London, England

For information about quantity discounts, email special_sales@mitpress.mit.edu.

Set in Stone Sans and Stone Serif by the MIT Press. Printed and bound in the United States of America.

Library of Congress Cataloging-in-Publication Data

Vision, Gerald.
Re-emergence : locating concious properties in a material world / Gerald Vision.
    p.   cm.
Includes bibliographical references (p.) and index.
ISBN 978-0-262-01584-4 (hardcover : alk. paper)
1. Consciousness. 2. Emergence (Philosophy) I. Title.
B808.9.V57 2011
126—dc22
                                                              2010045906

10 9 8 7 6 5 4 3 2 1

in memory of Sayra Vision

Contents

Preface

The presence of sentience in a basically material reality is among the primary mysteries of existence. How does it fit? How could it have come about? What could be the point of it? Working cognitive scientists, psychologists, biologists, and neural researchers in general tend to ponder such questions only in their off hours. To carry on, they need only acknowledge that material states, typically brain states, *subserve* conscious ones. Further detail about the character of this loosely specified relation will neither accelerate nor impede their inquiries, nor will it require any reformulation of carefully studied conclusions. This is not to say that their work has never been integrated with such inquiries, but that is not because it is unfinished without it, but because they have caught the philosophy bug. Empirical studies require no more to proceed than something suspended tentatively between causal dependence and identity.

Philosophers, on the other hand, are passionate about these differences. They cannot leave the issue in a suspended state. In the present philosophical climate many have been hard at work to show that conscious states and properties really are, at bottom, nothing over and above the matter that brings them about. For some time those well-motivated efforts have struck me as less than satisfactory, and thus I have undertaken to try to find the source of my discomfort and to see whether it withstands careful scrutiny. I have come to no more helpful a conclusion than that there is little more to be said than that material configurations can give rise to uncharted consequences. The result I arrive at is that conscious properties and states are *emergents*, and that, although they depend for their existence on their material bases (a dependence summed up by supervenience or realization relations to the material), there are no further details to explain that dependence. The more general message is that there need be nothing straightforwardly expectable about the gizmos that may result if one builds with enough materials in enough different configurations.

Not every serious philosopher shares the view that this is the best way to go about studying the nature of mental life. For example, even among those who agree that our mental life depends empirically on the physical, some affirm that once the mental takes off into complex emotions, moods, attitudes, humors, aspirations, or even grand ideas, it should be studied not by mucking about in our gray matter, but through the interrelations among such states or between them and our behavioral life. "It is simply wrongheaded to continue treating the mental as simply an exudation of matter!" There is no need to deny that there is something to this reaction. Given the less than stunning past performance of radical reductionisms, it is perfectly reasonable to map our mental lives in terms of relations such as those between longing and effort, inspiration and creation, frustration and desperation, hardship and motivation, and passionate affection and choices. Neural support may have only a minor part in such inquiries. However, that we have any conscious life at all calls for spade work that can't be carried out by starting from complexities within mental lives. Even if the critics to whom I have alluded think this general approach to mentality misguided, there are lessons to be learned from that enterprise.

Whether or not my assumption about the right starting point for this sort of inquiry is as plausible as I believe, I set out to show that conscious properties cannot be reduced to the physical reality on which they depend, identified with that reality, or given the right kind of materialist explanation in terms of that reality on which they nonetheless depend. In that sense, conscious properties have identities in tension with unconditional physicalisms. It is worthwhile to demonstrate that a measure of their autonomy survives even under those conditions. Any less of a defense of emergentism would be vulnerable to the charge that it is victorious only over a straw opponent. Thus, for argument's sake it may be conceded that conscious properties and states are realized by or strongly supervene on the physical. Indeed, I do not even rely on zombie or inverted-spectrum cases, in which conscious properties depend on the physical with only nomological necessity. Opposition to physicalism based on those cases has contrasted nomological with a more exacting metaphysical necessity. I raise no objection to the view that the sort of reliance the mind has on its physical base is only nomological. If that is the case, the dispute may continue on those grounds. However, there has been heated controversy over the intelligibility of thought experiments involving zombies and inverted spectra, which my approach is able to avoid. I am wagering that emergentism can be shown to be defensible under yet more stringent debating conditions. Should conscious properties metaphysically depend on their material bases, my claim is that the grounds for distinguishing the conscious from its base do not disappear.

The state of the current literature has made it convenient to state the emergentist's claims negatively, as a way to assail orthodox physicalism. That is but a partial picture. I hope emergentism is also viewed as a contribution to our understanding of conscious aspects. It strikes me that emergentism does a better job of coming to grips with conscious phenomena than the competing doctrines reviewed in part II. Of course, many will be unsettled by the fact that this leaves us with a primitive, brute relation between the conscious and the physical. Claims of simple, brute, or primitive relationships between entities have not fared well historically. But then neither have the classical alternatives: infinite regresses or vicious circularity. On the other hand, as I sketchily explore in the epilogue, the generic dismissal of brute relations may itself be no more than a bit of trade lore that has been carelessly taken on board. Moreover, the ensuing account is not intended as an analysis. Rather, it should be understood as a mapping of logical geography between the conscious and the mental. No effort has been made to lay out that relation in a sanitized vocabulary, or to avoid circularities. Indeed, I believe that, if conceptual circularities are broad enough and incorporate sufficiently diverse nodes, instead of being marks against an account they may be symptoms that we have reached rock bottom.

No one seems to me to have done more to advance our understanding of these issues over the past forty years than Jaegwon Kim. Nevertheless, his views bear much of the burden of the criticism I level against physicalism. However, I can do no better than to repeat a remark I recall reading somewhere. Although I disagree sharply with some of his views, if it weren't for Kim I would have no views at all on the subject.

Many people have offered me helpful advice on one or another part of this project. Those I can remember offhand include Steven Davis, Steven Hales, Eleanor Knox, Brian McLaughlin, Susan Schneider, Barry C. Smith, Michael Thau, Michael Tye, Todd Vision, Michael Weisberg, and Hong Yu Wong. I thank Temple University for a study leave to work on this material free from usual duties, and I am especially grateful to the University of London's Institute of Philosophy for providing an ideal setting under which this project was completed.

I Emergentism of the Mental Described and Defended

1   History and Background

1.1   Surveying the Landscape

Certain things commence in the most unexpected ways. According to Hippolytus, a Roman writer of the third century CE, Anaximander (fl. 571 BCE) held that living creatures arose from moisture evaporated by the sun. Given the crude state of science at the time, and that the leading alternative seems to have been that Prometheus and Epimethius created life on Zeus' command, this venturesome hypothesis warranted further consideration. Less worthy of consideration was a rumor, circulating in the seventeenth century, that if one put sweaty undergarments and husks of wheat together in an open-mouthed jar and waited 21 days, the action of the sweat on the husks would generate mice. Like the belief circulating among sailors that maggots were propagated by rotting meat, such speculations were not put to rest until Louis Pasteur's 1859 experiments undercut any basis for belief in spontaneous generation.

Those exploded claims were emergentist theses. Their common basis was that radically different sorts of things "emerged" from an ontologically simpler foundation in ways defying rational expectation. If that was emergentism's finest fruit, the view would be no more than a quaint historical relic. And, as we shall see below, more recently even sober emergentist claims have been derailed by scientific advances. But there remain open questions which seem to show that emergentist options still have a pulse in some quarters. The one I want to explore in this work is the question of conscious properties arising from brute, unthinking matter. Not only do I estimate that this is still an open question; I shall argue that there is no equally plausible non-emergentist alternative. Consciousness isn't the only live emergentist possibility. Normativity and color are two prominent instances of as-yet-unresolved and potentially unresolvable puzzles. Although each comes up later as a side issue (color in section 1.7, semantic norms in section 7.4), I will say nothing further about those prospects in this work. Rather, I will concentrate exclusively on the topic of conscious properties (more generally, conscious tokenings).

How to fit consciousness into a largely material world is—like "Why is there something rather than nothing?"—a perennial question that is hard to dismiss. Questions of this kind tempt some into supernatural resolutions. But, aside from the fact that a supernatural solution assumes the prior existence of what should be part of the question, they are too facile for thoughtful inquiries. There seems to be no alternative to carefully probing the natural world for an answer.

As a continuous school, emergentism entered Anglophone philosophy in 1843 with the publication of John Stuart Mill's *System of Logic*.[1] (The term 'emergentism' came later.) Its earlier advocates regarded themselves as staunch defenders of naturalism, although nowadays that may seem paradoxical. (On this change in fashion, see footnote 6.) Philosophical emergentists have always been in the minority, and had almost completely disappeared by the 1960s. But there has been a mini-resurgence of the view in some areas, especially those concerning a subclass of natural laws. However, the view I shall be recommending for reconsideration doesn't quite fit the mold of either the earlier or more recent versions. As I have noted, I am confining attention to emergentism in the philosophy of mind, and in particular to aspects of consciousness. Upon becoming aware of unwarranted assumptions that have made emergentism seem mysterious, I hope that it will be clear why this should not be unseemly even to the tough-minded.

I sidestep some basic questions about the phenomenology of consciousness or how we come to be apprised of it. I will rely on its self-evident character, without trying to decide whether awareness of consciousness is attained by introspection, knowledge without observation, natively, by intuition, or by some other method. Indeed, I can provide doubters no firmer demonstration of its reality than to suggest that they pinch themselves.

Salient recent accounts of conscious life that conflict with emergentism are considered in part II, where I discuss reasons for rejecting what I take to be their best versions. Here (and perhaps generally in philosophy), *a priori*

---

1. My quotations are from the third edition (1851).

demonstrations seem out of reach, but I believe we can achieve what Mill elsewhere (*Utilitarianism*, chapter I) called "considerations . . . capable of determining the intellect."

Before turning to concerns rooted in the philosophy of mind, a few remarks about the general character of emergentism are in order. This will be followed by a brief historical summary of what I am calling *classical emergentism*. The summary does scant justice to emergentism's contributions to metaphysics,[2] but I hope it will acquaint readers with both the similarities and the differences between that tradition and the view elaborated here. To orient the reader, I also describe some of the reasons the movement has fallen into disfavor.

1.2 Emergentism Depicted

Originally emergentism covered a broad array of topics, from chemical compounds to sensible qualities. Although it was never philosophically ascendant, for much of the first half of the twentieth century it was taken seriously even by those who opposed it.

Emergentists and their opponents generally shared a hierarchical picture of explanation, dependence, and the sciences—known also as a *layered conception of reality*. Suppose we proceed from relatively simple constituents and their interactions to their complex constructions. It is customary to think of the more complex as occurring at a higher level than the less complex, the lower infusing the higher with its features. Unfortunately, there may be no way of achieving a coherent unified portrayal of levels for every purpose to which this image has been put. Still, the picture has an intuitive pull, and for our purposes we needn't fuss over details. A generic hierarchy will simplify the exposition without placing any of the positions at a disadvantage. We might start with atoms as basic constituents—"swarms of atoms" for C. Lloyd Morgan (1923, p. 35)—and might then proceed to molecules, thence to chemical compounds, and eventually to macroscopic physical objects. Or we might go from individual molecules, to genes, organelles, cells, tissues, organs, and finally to organisms. Or perhaps, emphasizing a hierarchy of sciences, we might start from particle physics, then, omitting a number

2. For more thorough treatments, see McLaughlin 1992, McLaughlin 1997, and Kim 1992. For Mill's contribution, see also E. Nagel 1961.

of intermediate steps, proceed to chemistry, geology, biology, economics, psychology, and sociology.

From those bare materials, let's devise this rough sketch of emergentism: On some occasions, a novel outcome results from increased complexity in that outcome's base. To explicate the novelty in question, we might say that the lower levels on which emergent phenomena rest contain nothing that could enable one to anticipate the former's initial occurrence in terms of the lower level's types of intrinsic features, its structure, or a comprehensive examination of both.

Despite the fact that the view has been described in terms of what one can anticipate, the emergentism that will occupy us is intended as an *ontological* thesis. As the point is sometimes put, it is "over and above" its base. Various writers, among them Chalmers (2006) and Crane (2001), have distinguished an ontological variety of emergentism from an epistemological variety, regarding the latter as a worthwhile variation. However, a popular objection to classical emergentism has been that its ontological claims are transformed into an epistemic thesis about what one can expect. From that angle, the view is then readily dismissed as a form of temporary scientific ignorance. Whatever the value of an epistemic variety, the interest here is in ontology. The term 'emergentism' is nowadays tossed about regularly in scientific and philosophy-of-science circles. Those uses may bear to some extent on the brands of current interest, but in ways not easily summarized. Some of them, though not all, are epistemic. Moreover, classical emergentists have written in ways suggesting both kinds of view. However, the emergentism targeted here is an ontological thesis, and it is part of my task to distinguish that view from its epistemic kin.

Ordinarily what is taken to emerge is a *property* (or a feature, or a characteristic, or a quality). My treatment is focused largely on *instantiated* properties. Other versions might emphasize events (including static events or states), relational properties, processes, facts, or even individuals. However, most of the subsequent inquiry should be applicable, *mutatis mutandis*, to all, or many, of those aspirants; when the choice between them is not relevant, I often use neutral terms such as 'token' and 'aspect'.

Chemical compounds were once emergentists' favorite illustration. Various other things the view embraced at one time or another include life, organic functioning, lawlike generalizations (including stochastic laws), consciousness, (intentional) mental states, secondary qualities, norms, purposes, organized collectives such as nations, and other social or conventionally enabled phenomena. Items on this list do not share a common base from which each is supposed to emerge, although given the transitivity of supervenience some may claim that each is ultimately resolved into interactions among fundamental particles. Confining ourselves to immediate explanations, for some theorists life arises from structural properties of proteins, perceptual awareness from 40-hertz semi-oscillatory firings of neurons, colors from light and reflectance potential, norms perhaps from conventions, which themselves arise from tacit agreements (or acquiescences), and nations from the cooperative interactions of inhabitants. Certain emergentists have claimed that at least some of these phenomena are novel structures arising from material that lacked structures prefiguring their appearance.

Of course, not every first appearance of a complex aspect counts as emergent. Details matter. For example, if simple mereological composition will suffice to explain a complex constructed from its parts, the whole is not emergent. As C. D. Broad notes (1925, p. 62), if we have two forces acting on a particle at an angle to each other, we "find by experiment that the actual motion of the body is the vector-sum of the motions it would have had if each had been acting separately." Or, if two chunks of matter could be combined into a single aggregate, their combined rest mass would be the sum of the rest masses of the original chunks. A label that seems to have caught on among classical emergentists for describing the non-emergent is 'resultant'. Soon we will need a more rigorous statement of those differences, but this should be enough background to enable us to follow the movement's early development.

1.3 Classical Emergentism

Emergentism flourished from roughly the middle of the nineteenth century to the middle of the twentieth. Mill broached the topic by introducing a distinction between two modes of causal interaction: the mechanical and the chemical. He gives "the name Composition of Causes to the principle exemplified in all cases in which the joint effect of several causes is identical with the sum of their separate effects" (1851, book III, chapter VI, p. 374). This is intended to cover all mechanical causation, not only when causes augment one another, but also when one cause is partially thwarted by a second, thereby altering without obliterating the first's impact. Whereas the Composition of Causes is the general rule, there are exceptions; they issue in the products that later came to be known as emergent. According to Mill, "the chemical combination of two substances produces, as is well known, a third substance, with properties different from those of either of the two substances separately or of both of them taken together" (ibid., p. 374). Mill (ibid., pp. 377–380) mentions "heteropathic laws" as covering cases "in which the augmentation of the cause alters the kind of effect." Shortly after Mill, the contrastive term 'homopathic' was coined for mechanical causal laws. We can easily extend the heteropathic/homopathic distinction beyond laws to particular causes. In fact, without further explanation Mill uses the terms 'heteropathic causes' (p. 380) and 'heteropathic effects' (pp. 377, 381).[3] George Lewes later coined the title 'emergent', which eventually replaced Mill's 'heteropathic' as the consensus designation.

Mill's late contemporary, Alexander Bain gestures toward the same phenomenon when he distinguishes force, which is always mechanical, from collocation. He writes that "the mixing of materials, and its union of force, are not the same fact" because "we cannot fully predict the characters of the compound form [its] elements" (1887, p. 270). They "yield a new product, where the combining elements are not recognizable." Bain also acknowledges its broader range: "The analogy of Chemical Combination has been applied to mental and social combinations."

Emergentism was taken up as a more-or-less self-conscious cause early in the twentieth century. Its hallmark thesis was that emergent phenomena resist an expected mechanical explanation in their bases. Samuel Alexander, a leading figure in the movement, declared that such phenomena should be taken with "natural piety," which then became a watchword among those writing on the subject.[4] As Broad remarked with characteristic mordant wit, these results "must simply be swallowed whole with that philosophic jam which Professor Alexander calls 'natural piety'" (1925, p. 55). On the other hand, Charles Lloyd Morgan preferred a similarly reverent exhortation: when encountering emergence, "consider and bow the head" (1923, p. 4).

3. When first treating effects rather than just laws as heteropathic, Mill attaches a footnote reading "Anet ch. vii, §1." But I find no mention of heteropathic *effects* there or any earlier in Mill's *System of Logic*.

4. The phrase seems to have originated in the epigraph to Wordsworth's "Intimations of Immortality": The child is father of the man; / And I could wish my days to be / Bound each to each by natural piety.

Aside from Morgan, we may count Arthur Lovejoy among influential early-twentieth-century emergentists, and several notable authors joined him. Also, a group of present-day chemists, biologists, and philosophers of science declare themselves for emergentism. In some instances, their forms of emergentism are different, both in content and in ontological implications, from the present concern with conscious properties; in yet others, there is overlap. It would be unproductive here to try to cover the many varieties going under the title 'emergentism'. In what follows, I shall pick my way cautiously through that material for points and theses that intersect with our narrower concern, but shall focus only on several closely related views.

1.4 Problems and Refinements

It did not take long for emergentism's critics to find weaknesses. Indeed, some were spotted by its followers.

First, scientific progress has placed some of emergentism's former claims *in extremis*,[5] and typically they occurred in cases taken as emblematic of the movement. Chemical combination and organic life may be the first subjects that occur to most when thinking about classical emergentism, and for good reason. Although there were also emergentist treatments of the mental—and in spite of the title of Broad's celebrated opus *The Mind and Its Place in Nature*—in the view's heyday the examples of chemical compounds and living things (including evolutionary novelties) were its most prominent themes. But discoveries in quantum mechanics introduced explanations of chemical bonding via electromagnetism, and the disclosure of the DNA composition of genes has opened the way to explanations of crucial features of life such as self-replication, both of which emergentists had declared resistant to physicalist treatment.[6]

Next, objections have been raised to ways of defining the position. Of course, any attempt at a philosophical definition or analysis may be plagued by allowing in too few of the intended cases or too many of the unintended ones. Efforts to fill these gaps regularly end up in trivialization

5. McLaughlin 1992, p. 54 ff.

6. Taking life to be emergent was originally a *materialist* response to the doctrine of vitalism, which had explained life via immaterial factors such as *élans vital* or ectoplasms.

or vicious circularity, not to mention baroque qualifying clauses that can drain a view of its initial attraction. Emergentism is no less prey to those dangers than are the general run of attempts, with rare exceptions, to provide a challenged concept's illuminating necessary and sufficient conditions. But, beyond that, there have been complaints directed at distinctive aspects of emergentism. Here are two notorious examples.

A popular specification of emergentism latches on to underlining unpredictability upon first appearance. As was noted earlier, some have charged that this turns what was advertised as an ontological discovery into a claim about our current understanding. Our inability to predict an outcome upon first occurrence would be a fragile basis for the thesis, one that scientific progress has regularly overturned. This alone makes it unwise to transform emergentism into an epistemic thesis. However, leading emergentists didn't mean anything that chancy by 'unpredictability'. Predictability for them wasn't clearly distinguished from their notion of deducibility. The latter also bore an interpretation that by current standards is outdated: it included derivations requiring generous substitutions of terms. But it was not broad enough to collapse into an epistemic notion. For example, notice in the earlier quote from Bain, he writes that "we cannot *fully* predict the character of the compound" (emphasis added). Such qualifications were almost always at hand. This is not to deny that our current epistemic position, when carefully reflected upon, can be a useful clue to explanations not being in the offing. But the claim of current interest, and no doubt the one at which classical emergentists were aiming, is ultimately about the nature of external reality, not about current knowledge. Classical emergentists generally have been more guarded in their official pronouncements.

A tempered account of the intended doctrine seems to embody two requirements: (a) a complete, or ideal, characterization of the base from which the aspect emerges, and (b) an inability to deduce (or infer, or predict) an emergent aspect from that ideal base. This version of emergentism has valid historical credentials. The idealized explanations in (a) would disclose, in Broad's terms, what "can be deduced from the most complete knowledge of [the constituent properties] in isolation or in other wholes which are not of [their form]" (1925, p. 61).[7] But this invites the question "What belongs in a total explanation of the base?" Available answers

7. Also see Alexander 1920, volume I, pp. 46–47.

discover new complications. One method might be to build enough into requirement (a) so that its consequences would always be deducible. For example, suppose that a *complete* explanation of hydrogen includes "forming, if suitably combined with oxygen, a compound which is liquid, transparent, etc. Hence, the liquidity, transparence, etc. of water *can* be inferred from certain properties of chemical constituents." (Hempel and Oppenheim 1948, in Hempel 1965, p. 260) (Also see Beckermann 1992.) Similar dispositions or tendencies may be devised for inclusion in any base properties. With regard to pain, suppose its base includes the firing of C-fibers, activity in the somatosensory and prefrontal areas of the brain, etc. of a more complete organism. We might then ascribe to a complete or idealized knowledge of, say, C-fibers the conditional power to produce pain in its subjects when firing in the relevant conditions and background. That would enable us to infer pain from its dependence on nothing more than a combination of its base properties.

Emergentists were not unaware of this objection. Broad explains what he calls a "trans-ordinal law" as follows:

A and B would be adjacent, and in ascending order if every aggregate of order B is composed of aggregates of order A, and if it has certain properties which no aggregate of order A possesses and which cannot be deduced from the A-properties and the structure of the B-complex *by any law of composition which has manifested itself at lower levels.* (p. 78, emphasis added)

From there it is possible to claim that the exceptions, the emergent aggregates, all use laws which are unmanifested at a lower level. But it is ordinarily much easier to rule out certain clear violators than it is to devise a formula covering all and only acceptable aggregates. Or, given that the Hempel-Oppenheim objection relies on mentioning relational properties, another suggestion might be that at each level an aggregate include only intrinsic properties. But, alas, that move is doomed. It is difficult to take *structure* into account without relational properties, and we do need structure (that is, form) in our base: X inside Y is different from Y inside X. A further suggestion might be to allow certain relational properties as long as they don't relate aggregates at different levels. Aside from the difficulty of delineating a principled distinction between levels, this will prevent us from including any potential for combinations of items. One might settle for ruling out certain cases without requiring a general description of admissible versus inadmissible laws. It is a challenge to show that those exclusions are not *ad hoc*; another is to show why this is satisfactory in the absence of any principle.

Yet it could be the particular approach rather than emergentism itself that is problematic here. To get a better grasp of the state of the dispute, consider two ways, following Broad (pp. 24–25), of regarding the physical base properties.[8]

As the emergentist will insist, the physical base properties in certain combinations have the potential to issue in its emergent properties. Broad calls such properties when they are unrealized "latent." (This doesn't imply that *all* latent properties would, when realized, issue in emergent ones.) Taking our cue from that, we may regard a description of the (physical) base including both its manifest *and* latent properties as *the latent base*, or, if you prefer, *the latent description of the base*. An inability to show how to avoid taking the latent base for the base *period* fuels the Hempel-Oppenheim objection. However, a feature of this base as described is that no one is in a position to include its various latent properties until they have been combined in what Sydney Shoemaker (2002, p. 54; 2007, p. 76) has called "emergent-engendering ways."

The other way of regarding the base is to include only those properties that are manifest. In addition to its shape, color, size, weight, texture, and odor, this will include many if not all of the base's conditional powers[9]— what it can cause, again perhaps in combination with other properties, and what can cause it. For example, an object's having a certain bulk indicates that it can crush a fly, even if nothing with those manifest properties ever crushed a fly. Call this *the manifest base*, or *the manifest description of the base*. However, distinguishing a manifest base from a latent base in a principled way is fraught with difficulties.

The problems reviewed thus far have to do with achieving a respectable statement of the position. More particularly, they result from understanding what it is to be deducible from a physical base or from the requirement that we divide the physical base into two sorts and then rely on using only one of them (the manifest base) to bring out emergence's defining features. I introduce an alternative characterization in section 1.6, and elaborate it in chapter 2. Although it demands no such division of descriptions, it does

---

8. I am generalizing, as Broad intended, from his illustration of silver chloride and its components, Ag + Cl.

9. See Shoemaker 2003.

not escape other criticisms that have been leveled against emergentism. A final set of problems awaits all forms.

A leading problem has been how to find a causal role for *any* indepen-dent mental tokens. It is generally agreed that in order to have any effect, including a mental one, a mental property must have an effect in the physi-cal world. (For dissenting views, see Gibbons 2006; Stephan 2002; Craver and Bechtel 2007.) That involves the notorious problem of *downward causa-tion*, the causation of something at the physical level on which the mental depends. Moreover, every physical effect presumably has a physical cause, and it has been argued that the physical cause trumps the supposed mental one. Don't a mental property's causal powers reduce to those of the ulti-mate bases on which it rests? And if emergent properties have no causal role, what reason have we to believe there are such things? These questions are discussed in section 3.7 and probed further in chapter 4. One might also ask what it means for something constituted by its supervenience (or realization) base not to be identical with it. That question is also addressed in chapter 3. Powerful intuitions driving physicalism expose another chal-lenge to emergentism. Whereas some classical and recent emergentists have declared that their views are consistent with physicalism, forms of present concern sharply distinguish them. Physicalists of this stripe may claim that emergentism makes a mystery of its relation to physical reality. In part II I examine those and other leading naturalist views to see if they contain per-suasive grounds for rejecting emergentism. Here I simply note the battery of challenges that my highlighted position faces. Their cumulative effect may help explain why it is so difficult for current versions of emergentism to get admitted to the ranks of serious options.

1.5   Emergence and the Mental

Under *conscious* properties and/or states I include not only phenomenal consciousness, but also what Ned Block (1995, 1996) has termed "access consciousness." Phenomenal consciousness is the undergoing of a con-scious state.[10] Leading examples are sensations such as a headache, a tingle in one's leg, an itch, drowsiness, orgasm, an after-image, and perceptual

10. Although I take this to be nothing beyond undergoing a first-order state (e.g., Block 1995; Dretske 1993), these points are not in conflict with the view that con-sciousness is a second-order monitoring of its first-order episode.

experiences such as of a blue patch or the taste of cinnamon. Some of these states are representational, but, it is contended, there is a "what it is like" (Nagel 1974) that resists consignment to their representational contents. Access-conscious properties are those that one has directly available for use in reasoning and in other (verbal and non-verbal) behavior. Block calls them "inferentially promiscuous." They contrast with phenomena, such as blindsight or a Freudian unconscious, in which a subject's behavior might be directed by intentions and motives to which she has no unmediated access. Although for the bulk of this essay my choice of examples will concentrate on phenomenal properties (and then mostly on pain, because it has been focal in these discussions), the points raised are intended to apply to both forms of consciousness. Access consciousness isn't seriously contemplated until chapter 5.

No special note needs to be taken of the occasional claim that access consciousness already involves phenomenality. The point to be emphasized is that the mental phenomena that concern us cover this spread of cases, its extension. In fact, if access consciousness is just a species of phenomenal consciousness, that should make it easier to draw lessons for the former from the conclusions reached about the latter. Indeed, it may even extend those conclusions to the bulk of mental properties.

1.6 Relevant Emergentist Theses

Finally, here is the version of emergentism that constitutes our central topic. It can be summed up in three theses, to be elaborated as the discussion proceeds.

Imagine that E is a representative sample of the properties of concern. To be emergent, E must meet the following set of conditions:

(1) E is *dependent* on different sorts of a non-emergent base in a way made manifest by E's *supervenience* (or *realization*) on those same properties.

(2) There is *no* further (minimal) *explanation* of why E is supervenient on (or dependent on, or realized by) that non-emergent base, viz., the relationship is brute.

(3) E is a cause (of both mental and physical aspects) in ways in which there is no sufficient cause in context at the levels of E's non-emergent base(s).

I leave open whether the supervenient or realization base is itself a property, a collection of properties, or something else. Our dealings are predominantly with properties, but we need make no commitment on the general issue.

Each of the three conditions cries out for further clarification and defense. Beginning with (1), there are a number of distinguishable forms of supervenience. To what extent does (1) depend on which of them is chosen? Why suppose that any of the forms establishes the dependence of the supervening property? In fact, as we shall see in chapter 3, realization turns out to be more central to emergentism than supervenience.[11] (The realization relation of concern is that in which something is realized *in* something else, as a statue being realized in marble, not that in which something is realized *by* something else, as Smith's profit being realized by last year's investment.) Regarding (2), the claim is that *no* further minimal explanation exists. This is required to distinguish the present view from the epistemological interpretation stating that we do not possess (or will never possess) the desired explanation. That view was set aside earlier. Still it remains that our never being able to achieve an explanation could result from our limitations rather than from the nature of cognitively indifferent reality. Only the latter is of interest for the ontological thesis now being examined. Two additional questions are pertinent: How can anyone in our present circumstances claim with any confidence that *there is no* further explanation? What can be meant by the *sufficiency* of a cause? Questions of this order concerning supervenience and explanation are addressed in chapter 2 to the extent that our limited concerns dictate.

Conditions (1)–(3) isn't the only form in which emergentism appears in the current philosophical literature. Some emergentists reject (1) on the grounds that once an emergent aspect arises it radically transforms the base on which it depends; the base then disappears and is absorbed into its emergent product. Earlier, Alexander (1920, volume II, p. 9) suggested as much: "The neural process which carries thought becomes changed into a different one when it ceases to carry thought." (Recall also Bain's remark that "the combining elements are not recognizable" in the collocation.)

---

11. Distinctions between supervenience and realization are explored in chapter 2. However, because the extensions of each in cases of present interest overlap almost completely, we are able to overlook their differences for much of this discussion. What matters is a constitutional dependence in both.

Others (e.g., Gillett (2002)) suppose that (3) by itself, or (3) with the addition of (1), suffices for emergentism. Those views are compatible with some robust forms of physicalism. Finally, minimal forms of emergentism, called "weak emergentism" by Bedau (1997), need only (1) and (2). Some of those variations are considered in subsequent chapters.

We may illustrate weak emergentism with a favorite ploy of opponents of physicalism: the possibility of zombies. (See Chalmers 1996.) Zombies are physically, and perhaps behaviorally, indistinguishable from us, but lack phenomenological properties, commonly known as qualia. Their behavior is directed by their physical components, and if it is possible to have beliefs without qualia, zombies may even falsely believe that they have conscious states and properties. If we are not zombies, it must be by virtue of non-physical features we possess. Under (1) those features do not float free of the physical world, and on (2) their intrinsic nature is not explicated by the features of that world. But nothing about our differences from zombies shows our additional features to have any causal powers that are not contributed by our physical bases. For that we need condition (3).

Weak emergentism has been too timid a view for most emergentists, indeed even for typical non-emergentist commentators. On the weak view, despite our differences from zombies, our distinct mental lives might be epiphenomenal, and this, it has been held, is unacceptable. (See below.) Any form of the view that includes (3) could be known as *strong emergentism*,[12] which I shorten to *emergentism* because the only versions seriously considered in this work ascribe causal relevance to emergent aspects. But, as I noted earlier, any emergentism incorporating (3) encounters serious problems about the causation of the mental. Before tackling that issue in earnest (in chapters 3 and 4), a few initial remarks about causation may be in order.

An additional distinction is relevant to article (1). Supervenience, or realization, is synchronous with what supervenes on it or is realized by it. We are concerned here only with varieties of emergence meeting that requirement. This isn't an arbitrary stipulation; it captures what seems to me to be the main tendency of the current view. Certain classical emergentists may regard the base as preceding its emergent. It hasn't even prevented some current emergentists from making similar claims. For example, in

12. This differs from Chalmers' (2006) taxonomy, in which 'strong' and 'weak' designate, respectively, ontological and epistemic emergentism.

evolutionary versions of the doctrine, the base may be an earlier form of plant or animal giving rise to a novel form. In yet other versions the base is specified as the (efficient) cause of the emergent, and it is generally supposed that a cause precedes its effect. Those variants aren't ruled out, but they aren't part of the view under discussion. Our concern is with a theory in which the emergent is supposed to supervene on or be realized in its base, both synchronic relations. This doesn't discharge all criticism of (1). In the next chapter I will briefly discuss a challenge to (1) that raises an objection to an independent base, but it concerns only the interplay of synchronous factors.

Recall that the discussion largely concerns *properties*. One may wonder how, when the topic turns to causation, properties, rather than, say, events, can be the relata of prime interest. However, this treatment of properties is meant to cover tokens or instances of properties as much as their types. The properties under consideration, unless we are discussing type-type identity theories, are instances, also known by some as 'tropes'. They are as individual as the particulars to which they are ascribed. Our interest is in the red of *this* tomato, not redness in general or the redness of tomatoes as such. When broaching the topic of causation, my remarks should also apply, *mutatis mutandis*, to events and states. Depending on one's further views, the difference may turn out to be merely terminological. On one popular account, events are instantiations of properties. That interpretation creates a convergence between issues about the causal prowess of properties and states. If we are to remain resolute realists about causation, the particular case ought to be of special interest. Our properties and/or states must be causally efficacious (or causally relevant) if our causal generalizations are to have this realist bite.

Although this affords us some latitude in discussing issues interchangeably in terms of properties and events, we needn't suppose that the difference between an event and its property is *never* relevant. But the differences would be more pronounced if, as in many discourses, it had been assumed from the start that the events discussed were all particular occurrences and properties were all universals or types.

Sticking with the theme of causation, consider epiphenomenalism of the mental—the view that it never causes anything, although it is an effect of other causes. That doctrine is not without advocates, but it also has a considerable dialectical burden. One solution to the causal difficulties besetting the mental is the view that a mental property gains a causal role by virtue of its identity with a physical property. If so, the causal efficacy resides in the property under its physical description, not in its mental aspect—what has been called "type epiphenomenalism." The problem—known sometimes as the qua problem (Maslen et al. 2009)—was noted by Broad (1925, p. 473): "Epiphenomenalism . . . simply says that mental events either (a) do not function at all as cause-factors; or (b) that, if they do, they do so in virtue of their physiological characteristics and not in virtue of mental characteristics."

Why should epiphenomenalism seem so implausible here? On a popular account, I can become *empirically* acquainted with an X only if X figures causally in my experience.[13] Suppose the same is true of our conscious episodes. If they could not be causes of our judgments about them, it would be perfectly mysterious why we ever supposed we had them in their mental semblance (or, for that matter, how we could "suppose" anything at all). Against this, some have claimed that conscious phenomena are different; there is no internal sensory faculty by which to detect them. A few have even claimed them to be *a priori* and thus not regulated by the conditions governing experience of the empirical world. However, these differences fail to shake the conviction that if conscious properties couldn't play any role in a self-awareness of them, it would be hard to see how we should have happened upon the belief that there were such properties. Even if a conscious property's empirical credentials are tainted, it is only a *contingent* truth, say, that my thumb hurts. Thus, it is not something I can excogitate in the manner of a typically necessary *a priori* truth, such as that $2 + 3 = 5$. It would be the contingency of the pain, rather than its paradigmatic empirical character, that would demand its causal role here. Even if, as some suggest (e.g., Horgan and Kriegel), awareness is an intrinsic feature of an occurrent phenomenal state, the second-order knowledge of that state would invoke a causal connection to the state.

I have yet to complete this initial summary of emergence. But before attending to that, perhaps a quick review of the variety of positions in the last century or so on the nature of the mental, painted in very broad strokes, will locate emergentism more definitely for the ensuing discussion.

13. A thesis defended in Vision 1996.

1.7 Theories of the Mental I: Eliminativism

Strictly speaking, eliminativism declares that nothing in the empirical world correlates closely enough to our mentalist vocabulary to warrant taking the latter as more than a useful fiction. Occasionally the view is explicit, often only implied. But in each embodiment it constitutes an *irrealism* about mental, including conscious, properties. Here I use the term 'eliminativism' broadly to cover an aggregate of irrealist options that may go under titles such as instrumentalism, error theory, and even some forms of functionalism. With the exception of a certain relevant form of functionalism, these options also tend to be physicalist in spirit; but unlike the physicalisms sketched below in sections 1.9 and 1.10, they reject outright or diminish beyond recognition the reality of conscious aspects. In a more comprehensive review one would be obliged to examine this collection in greater detail, but nothing that encyclopedic is undertaken here. One reason is that it would distract us from the main target of the exposition, the standing of emergentism. Another reason is that the zeitgeist seems to indicate that the realist alternatives are the leading naturalist views when issues relevant to emergentism are aired. This section contains some further remarks on the irrealist alternatives, but afterwards eliminativism largely drops out of my deliberations (save for a brief reappearance in the epilogue). However, readers may justly wonder what entitles me to be so cavalier in dismissing this view. So as an apologia I set forth one reason for not pursuing it further: namely, once phenomenal experience enters the inquiry, it is a mistake to offer an account of it, including a debunking one, that omits the 'what it is like' of phenomenal states.

First, a qualification. There is a vast literature on consciousness, and a substantial portion of it contains a much more extensive and thorough treatment than I can offer here.[14] In fact, it would be a mistake to take what I say in this section for anything as grand as an account of phenomenal experience. But I can briefly explain why the 'what it is like' of conscious experience is indispensable to any competitive theory in which implications are drawn regarding it. This still leaves in the field a number of competing views, including dualism and other physicalist theories described below. My reasons rule out only what I have labeled as irrealist views about the qualia of conscious sensation.

14. For a list of the ways in which 'conscious' has been employed, see Lycan 1996.

Irrealism diagnoses sensations such as pain very poorly. To illustrate, compare the options for one's theories of pain qualities with those for heat and color.

It is a fair guess that humans first became acquainted with heat as a sensation, ranging in intensity from comfortable warmth to extreme hurtfulness. Even if this isn't an accurate history of the race, it certainly seems to be the way young children come to understand heat. If adults warn "Hot!" as they point to items such as a stove, a pavement, or boiling water, how might that register for young children before they have had an unpleasant sensation? Despite this manner of becoming acquainted with heat, the common heat found in our workaday environment has been discovered to be molecular motion. Although we are introduced to heat via a range of feelings, it is in fact a wholly non-subjective feature. We have, as John Searle put it (1992), carved off the surface features of heat to uncover our definition.

An extension of this reasoning to the sensation of pain may appear to establish irrealism about pain's inherent phenomenology. Just as scientific progress led to marginalizing the feeling of heat, it should do the same for pain. But now consider color. While color is also consciously experienced, the question of whether it is a mind-independent feature of the world remains *sub judice*,[15] both in philosophy and in the relevant sciences. It is not that we lack sufficient information about the physical basis of color experience. Our knowledge here is not inferior in kind to that which we have for heat. If it were merely a question of discovering color's objective correlates—say, surface reflectances for non-luminous objects—everyone should agree, as they do for heat, that this is what color *is*, nothing more. But the debate still rages about whether these mind-independent features are the colors themselves or, as in the case of secondary-quality and error theories, merely experiential contents triggered by an object's non-chromatic features. This is not the place to try to resolve that dispute. But if heat exemplifies the standard by which to decide these cases, the philosophical issue should dissipate once there is general agreement on the scientific facts. Nevertheless, the dispute over color continues even in precincts in

15. X is mind-dependent $=_{df.}$ X is not (/no longer) cognized $\rightarrow$ X is not (/no longer). (Variations in accounts of mind-dependence will depend on the modal strength of the implication, on how dispositions to cognize are viewed, and on one's views about that definition's tensed forms.)

which there is broad agreement on the science. For whatever reason, some consciously felt properties already have a built-in slot for the non-subjective qualities with which they are to be identified even before the science arrives, whereas others do not.

Why does the objective or mind-independent definition of heat make sense? A possible explanation is that heat does many things other than cause sensations. It fries eggs, expands metals, starts fires, dries up puddles, boils water, melts ice, blisters fingers, both nurtures and kills plant life, and so on. This enables us to intelligibly imagine a world in which an isolated race of intelligent beings have in their environment the same variations in kinetic molecular motion, but do not feel it, never have felt it, and have no inkling that there might be creatures who do feel it (save by conducting Nagelian-like thought experiments about, say, possible bat-like creatures that might have a sense to detect it). Of course, this 'thing' still burns and causes injuries, nourishes these beings, and in sum has all the non-sentient effects on their bodies that heat has on ours, which undoubtedly causes them to take note of it just as we take note of the effects of vitamins. Moreover, we can also imagine that they have the word 'heat' in their vocabulary, signifying the same phenomenon that our similar-sounding word signifies. They simply do not detect its presence or absence in their sentient lives.

I find no reason to suppose that this scenario is incoherent, either intrinsically or in conjunction with current thermal physics. Chalmers (1996, p. 45) claims that in leaving out the sensation of heat "part of the phenomenon is left unexplained." But how does this leave the account any more incomplete than if we had left out instead its ability to blister skin? Was there no heat before there were sentient beings? Or was the mere disposition to cause a sensation if there were sentient beings sufficient for the concept? Indeed, doesn't our current understanding of heat already leave out what may be many equally standard features of it, such as its capacity for interacting with the potentially vast number of elements in the universe with which we are likely to be unfamiliar? My imagined scenario seems to demonstrate that heat sensations are historically and epistemically important for heat's discovery, but not any more significant than its other features for an account of what heat *is*. (Again, it is not obvious that a comparable imaginary setting replacing heat with color would have a similar result, at least according to secondary-quality theorists. Could they allow that there were colors in any but the most attenuated dispositional sense in a world with no sentient creatures?)

Now let us turn to pain. I can't imagine a similar race of beings who *had* pains, but were constitutionally unable to feel them. Unfelt pain, as many have held, makes no sense. This is not a question of whether peripheral cases in our world might accommodate a sincere report of not feeling pain to be outweighed by neural evidence to the contrary (see, e.g., Lamme), a view on which we needn't take a stand, but whether we could imagine a possible world in which *no* creatures *ever* felt pain, knew of no other creatures who did feel it, but in which nevertheless there were pains only because there were the neural states that currently subserve our pain. If, as I believe, this is not imaginable, we cannot skim off the subjective features of pain and still retain what we thought of as our concept of pain. Some have held that pains have a content to the effect, roughly, that the body has been damaged. This isn't ruled out by the requirement that pain be felt. But bodily damage or its danger cannot be the moral of the tale. We are familiar with very many instances of bodily damage that aren't painful (e.g., various tumors or certain of their stages, the debilitating effects of brain deterioration in senility, leprosy, clogged arteries, or poison ivy damage which causes only itching), so we cannot retain our concept just by hiving off the subjective element and defining it via its tendency to be induced by bodily damage or distress. Indeed, this illustrates an important difference between heat and pain. Heat, as we have seen, comports with its physical manifestations; but the concept of pain persists despite a considerable disconnection with instances of bodily damage. It seems perfectly clear that any concept of pain that indicated *only* bodily damage without sensation would be an altogether different concept from the one we have now. An isolated race of creatures unable to feel pain wouldn't be in pain in any previously recognizable sense.

This is not to say that we are prohibited from redefining pain. We can redefine any concept. But if we do so for pain, it is evident that we have crossed a line that was not crossed for heat. It is not necessary to latch on to any one competing account to explain why this is so. This difference in our treatments of heat and pain may have something to do with the fact that heat manifests itself in so many other salient ways, whereas pain does not. However, the difference is more robust than these remarks; *qua* phenomenon it outlasts all failures in our feeble efforts to explain it. There is certainly a strong inclination to hold that pain must be felt in all but perhaps a few exceptional cases, whereas sensations of heat seem to us, and should have seemed to us even before the advent of modern science, only contingently related to heat. There may be some who are ready to reject the intuition about pain, courtesy of overarching metaphysical or semantic commitments. But, as Wittgenstein admonished (1953, I, §66), "don't think, but look!" The rest is speculation.

Nothing in this rules out physicalist reduction. It remains possible to discover that pain is identical with physical, functional, or representational X. What is precluded is only that, perhaps per impossibility, Xs without consciousness of pain would no more be pains than Mark Twain without Samuel Clemens would be Mark Twain.

Searle agrees; however, he also states that the difference is trivial, boiling down to the pragmatic fact that we are more interested in the subjective character of pain: "where the phenomena that interest us most are the subjective experiences themselves, there is no way to carve anything off" (1992, p. 121). Following Searle, I believe it is true both that (a) pain's subjective character is its inescapable feature and, apparently unlike heat, (b) the subjective character is what interests us most. But it does not follow that (a) *because* (b). For all Searle says in defense of this pragmatic solution, it falls into the category of an all-too-frequent philosophical defense that we may label "just can't think of anything better." Wherever the explanation has nothing going for it other than the fact that it is the least bad thing we can think up, as philosophers I believe we are well-advised to remain agnostic. Indeed, we could just as easily have said that the reason why the subjective interests us is precisely that it is a necessary truth, and thus impervious to further explanation, that pains are felt. Although this explanation is avoided because it is an unfashionable appeal, at least it has the support of an impressive intuition. Still, even if it is mistaken, the evidence entitles us only to the combination of (a) and (b), not to the second accounting for the first.

Thus I bypass any further examination of irrealisms about consciousness. Let me turn instead to the most popular realist alternatives to emergentism. Of course, substance dualism is the realist view *par excellence*. I shall say something about it, but shall pass on quickly to what I take to be the main realist competitors to emergentism: various forms of physicalism. They are only briefly sketched here to give us a background. After laying out the case for emergentism in chapters 2–5. They are examined more fully in part II.

1.8 Theories of the Mental II: Dualism

When one speaks of dualism in connection with the philosophy of mind, the original Cartesian variety first comes to mind. It is what I shall mean by plain 'dualism' unless specified otherwise. Historically it spurred the concern with mind that evolved into our current problematic. Dualists state that each person consists of a space-occupying material body plus an immaterial substance, the latter being a non-spatial "receptacle" containing the whole of one's mental life, though dualists customarily allow that *impure* mental states (e.g., answering thoughtfully, driving carefully) also involve bodily motions. On this account there are two major components of the mental realm: a substance and the transient aspects proper to it. Phenomenal and access-conscious states are not themselves immaterial substances, but items that, according to dualists, are capable of taking place within or with the cooperation of their immaterial substances. Pure mental states are not minds, but occur "in" minds. Various other names for immaterial substance have graced the literature, among them 'soul', 'psyche', 'spirit', and 'res cogitans'.

For a dualist, 'mind' denotes something quite distinct from the brain or any other material entity. In spite of the metaphysical distinction between substances, Descartes believed that two-way traffic between them is rife. But problems of causation, cited earlier in connection with emergentism, recur. In addition to those, many have been baffled by the notion of something in a wholly immaterial realm affecting a state of affairs in the material world (e.g., raising one's arm), or even by brute matter influencing mental life (e.g., perceptual experience).

However, substance dualism plays a minor role in what follows. This is not primarily because of widely circulated misgivings about interaction between antipodal material and immaterial substances, but because the notion of such an immaterial substance, if it is not idle, strongly suggests that one's continued identity depends on the identity of one's soul; and this is extremely tenuous, as witnessed by insuperable difficulties over such a substance's identification, re-identification, and principles of operation.

The use of the word 'mind' in the sequel doesn't denote an immaterial substance, but refers to mental life in general, however analyzed.[16]

Another set of positions in the literature has been called "dualism," sometimes as a disparagement by physicalist opponents. Those views might also be labeled "dual aspect theory" and "property dualism." Proponents acknowledge that there is at most one substance, but maintain that in addition to physical properties, that substance also has irreducible mental properties. While this does not resolve the initial enigma about how the mental and the physical can causally interact, the difficulty is now subtler. The mental properties in question have a foot in the physical world; they may be properties of, say, the brain or its activity.[17] The contrast isn't as stark as it would be on Cartesian dualism. But neither is it an issue we can avoid because emergentism is a variety of dual aspect theory, as are certain forms of non-reductive materialism.

Emergentism may have been originally put forward as a more scientifically attuned alternative to dualism, but its scientific standing has since evolved; emergentism's present task is to find a slot alongside the physicalist alternatives that now dominate cognitive studies. Let's complete this rough taxonomy by looking at various physicalisms.

1.9 Variations on Physicalist Themes

A clear majority of cognitive scientists and mainstream philosophers of mind reject substance dualism. Most seem to converge on a loose and tolerant materialism. Beyond that, paths diverge. The basis for calling this consensus "materialist" is that these philosophers agree that our reality bottoms out in material world.[18] Perhaps not everything is explicable; but to

16. This summary doesn't cast a net wide enough to catch every fish. For example, Nida-Rümelin (2007), among others, combines substance dualism with emergentism. Those accounts offer bottom-up theories of experiential subjects as distinct from the subjects' bodies or brains, the latter two being incapable of having conscious properties. (See chapter 2 below.)

17. On certain assumptions about substance, perhaps we should opt for neutral monism. (See Schneider, forthcoming.) That will not require modifying our supervenience thesis.

18. It is hard to know how to classify neo-panpsychists, who speculate that we may find the primordial elements of consciousness at the same fundamental level as the particles of physics. Chalmers (1996, 2002) entertains that hypothesis.

the extent that we have well-grounded explanations, they will contain at least traces of their physical origins. Some hold that the direction of science inexorably points toward the bases of everything else being discoverable in interactions between the most fundamental particles, a thesis sometimes dubbed The Standard View. Stephen Weinberg summed it up in 1974 as follows: "at the present moment the closest we can come to a unified view of nature is a description in terms of elementary particles and their mutual interactions" (p. 50). And nothing in the past 35+ years has undermined a reasonable expectation that things will progress in that direction. Indeed, Sydney Shoemaker considers it an integral part of physicalism. He assumes "a physicalist view according to which all of the facts about the world are constitutively determined by . . . facts about the properties of basic physical entities and how they are distributed in the world" (2007, p. 33). But one need not go to those lengths to reject dualism or emergentism. Various forms of physicalism demand only that the mental be ultimately reducible to, identical with, or explicable in terms of something or other physical. However, for the views of current interest, materialist philosophers have left room for the singular qualitative, first-person features distinctive of our mental lives—that is, qualia. This form of physicalism embraces phenomenal realism.

With only rare exceptions, phenomenal realists who consider themselves physicalists share the view that each mental token is either identical with or fully explained by a physical token. Type physicalists maintain that these identities or explanations can be reductive; token physicalists hold that reductive accounts are not in the offing, although identities or explanations between instances of conscious properties and their bases are realizable. Others may take the supervenience of the mental—emergentism's thesis (1)—to be *sufficient* for physicalism. A physicalism making no additional claims remains compatible with what I am calling *emergentism*. If the supervenience or realization relation is brute (that is, admits of no further account beyond the fact of supervenience or realization), this unadorned explanation of why the mental is really physical is in most estimates disappointing; it falls short of delivering the unified ontology that has been a credo of the dominant strain of materialism. Thus, I concentrate for the most part on brands of physicalism that assert the identity of the mental and the physical, either reductive identity (as with the general run of type physicalisms) or non-reductive identities (as in token or non-reductive physicalism).

Henceforth I'll refer to the view that proposes an identity between mental and physical properties or states at the level of types as *plain*, or *type*, or *old-school* physicalism. As earlier, identity is a stronger requirement than is needed for physicalism, although an identity thesis is its commonest form. Strictly speaking, a physicalist need hold only that physical aspects are able to *explain*, *replace*, or on some versions *necessitate* mental ones. And mere explanation or necessitation has sometimes been regarded as adequate for reduction, a view explored more fully in chapter 8. But it is a delicate balance, perhaps too delicate, to find an intermediate sort of explanation that is strong enough for type physicalism's reductionist ambitions but not sufficient for identity. In fact, those problems mirror the ones that impair the role of the *bridge principles* central to earlier conceptions of theory reduction.[19] It has been observed that, if those principles fall short of stating identities, they are too weak to serve their purpose, and, indeed, that they presuppose an independent existence for the reduced theory and psychophysical laws relating it to the reducing theory.

However, even for physicalism with type identities, further distinctions are in order. One species, commonly known as analytic behaviorism, encounters what are widely regarded as insuperable difficulties; none of its varieties is generally taken to be a live option nowadays (as always in philosophy, ignoring the rare exception). However, a brand of old-school physicalism is still very much alive. It is a descendant of the earlier central-state materialism of Herbert Feigl and J. J. C. Smart, who claimed that we could achieve an identity between mental states or processes and those in the brain or other intrinsic bodily states. That view is the centerpiece of chapter 6. But there are also other forms of physicalist-leaning theories that deserve mention. I begin with a brief glimpse at *representationalism*, or, as it is known in at least one instance, *representationism*.

Representationalists hold, first, that all mental aspects, including phenomenally conscious ones, have intentional or representational contents, and, second, that conscious aspects are features of their contents, sometimes accompanied by limited additional factors. For example, the pain felt upon stubbing one's toe may have an intentional content representing in a particular way damage to or distress in one's toe. Another pain may represent, say, damage or distress to one's shoulder. On a teleological version of the

19. See, e.g., Kim 2000a.

thesis, pain may be designed—say, by evolution—to represent that a certain part of one's body requires attention. Many representationalists, though not all, are semantic externalists (or anti-individualists), holding that environmental, sociolinguistic, or evolutionary forces are central constitutive factors in those intentional contents. Moreover, not all representationalists are, strictly speaking, physicalists. Some settle for a more relaxed brand of naturalism. I list them here, first, because certain of their number consider representationalism as a doorway to physicalism, and, second, because even those who reject physicalism hold views incompatible with forms of property dualism. They are committed to rejecting the notion that the state exhibiting the intentional content has a distinctive intrinsic nature, a something it is like, independent of its content. That content, with perhaps a few minor additions, exhausts the nature of conscious properties. (Here again, Chalmers (1996, chapter 6) creates headaches for taxonomers.)

Two qualifications are in order. First, because the external world is wildly diverse, even physicalist representationalists can reject *typal* identities. While they all "reduce" qualia to intentional contents, some are uncommitted on further physicalist reductions. However, on the basic differences with emergentism, the representationalists of concern are one with physicalism. Second, it should not be supposed that all semantic externalists are physicalists, or even naturalists. For example, Tyler Burge (1979; 2007b,c) distances himself from physicalism and representationalism by denying that the sociolinguistic information definitive of our phenomenal states is tantamount to intentional content.

A popular view, making up yet another branch on our tree of physicalist options, is psychofunctionalism (plain 'functionalism' here). On it, mental properties are *defined* in terms of their abstract functional roles. If M is a (type or token) mental property, it is delineated via its typical relations to (a) stimuli, such as perception or hearsay, which give rise to M; (b) interactions with other mental properties—say, M', M'', M''', etc.—by way of inference, causation, and other associations; and (c) behavior, including reasonings, made more probable by (a) and (b).

On this account, M has been exhaustively characterized in terms of its extrinsic features, its relations with the environment, other mental properties, and the behavior in which it issues; no mention is made of any intrinsic (non-relational) features it may have. Because of this, the most favorable candidates for functionalization are the properties most receptive to dispositional components, such as beliefs and desires.

For conscious properties, standard functionalism appears at first glance to ignore the something it is like of conscious experience. If that is the final draft, functionalism is among the class of the eliminativist theories set aside for reasons aired in section 1.7. (Although it is useful to distinguish forms of reductionism, which that sort of functionalism would exemplify, from eliminativism, reductionism differs from eliminativism chiefly in name. As Chalmers (1996, p. 165) has noted, it does no more than retain the title 'experience' for its explananda whereas eliminativism does not.) However, that assessment of functionalism may be premature. Pioneering functionalists regarded their views as doing no more than introducing "topic-neutral" translations of mental terms in an attempt to overcome initial resistance to locating what may seem to be extra-physical in a physical framework. After surmounting this obstacle, a physicalist identification or definition is a natural next step. Recently the procedure has gone as follows: following functionalization, we identify the functional (mental) property with whatever physical realizer is responsible for that property's behavior (Lewis 1983c; Kim 2005). That form of functionalism is squarely physicalist.

On the other hand, there are philosophers who believe that our labors terminate with the functional definitions. That view resists physicalism. Physicalists have recourse to the foregoing considerations: What matters are not the definitions obtained through functional analysis, but the identities with whatever physical aspects fill the causal roles specified in the analysis. Those realizers of mental aspects defined by their functional roles are invariably physical. That is the sort of functionalism that has a place in our consideration of physicalist options.

This brief review shows that the different takes on the physical bases of the mental present a crowded and messy field. Nonetheless, we may identify major lines of inquiry and clearly delineate views in that broad category as distinct from the variety of emergentism under consideration, or, for that matter, from any other variety of it with which I am familiar. Two qualifications will help to round off this initial characterization of physicalism.

First, I bypass the question of what counts as physical. Various suggestions, ranging from the spatially extended to the inanimate to whatever is non-mental, have been offered. As Noam Chomsky famously remarked, the notion of a physical explanation is guaranteed to cover *all* explanation that becomes accepted "for an uninteresting terminological reason, namely that the concept of 'physical explanation' will no doubt be extended to incorporate whatever is discovered in this domain, exactly as it was extended to accommodate gravitational and electromagnetic force, massless particles, and numerous other entities and processes that would have offended the common sense of earlier generations" (1972, p. 98). Here I simply rely on the fact that none of the physicalist-leaning views examined in this work hinge on the sorts of borderline cases that would compel us to be more precise about inclusion in the physical. (But see section 5.2.) Physicalists, functionalists, and representationalists alike tend to regard their views as offering reductionist, objective (that is, third-person) identifications of the mental. Put otherwise, upon successful completion of the view we are entitled to claim that a given mental aspect is "nothing but a(n) ___" (the blank to be filled in as directed by one's favored theory), in contrast with its being "something over and above" the physical. That will suffice to contrast those theorists with emergentists, and to entitle them to full participation in the discussions that follow.

Next, whereas any physicalist doctrine can limit its scope to a mere selection of mental aspects, our interest is in a comprehensive physicalism. The inability to include some conscious aspects in its identities or reductive definitions counts as a failure of the view. Such partial views are to be regarded as unsuccessful attempts to disguise counterexamples.

With the foregoing qualification in mind, we still need a representative version of physicalism to play off against emergentism. For that purpose I shall adopt old-school physicalism, which identifies kinds of mental phenomena with bodily states, etc., almost always spiking activity in the nervous system.[20] David Lewis (1999, p. 291) writes: "I am a realist and reductive materialist about mind. I hold that mental states are contingently identical to physical—and in particular, neural—states." Roughly, this is a view to which physicalists across the board might subscribe, although old-school physicalists may differ over whether the thesis is contingently or necessarily true. Moreover, old-school physicalists who pursue central-state identities or necessities may divide into chauvinists, who hold that only creatures whose anatomy resembles ours in certain respects have consciousness, or pluralists, who grant consciousness, but only in a different sense, to creatures anatomically or materially different from us. Details of that distinction are provided in chapter 6.

20. This expositional convenience is not intended to rule out externalism. Perhaps conscious states with contents have identity conditions referring to the subject's external environment or language community.

1.10   Non-Reductive Physicalism Contrasted with Emergentism

Thus far, the salient realist options still in view are emergentism, representationalism, and old-school physicalism. The last is a natural ally of forms of reductionism. However, it should also be noted that it is not mandatory in general to discard whatever gets reduced (see, e.g., Sober 1999). For example, we continue to determine amounts of heat and pressure with the Boyle-Charles law despite the absorption of thermodynamics into statistical mechanics. However, when we are discussing the reduction of mental to physical properties in philosophy, what stands out is not the ability to streamline our equations, but that the reduced class takes an ontological back seat. Thus, for the cases of current interest, an identity for a target class of Xs with Ys is intended to enable the claim that Xs are nothing but (or over and above) Ys. Some reductive physicalists hold, even more radically, that the identities are an important lemma in a demonstration that the relationship is not like that of thermodynamics to statistical mechanics, but rather like that of phlogiston to oxygen (viz., of alchemy to chemistry). Physical distinctions may then be viewed as "wip[ing] out familiar distinctions [between mental aspects] as spurious" (E. Nagel 1961 p. 340).

A point to bear in mind is that only identities between the generic or the abstract, such as laws or types of properties or entities, lend themselves to reductive analyses. And not even all of those hold out prospects for reduction—consider baby buggies and perambulators. Contemplating reduction is more prevalent where laws are directly involved, less so when what is identified are different names for the same general types. Thus, distinct names for a single species, such as 'The Grizzly Bear' and 'Ursus Horribilus' or 'Brontosaurus' and 'Apatosaurus', simplify one's ontology without thereby reducing either type to the other. Nevertheless, it appears that every identification that is fodder for reductionism is with a type or with the respective membership lists of types.

On the other hand, many physicalists are not committed to such type-level accounts. These are non-reductive or token physicalists. They reject identities between specific types of mental and physical phenomena, but accept a physicalist account of some sort at the level of tokens. Non-reductive physicalists—e.g., Davidson (1980b)—typically hold that there are token identities between mental and physical aspects, but some—e.g., Horgan (1993), Pereboom (2002), Wilson (2002), and Antony (2007)—appear willing to settle for non-identity where the mental token can be robustly explained by a physical one.

Identities between individuals—say, between Charles Lutwidge Dodgson and Lewis Carroll, between Constantinople and Istanbul, or between The Crimean War and The Eastern War—do not lend themselves to reductions. They may commit their holder to only one thing where she might have previously taken there to be two, but the items in question provide no simplification or streamlining of one's ideology. If there are *reductions* at the level of particulars (say, 'That's light reflected on the stream, not a fish'), it isn't clear that they are identities. Moreover, if they were identities, they would not be those of interest for the notion of reduction in science and philosophy. Thus, the acceptance of individual identities between mental and physical instantiated properties, although incompatible with emergentism, doesn't by itself advance reductivist aspirations.

Like emergentism, token physicalism rejects identities between various mental and material property types and may hold that the mental is dependent on the material in ways to be spelled out by supervenience or realization. Indeed, token physicalists are sometimes erroneously taken, especially by critics, to be emergentists. Whereas token physicalists form a mixed collection, as a group they are distinguished from emergentists by being committed to one or both of the following:

(i) *Token identity.*   Each token mental property is identical with some token physical property.

(ii) *Explanatory access.*   Each mental property is explicable in terms of some physical property *in a way that goes beyond the fact* that the mental property supervenes on or is realized by that physical property.

A parallel disjunction may be constructed in terms of states. And some—e.g., Loewer (2007) and J. Wilson (2002)—may prefer to frame our second disjunct in terms of the physical's *necessitating* rather than *explaining* the mental.

In its commonest incarnation, token physicalism opts for (i) above (that is, token identity) or for both (i) and (ii). But, as (ii) demonstrates, one can be a token physicalist and reject all such identities. Earlier I mentioned problems for type physicalists who sought to replace identities with explanations or necessitations. Those particular difficulties need not vex token physicalism's exclusive appeals to explanatory relations; it bears only on views with reductionist ambitions. However, a token physicalist taking this route must hold not only that mental aspects supervene (or are otherwise dependent on) physical ones, but also that we are able, or should eventually be able, to explain *why* the mental supervenes on the physical. That may engender a different set of problems.

The emergentist now under discussion (see (1)–(3)) rejects both (i) and (ii). Another way of putting the rejection of (ii) is to state that the relation of, say, conscious properties with their physical dependency base is brute or primitive. Samuel Alexander writes of emergent qualities as "under the compulsion of brute physical fact" (1920, volume I, p. 46). Of course, there are always further things to say about anything. But the emergentist holds that there is no further minimal explanation of the fact that mental state *m* depends on (or supervenes on, or is realized by) its physical base *p*.

These features make it easier to put in relief the differences between emergentism and non-reductive physicalism. Consider again my tripartite statement of emergentism for property E:

(1) E is *dependent* on different sorts of a non-emergent base in a way made manifest by E's *supervenience* (or *realization*) on those same properties.

(2) There is *no* further (minimal) *explanation* of why E is supervenient on (or dependent on, or realized by) that non-emergent base; viz., their relationship is brute.

(3) E is a cause (of both mental and physical aspects) in ways in which there is no sufficient cause in context at the levels of E's non-emergent base(s).

Both parties can accept (1), subject to the proviso that token physicalists may demur at regarding token identity as a kind of dependence. It is clear that emergentism parts ways with non-reductive physicalism at (2). Whereas (3) is an issue for emergentism, token-identity materialists have no need, or less of a need, to respond to criticisms of mental causation. If they accept (i), a mental cause is always identical with one or another physical cause. If they reject (i), explanations via (ii) in terms of physical causes can still be substituted for those in terms of mental causes, providing at least partial relief from the difficulties raised for mental causation.

1.11 Conclusion

I began with a brief history of emergentism, exploring both its ontological aspirations and the reasons for its general repudiation and subsequent neglect. This classical emergentism was then contrasted with the restricted emergentism to be developed in these pages. Finally, I produced a quick sketch of the major theories that compete with emergentism, several of which will be explored in greater detail in part II. Thus, we now have before us a roughly sketched map of the issues. With that in hand, I turn to the task of elaborating emergentism and the beginnings of an explanation of why I take it to be a defensible view of mental life.

2   Fleshing Out the View

2.1   Elaboration of Supervenience and Explanation

The task of this chapter is to elaborate and clarify the first two theses of the emergentism first specified in section 1.5. To wit: For emergent property E,

(1)   E is *dependent* on different sorts of non-emergent properties in a way made manifest by E's *supervenience* (or *realization*) on those same properties.

(2)   There is no further (minimal) *explanation* of why E is supervenient (or dependent) on that non-emergent base, viz., the relation is brute.

The "realization" option in (1) is deferred to the next chapter. Pros and cons concerning the third thesis, emergent causation, are taken up in chapters 3– 5.

Thesis (1) introduces the sometimes embattled notion that supervenience provides a kind of dependence. This claim warrants closer attention. Thesis (2) immerses the view in knotty issues surrounding explanation, which also call for amplification. However, the defense of a plausible theory of explanation would go well beyond anything needed for these limited purposes. For the present, it is important only to be sufficiently expansive about explanation's role while sidestepping the more divisive issues over which the competing theories lock horns. Thus, I am counting on the remarks about explanation assembled unsystematically in section 2.4 to quell popular misgivings about explanation's role in (2) while still remaining compatible with a broad selection of such theories. Indeed, that notion's present employment could be served with little more than Michael Scriven's (1962) quip that an explanation is whatever fills a gap in the understanding. Once these clarifications are before us, we can begin exploring further two contentious features at the forefront of emergentism:

its distinctive place in the pantheon of views about mentality and, once again, its claim to an independent causal role.

2.2   Supervenience Essentials

A class of A properties supervenes on a class of B properties if and only if there is no change in the A properties without a change in the B properties. Among their customary applications, A properties might be normative and B properties natural; or A properties might be secondary qualities and B properties primary qualities; or A properties might be group behavior and B properties individual behaviors. In our case, the A properties are conscious and the B properties are physical properties and their interactions.

Despite some earlier uses, supervenience's steady employment in philosophy can be traced to G. E. Moore's (1903) use of 'criterion'. According to Moore, nothing can be "a good X," a normative notion, without satisfying certain naturalistic criteria. Supervenience is the converse of Moore's criterion (viz., Bs are the criteria for As if and only if As supervene on Bs). For example, to be good an apple must have properties such as being red, ripe, and juicy (Urmson 1959). Its goodness cannot alter without certain changes in the latter set. Donald Davidson later imported supervenience into the relations between the mental and the physical, where it has since flourished.

Of course, supervenience may be found in many areas that are not so directly philosophically charged. For example, it is widely employed as a mereological notion. If a sheet of some material is (roughly) square, this will supervene on its parts and their arrangement. Change the number or arrangement of those parts in various ways and the sheet will no longer possess that shape. A collection of molecules will supervene on its constituent molecules, a single molecule on its atoms, a span of time on its constituent moments, a numerical series on the arrangement of its numerals. The supervenience relation lends itself to the layered conception of reality, with a lower level of subvenients "giving rise to" an upper level of supervenients.

No doubt a leading reason why supervenience has thoroughly captivated the imaginations of writers in hotly contested areas is that it appears to supply a kind of dependence of apparently problematic areas on settled ones while remaining neutral on the further reduction to or identity of supervenients with their bases. The problematic area might be the normative or the mental; the unproblematic base might be the natural or the physical, respectively. Moreover, this neutrality enables both sides to develop their views in their preferred directions. It does not prohibit further reductionist theorizing. In fact, if property A is identical with property B, or state X with state Y, or even instances of those (a and b and x and y, respectively), each supervenes on the other. In sum, supervenience subsumes identity. Identity following from supervenience has been a common step in arguments for reductions. The identity of supervenients with their bases is compatible with every formulation of supervenience with which I am familiar and is preserved in those presented below. On the other hand, supervenience per se is not identity or reduction. Thus, for those who, like emergentists, regard further reduction as unpromising, but who hold that properties of a certain class are not free floating, supervenience has seemed to supply enough dependence to satisfy them. If conscious properties are not independent of their subjects' physical constitution, this can be specified by the former's supervenience on the latter. For non-identicals, some changes in subvenients need not be reflected by changes in supervenients.

There are various forms of supervenience. Among those frequently mentioned are weak and strong individual supervenience, weak and strong global supervenience, and regional supervenience.[1] The discussion below is conducted in terms of strong individual supervenience, which is compatible with a substantial emergentism and states only what each of the warring camps can accept. (Our results can be easily enough restated for the other forms.) We may formulate our version as follows:

(MSS)   A properties strongly supervene on B properties $=_{df.}$ necessarily, for any property $\alpha \in A$, there is some property $\beta \in B$ such that the possessor of α has β, and necessarily whatever has α has β.

Occasionally strong individual supervenience is stated in terms of possible worlds:

(PSS)   A properties strongly supervene on B properties $=_{df.}$ for any possible worlds w and w^*, and any individuals x in w and y in w^*, if x in w is indistinguishable in its B properties from y in w^*, then x in w is indistinguishable in its A properties from y in w^* (Bennett and McLaughlin 2005).

1. For comprehensive reviews of supervenience, see McLaughlin 1995 and Bennett and McLaughlin 2005. For present purposes, we may ignore further bells and whistles (e.g., centered worlds).

Whereas on natural assumptions (MSS) implies (PSS), on a commonly accepted reading (PSS) does not imply (MSS). Two individuals, say x and y, are indistinguishable in their B properties if they lack all B properties. However, (MSS) affirms the existence of B properties.[2] Because our interest in the supervenience bases of conscious properties is limited, we may ignore these differences. We may assume that all conscious properties have physical realizations on which they thereby supervene, although the class of B properties may be quite large and varied.

A number of other details of the interpretation of these formulas weigh in the balance. For example, necessity comes in different flavors, including, for our purposes, nomological and metaphysical. This sort of difference will determine which possible worlds are accessible for evaluating claims that one sort of aspect supervenes on another. For the most part, the first occurrence of necessity in (MSS) is taken as applying broadly. But, as we shall see, a question has arisen over how an emergentist should regard its occurrence in the concluding phrase "necessarily whatever has α has β." Also, the assumption that supervenience implies the dependence of A properties on B properties is questionable. I temporarily set aside these issues in order to examine supervenience's ostensible role in physicalism.

As was noted in the preceding chapter, some writers have taken the supervenience, or realization, of the mental on the physical as sufficient for physicalism.[3] I am assuming that they intend their physicalism to rule out any form of property dualism, including emergentism. Working on that assumption, my thesis (1) is incompatible with emergentism. Nevertheless, taking as their inspiration a remark found in Kripke 1980 (pp. 155–156), Block and Stalnaker (1999), Jackson (1993, 2007), and Loewer (1997, 2007), among others, characterize physicalism as the view that, to create the world, God need only create the physical stuff and its modes of composition. If a mental aspect supervenes on the physical, we thereby get the mental *gratis*. However, if physicalism is meant to exclude property dualism, this characterization of it is patently inadequate. That the emergent

2. McLaughlin 1995.

3. Kim (2000a, p. 38) writes that such supervenience "could be usefully thought of as defining minimal physicalism," but adds immediately afterwards that "emergentism, too, is arguably committed to mind-body supervenience." Thus, for Kim, either emergentism is a form of physicalism (*pace* Kim 2005) or else "minimal physicalism" is not physicalism.

comes along with the physical, so that it doesn't require extra exertion on God's part, does not make its qualitative character any more physical than it would have been otherwise. In other words, the scenario says nothing about whether the mental properties that supervene on the physical are distinct from them, or are even explicable in their base's terms beyond the fact that they are brought into existence by that base. Kripke (1980, pp. 155–156) used the vivid image of God's minimal labor to illustrate only a necessary condition for physicalism. That illustration is innocent enough. But as a sufficient condition either God's minimally effective labor plainly fails or, *pace* the intentions of those exponents, it installs a form physicalism consistent with property dualism. Although physicalism of that stripe does appear in the literature, it is not the variety in which we are interested.

Equally important, an analogous blemish spoils a less fanciful statement of physicalism. It is the view that any possible world that is no more than a minimal physical duplicate of ours is a duplicate of ours, period. (See, e.g., Jackson 1998, p. 12.) This formulation disguises, but doesn't eliminate, a closely related problem. Let us ask whether the minimal physical duplicate includes whatever supervenes on it. If it does, then, on the current definition of emergentism, those aspects, if there are any, will be included in a minimal physical duplicate of our world. That would disqualify the view for our relevant form of physicalism. If it does not, and we don't count any form of supervenience among its "modes of composition," even ordinary items such as pandas, glaciers, fungi, stars, and seas will be excluded. Perhaps excluding such prosaic items of worldly furniture conforms to the views of certain metaphysicians who favor the most austere inventory of physical reality, but I suspect it isn't a welcome implication for typical proponents of the current form of physicalism.[4]

I noted in chapter 1 that some self-styled emergentists have held that their version is compatible with physicalism. Unlike other physicalists, they can accept either of the characterizations of physicalism in the last two paragraphs. Their emergentism, as was noted, is simply the view that certain higher-level physical complexes have novel causal roles, a variant of tenet (3) for the non-fundamental physical. There is little point in disputing that terminology. (Nevertheless, it conflicts with what orthodox

4. Cf. Jackson's remarks on four-dimensionalism (1998, pp. 42–43), which are pertinent because of his view that conceptual analysis should not be *radically* reformative.

physicalists take to be a defining article of their physicalism; see section 4.6.) The physicalist project of concern is advanced by reduction, non-reductive identification, or further explanation of the mental in physical terms. That sort of physicalism is the only kind considered in these pages because it forms an instructive option to play off against emergentism. Thus, I ignore the sop thrown to physicalism by versions of it that are compatible with emergentism.

2.3   Supervenience and Emergentism

There are more issues about supervenience's role here than I can canvass, but by addressing points that are fundamental for clarity and defensibility I am hopeful that the four salient ones on which I have chosen to comment will put the intended relation in proper perspective. In brief, they are the following:

(a) supervenience versus realization

(b) the mode of necessity underlying emergentism

(c) emergentism without supervenience

(d) supervenience as a kind of dependence.

Let us begin with (a). Put bluntly, the physical realization of conscious properties is more central to our concerns than supervenience. A supervenience base, unlike a realizer (with an exception discussed below), needn't ultimately belong to the same subject as its supervenient property. Disraeli's knighthood supervenes on the Queen's going through a ritual, but the Queen's ritual doesn't realize—that is, physically embody—Disraeli's knighthood. Xantippe's widowhood supervenes on Socrates' death,[5] although her widowhood isn't realized in Socrates' death. This is consistent with the (MSS) condition that the possessor of α have β. Disraeli must possess the relational property of being the recipient of the Queen's bestowal of knighthood. But his knighthood also supervenes on the property of the Queen's going through a certain ritual, which is non-relational.

5. Some have denied that the dependence of Xantippe's widowhood on Socrates' death is a case of supervenience. But it seems, like Disraeli's knighting, ideally suited to the formulas for supervenience. Could the same be said about the dependence of Xantippe's widowhood on something described as "her husband's death"?

Realization, unlike supervenience, is irreflexive (viz., nothing realizes itself) and anti-symmetrical (viz., if A realizes B, B does not realize A), and it is debatable whether realization is transitive. But on virtually all of the strict definitions with which I am familiar, if A = B, thereby satisfying all three relations, then A and B supervene on each other. However, there is a good deal of overlap between the extensions of realizers and subvenients of mental properties; in cases of interest they largely coincide. Thus, I follow the discussion's dominant trend in framing this constitutional dependence of the mental in terms of supervenience, and in context I freely interchange supervenience with realization. Properties generally satisfy both conditions when relevant questions are raised. Occasionally, when it irrelevant to the specific discussion which of the two matters, to avoid the clumsy phrase "supervenient or realization base" I write simply about a property's base. In this chapter, I am primarily explicating supervenience. In the next one, where the focal issue is the nature of constitution, the idiom of realization is more convenient. Readers shouldn't suppose that the implications for our topic have changed significantly just because the term has.

An exception to the view that the realizing and realized property are always properties of the same thing is supplied by certain cases of coincidental objects. (See Shoemaker 2007.) For Neo-Lockean personal identity, a human and a person are different entities, although the mental properties of the person are realized by physical properties of its biological (that is, human) self. In this spirit, I argue in chapter 3 that the properties of a statue are realized in the properties of its matter, and share some properties, although the statue and the matter are different subjects. However, for supervenience, a property may supervene on the property of something that neither is the same as it nor coincides with it.

We now turn to (b). What is the strength of the necessity operators in (MSS)? (The question is reflected in (PSS) by asking which possible worlds are accessible for assessment.) The two leading candidates are nomological (that is, natural) and metaphysical necessity. More than a few writers have supposed that only nomologically necessary supervenience suits emergentism. One reason is that the zombie hypothesis (see section 1.6) has been a bedrock of non-physicalist thinking.[6] On the natural laws in

6. See, e.g., chapter 3 of Chalmers 1996. An inverted spectrum is another favorite example. Potential illustrations of the latter come in various strengths; on at least some of them, the undetectability of the inversion doesn't depend on a difference to the natural laws holding for normal perceivers and inverts.

operation, conscious states (and properties) are lawfully connected to embodied neurological activity. Zombies are possible only in a world in which those lawful connections are severed. Nomological necessity leaves space for that connection to be violated.

On the other hand, metaphysical supervenience covers as many possible worlds as logical or conceptual necessity. It differs from logical necessity (a relation of formal or syntactic implication) and from conceptual necessity (which also includes implications in which expressions or concepts are substitutable a priori for others) in that it also embraces cases of a posteriori necessity. Thus, 'H_2O' is not synonymous with 'water', but on the supposition of that chemical lore 'If x is water, then x is H_2O' holds in every possible world accessible to logical and conceptual necessity. For the inhabitants of Twin Earth, if the clear, flowing, potable liquid in their "lakes" and "rivers" has the exotic chemical makeup XYZ, they are not familiar with water even though in their tongue XYZ is called 'water'. Although statements made with sentences such as 'Water is H_2O' are necessary truths, their necessity is not conceptual or formal. Nevertheless, the same comprehensive set of possible worlds with which we assess formal implication is in play for evaluating metaphysical necessity. If A is metaphysically dependent on B, no logically possible world will have a token of A without a corresponding token of B, and no logically possible world will have a token of B without a token of A. Put otherwise, if the occurrence of A metaphysically necessitates the occurrence of B, then A semantically implies B. It is worth noting that semantic implication is emphasized in cases in which supervenients are identical with their bases: water is not only implied by H_2O, but is H_2O; lightning is not only implied by a discharge of electrons, but is a discharge of electrons.

It has seemed to some that to preserve the distinguishability of emergent properties we must avoid interpreting the necessity in (MSS) as metaphysical. Nevertheless, I propose that we understand (1) so that the second occurrence of necessity is metaphysical. The desire to preserve the possibility of emergentism through nomological necessity marks no crucial distinction for the current project. Either, as some have suggested, the metaphysical collapses into the nomological, or else it accesses a broader range of possibilities. If the former, there is no need for their distinction because the zombie case fails. Moreover, there is a raging controversy in the literature as to whether zombies are indeed conceivable, in which it would be tactically advantageous to avoid entanglement. Thus, this defense of emergentism needn't rest on the conceivability of zombies. If they are conceivable, fine. It is one more bit of evidence in favor of emergentism. However, I am granting, *arguendo*, that emergent aspects supervene with metaphysical necessity on their bases in this defense, whether or not metaphysical and nomological necessity come apart.

A further word on this choice is apropos. Aside from the fact that the zombie hypothesis involves an avoidable controversy—some (e.g., Tye (2007)) deny that it makes sense; others even question the grounds for a belief that we are not zombies (Dretske, manuscript)—the metaphysical necessity of the conscious on the physical does not abolish the distinction between the third-person access we have to neural activity and the first-person transparency of experience. No doubt, matters do not end there. For example, suggestions have been made to regard those differences merely as distinct "modes of presentation," conceptual rather than property differences. More is said about this "conceptual gambit" in section 2.5, although its upshot is that we must probe physicalist recommendations further to moot that issue. However, a leading reason for staying with emergentism under this more daunting requirement is that the present version is defended for rather different reasons. Explaining those reasons at this stage requires anticipating some matters that can be properly explored only in the sequel. But here, at any rate, is a rough outline of the drift of the argument that will follow.

Metaphysical supervenience of the conscious on the physical is compatible with multiple realizability, and multiple realizability has been a weapon against identities between mental and physical types. That objection has been challenged, but in chapter 6 I hope to show that it holds its ground against the opposition. At this stage, it serves merely to explain why metaphysical necessity need not establish type physicalism. Now, even if multiple realizability precludes identities of types of varying generalities, each conscious property may still be realized by some or other physical property, which leaves open the prospect of token identities. That is equally fatal to emergentism. However, once type physicalism and some of its grounds have been scrapped, and the leading arguments against mental causation have been neutralized (chapter 4), the only handle we have both for grasping the nature of token identity and supporting instances of it will be the implicit conditions guiding its familiar paradigms. Call an arbitrary quale

'Q' and its neural aspect 'N'. It may then be argued (chapter 8) that any tokens of Q and N fail to satisfy the conditions for their identity (or even for understanding what is claimed by it). That too is not the last word on the subject. Perhaps type or token physicalists will settle for something less than identity, say explanation of the conscious in terms of its physical base. To complete the argument we must show that this avenue too is closed. If we can achieve all that and overcome the resistance to mental causation, a full defense of (1)–(3), even with metaphysically strong supervenience, is complete.

A subsidiary reason for preferring metaphysical to nomological necessity has little to do with emergentism per se, but rather with the smooth operation of one's account of supervenience. Speaking locally, Q's instantiation doesn't appear to depend on all the natural laws, only on those that are relevant to the production of Qs. Call those laws m, the whole set of natural laws n. If $m < n$, then Q may be supervenient on N in a world in which a comprehensive body of natural law is incomplete but still operating in other respects. Whereas it seems conceivable that some natural laws might be absent from our body of laws, the absence of our entire body of natural laws is difficult to conceive. That situation seems impossible to describe in our current terms, and unthinkable with our current concepts; our very classifications are thoroughly intertwined with categories whose terms can be understood only within the theories supported by those laws. Total violations of nomological necessity are indiscriminate; they conceive of the entire body of natural law failing, not of minor deviations. But there is no warrant in the zombie hypothesis for supposing that its possible worlds might not be relatively minor deviations from the body of natural law. The non-specificity of the part of the body of natural law involved here is no longer a structural defect in the form of supervenience itself, but, as it should be, a mere local matter. The violation of nomological necessity as such seems too indiscriminate to focus on what the zombie hypothesis seeks to specify.

Let's move on to (c), a consideration of emergentism without supervenience (perhaps even without realization). While it is customary to emphasize the supervenience of mental properties on the physical, some emergentists reject it. Even some physicalists[7] deny that phenomenal

7. E.g., Schiffer (1987) and Grimes (1988).

tokens, or any other mental ones, supervene on the physical. Their complaints usually center on the notion of supervenience itself. Of course, emergentist rejectionists would disagree with my formulation of that view.

No doubt it would be self-refuting for emergentists to deny that their aspects depend on a physical base. Those properties must "emerge" from something if the title is to mean anything. But a somewhat common thread among them is that once the emergent property appears it radically transforms its physical base, so that the base no longer persists as a support. What was once the base is now fused into the emergent aspect. Paul Humphreys puts the point as follows:

> In the course of fusing [the earlier properties] become the [emergent property] instance, rather than realizing the [emergent] property in the way that supervenience theorists allow the subvenient properties to continue to exist at the same time as the supervenient property instance. (1997, p. 10)

Why shouldn't all emergentists accept this? For starters, consider that any emergentist thesis requires at the very least that emergent aspects *depend on* the physical in a way that highlights the sort of asymmetrical dependence for which supervenience was originally invoked. A subvenient or a realizer is intended to provide a non-causal sufficient (and sometimes necessary) condition for the emergent. In a broad sense the base *constitutes* the emergent aspect. The notion I have in mind is rather commonplace: something's constitution either discloses what it is "made of" (as in a hut's being constituted by a collection of twigs) or gives the non-causal conditions for the thing's being so (as a fact constituting the truth of a proposition). Realization is one form of this, although constitution is broader than both supervenience and realization. (Presently I distinguish a narrower sense of *constitution* in which a base needn't constitute its emergent aspect.) Also, even emergentists who reject supervenience for the above reasons seem to admit that the base is recoverable. According to Humphreys, the emergent property can be "decomposed" into the properties from whose fusion it emerged. In a crucial sense, the base hasn't really disappeared.

Two further points strengthen this one. In the first, I concentrate on a line of argument, exemplified by Humphreys, for eliminating a supervenience base. It is directed at a challenge thrown up by physicalism for rejecting independent mental causation. Although he identifies a definite threat to emergentism (which I address in chapter 4), Humphreys' attempt at rectifying the situation fails. The second, more general point introduces a distinction between forms of emergentism that will guide us throughout the rest of this study.

First, it has been argued that supervenience of the mental is incompatible with a causal role for emergent properties. Two objections are produced to show that mental causation would violate an important feature of causation; in chapter 4 I label that feature descending support. Causal relevance is declared otiose for emergent properties by the causation that takes place between fundamental particles. Against this claim Humphreys observes, plausibly enough, that if this argument blocks emergents, or any mental properties, from causal efficacy, it equally blocks the causal efficacy of tokens of special sciences. This is known as The Generalization Argument. (See section 4.5.) Humphrey's solution abolishes the hierarchy by denying that a supervenience base underlies emergent properties.

One problem with this solution is that the same reasoning can be deployed to deny that anything supervenes on anything else. For example, once a property is biological or chemical we might conclude that it is no longer physical—that a symphony is no longer a collection of notes, a house is not composed of bricks and mortar, or a normative feature no longer possesses its natural properties. Alternatively, one might search for a mark to distinguish all and only the relevant cases from legitimate applications of supervenience. But the prospects for finding one are not promising, and we are still left with the causal impotency for any supervenient tokens. Undoubtedly the challenge of descending support must fail if emergentism is to succeed: an independent mental causation is a direct consequence of tenet (3) of our emergentism. I take a different approach to meeting the challenge in sections 4.5 and 4.6, in which supervenience on the physical remains intact. On the other hand, Humphrey's solution has these untoward consequences.

A second and more general reason for dissenting from a non-supervenient emergentism arises from the need to distinguish different relationships that emergent properties may bear to their bases. Some are composed of their base whereas others may be emitted by their base. Philosophers and scientists influenced by failed attempts at reductions within a given science might want to argue that emergent properties composed of the properties of their bases are causally efficacious in ways in which a lesser combination of any of their compositional properties are not.[8] Or cell biologists may

8. See, e.g., Gillett 2002.

claim that combinations of cells can influence development by affecting individual cells. They may argue that some causal laws exist exclusively at levels of greater complexity and are instantiated by individual causes at that level. Because the emergent properties are composed of those in their bases, this may lend itself to pondering whether the base properties are still independent elements of the resulting product. This is not an issue on which I have chosen sides. I merely note that non-supervenience is a greater temptation when one thinks of emergence as a compositional property.

On the other hand, some emergentist claims are for properties that aren't aptly described as "composed of" their bases. The relationship of a conscious property to its neurological base is just such an instance. A conscious property need not be thought of as a supersized state (or a complex property) of the brain, but non-physicalists allege that it is something altogether distinct from its underlying brain token. At least that intuition is a fundamental inspiration of property dualism. Not only should the base property for emergents be relational (after all, part-whole is relational); it should produce discrete tokens. I can't think of a wholly satisfactory label for this sort of transaction, so I have chosen the clumsy notion of emission, on a very partial analogy with a chemical giving off an odor. Another useful analogy might be the notion of "setting off," as, say, when conflict in the Middle East "sets off" a panic on Wall Street. These suggestive analogies are only rough guides. They are causal notions, whereas the relation of supervenience or realization to what it "emits" is constitutional. There is an echo of this difference when we trouble over whether it makes sense to give a conscious property instance a spatial location—the sort of location we give, say, to its underlying brain state. That issue is raised in chapter 8. I do not claim that it makes no sense to locate a conscious property spatially in the brain, but I claim that this can be achieved only through identifying it with the location of its base. A conscious property cannot be located as directly as a neural configuration without first identifying a base with which it is identical or in which it is realized. Nevertheless, the fact that it is even natural to raise a question about the localizability of conscious properties illustrates the distinction between these claims and those of emergentist thinkers whose focus is on compositional emergent properties or states. Other emergentist claims that may fall into this second, emission class are those for normativity and those for secondary qualities. Where the emergent property is not conceived as compositional, there is no *prima facie* temptation to suppose that its base fuses with it, thereby losing its identity *qua* base.

To press the analogy a step further, when, say, Limburger cheese emits an odor, the cheese does not disappear, and what is emitted is no longer part of its bulk. One reason this model may get short shrift is that it is so easily assimilated to compositional cases. But a second and equally important reason for its neglect is that it is easy to conflate what I am calling constitution (used here broadly) with composition. Although I believe the distinction can be understood in terms of our common, loose use of these terms, that doesn't matter to me as long it is there to be made. Composition in my sense is a mereological notion. Constitution is its genus, but is more sweeping. There is a perfectly good sense in which an emergent property's base constitutes that property. In fact, realization is a straightforward species of constitution. However, one thing may constitute another without thereby absorbing or composing it. Once again, Socrates' death may constitute Xantippe's widowhood, or the Queen's enacting a ritual may constitute Disraeli's knighthood, without either composing its outcome. Or a state of affairs may constitute the truth of a proposition without thereby composing that truth. Indeed, it is difficult to see how the state of affairs could compose what it makes true[9] if it is distinct from the bearer whose truth it constitutes. On some accounts, hinging on one's view of truth-bearers, there can be a world of states of affairs without truth-bearers. Our Precambrian world may have been just such a place. This alone would not prevent a worldly state of affairs from constituting the truth of an existing proposition. But there need be no proposition for the state of affairs to compose.

None of this establishes the plausibility of emergentism, but it helps us to sort out what is at issue. It is important not to assume that every property that is a candidate for emergence is compositional. No doubt those who describe, much less defend, emergentism are not committed to acknowledging both compositional and emission versions of it. For present purposes, however, if the emergence of conscious properties works for anything, it works for an emission view. It is difficult to see how conscious properties could emerge by composing neurological ones. That would make a conscious property a super-sized neurological one. The mistake is not in

9. Save for those who hold an identity theory of truth.

the outright refusal to accept the emission model (an option for anyone prepared to argue for it), but either in conflating it with the compositional model or in neglecting to reserve a slot for it in a comprehensive overview of emergentism.

The emission model doesn't demand that conscious properties supervene on their bases. It leaves room for Humphreys' notion that the base is transformed into the emergent property. The reasons given above for rejecting the non-supervenience view are orthogonal to the compositional/ emission distinction. Not only are there forms of non-causal dependence other than supervenience; as we are about to observe, supervenience's ties to dependence are questionable. However, supervenience is a reasonable first approximation to bring out the kind of dependence appropriate for emergent properties, as is made explicit in my formulation of condition (1). Unlike traditional substance dualism, emergentism is a bottom-up alternative to physicalism. Supervenience is a natural way to locate the base from which emergent properties must emerge. Of course, the supervenience of conscious properties may be less critical for issues surrounding emergentism than its physical realizations. However, our current approach needn't force us to choose between them.

Finally, what of the relation of supervenience to dependence, item (d) on our roster of theses clamoring for elaboration? Much has been made of the fact that not only does a supervenient property vary with its base, but the former depends on and is explained by the latter. When supervenience has played a central role in recent definitions of emergentism, it has drawn its interest from the supposition that it elucidates the unidirectional dependence of the mental on the physical. However, upon closer inspection it is clear that 'X depends on Y' is wholly independent of 'X supervenes on Y'. Davidson (1980b, p. 214) implies that supervenience is at least a species of dependence when he declares that "mental characteristics are in some sense dependent, or supervenient, on physical characteristics." Nonetheless, Kim (1993b, p. 148) notes that supervenience, "even in the form of 'strong asymmetric covariance', does not give us dependence; in that sense, dependence is an addition to supervenience." Of course, there are dependents that do not supervene on their bases; the only question is whether there are supervenient properties not dependent on their subvenients. Here is a recipe for some cases: If X and Y each depend on Z, but not on each other, we may have a situation in which there can be no change in

X without a change in Y, the hallmark of supervenience. To get around this, I include dependence as an explicit add-on in condition (1). At worst, this is a harmless circumlocution because the only supervenience relations of interest in this context are those that intersect with the relevant dependencies. Still it seems clear that unadorned supervenience guarantees no more than the covariation of properties.

These remarks are not intended as an account of supervenience as such. They purport only to cement a basic understanding of its role in our more narrowly circumscribed deliberations. Let us then turn our attention to explanation.

2.4   Explanation Essentials

The explanatory shortfall declared in (2) distinguishes emergentism from competitors such as type and token physicalism, representationalism, and popular forms of functionalism. For the latter camps the instantiations of conscious properties are either *identical with* or *explained by* their material bases. Questions about identity and its relation to realization are broached in the next chapter, and the topic gets a fuller airing in part II. In this place I address only the absence of explanation cited in (2). Again, I have no overarching theory to propose. Still, the notion *explanation* is contentious enough so that its unceremonious employment could set off alarms. What I can offer is a certain measure of elucidation about its role in (2).

I intend my remarks to be compatible with a broad swathe of accounts of explanation. For example, my use of explanation should be neutral between ontological theories and communicative-act theories, that is, between those in which an explanation is a state of affairs in the world, which needn't be apprehended, and those in which it is nothing beyond the content of a speech act of explaining.[10] However, even if we are restricting ourselves to the ontology of explanations, context cannot be ignored. An explanation must always cite a genuine state of affairs, but not every state of affairs will be relevant to the circumstance resolved by an explanation. (See, e.g., Lewis 1986d, pp. 229–30; Menzies 2004, pp. 145–151.)

Nevertheless, ontological accounts make an important point for present purposes. Article (2), that there is no further explanation, could be

10. For further elaboration of this difference, see Strevens 2008.

restated as claiming that this supervenience relation is brute or primitive. Explanation needn't be mentioned, because the primitive character of the relation guarantees that nothing in reality could supply an explanation of the required sort. Moreover, talk of brute or primitive relations is unmistakably metaphysical, which is how things should fall out for this view. I place explanation up front only because it seems a more transparent way to introduce the point. Moreover, stating the bruteness in terms of the limits of inquiry may add heft to each of two contentious notions in philosophy by showing that our condition can be explicated in complementary ways.

The objective side of explanation shows up when we note that it is like information, another objective quantity whose existence does not depend on anyone's possessing it.[11] But this should not mislead us into inferring that how an explanation is stated makes no difference. Whatever one's ontological or communicative preferences, although 'A caused B' may be a candidate for an explanation in ordinary circumstances, and 'A = the cause of B', the utterance 'The cause of B caused B' shouldn't count as an explanation in anyone's estimation. It is inadmissible as an explanation because it conveys no more than that B has some cause or other.

This restriction might be contested by those who regard 'The cause of B caused B', (or, better yet, 'The cause of B causally explains B') as generating either an intensional or a compound context of a sort that invites scope distinctions.[12] It could be argued that if the phrase 'the cause of B' were given a wide-scope reading, it might serve as an explanation of B's occurrence. This doesn't strike me as sufficient to overturn a specification requirement. At most it indicates that the phrase 'the cause of B' points toward the existence of material available for an explanation, but doesn't yet specify it. What more does it say than that some explanation or other exists? It is akin to describing a building as a thing having some description or other.

No doubt the bare fact that A supervenes on B is itself something of an explanation of A. However, supervenience is an explanation of A's occurrence, existence, or instantiation, not, as such, of A's character, makeup, or (intrinsic) nature. Even claiming that B bestows on A its status doesn't remove the ambiguity between these readings. Given supervenience, the more robust explanation of A's nature would be what has been labeled

11. See Dretske 1981.

12. Thanks to Michael Weisberg for bringing this to my attention.

"superdupervenience."[13] In effect, (2) states that emergent properties aren't superdupervenient, and that is how I shall understand the claim that there is no further explanation of the supervenience of an emergent property.

Thesis (2) doesn't imply that the emergentist is committed to its properties' lacking all further explanation, only their lacking a further explanation of why those properties supervene on their bases. That leaves open the possibility of lateral or higher-level explanations, or perhaps further tie-ins with other properties at the level of the base or lower. For resultants (viz., non-emergents) there is an answer to the question why a property is supervenient on its base, even if the explanation isn't at hand. A mereological aggregate, for example, is explained by the assemblage and structure of its parts. C. D. Broad mentions a clock's movements resulting from those of its component parts. The way the base puts its parts together removes any mystery about why the whole exhibits its properties or propensities. And a functional property is explained by its role. Although emergent properties in my sense are supervenient on non-emergent properties, nothing in that fact sheds further light on why it is so.

It has been suggested that resting emergentism on the absence of explanations transforms a putatively metaphysical issue into an epistemological one.[14] The inclusion of the ontological conception of explanation and its gloss in terms of the brute nature of the supervenient dependence are inserted precisely to prevent this misunderstanding. But even an ontological conception of explanation should come with the proviso that the explanatory state of affairs be understandable in principle. To complete the case, it should be added that the intended lack of an explanation is the result of (a) the world's not containing one rather than the result of (b) limitations on human cognitive capacities preventing our species and its successors from being able to grasp a genuine explanation, which, for all that, is in principle apprehensible by other possible creatures. It is the world rather than the class of rational beings that lacks the wherewithal for explanation. This is the way Samuel Alexander (volume I, pp. 46–47) understood our predicament. I am content to follow him there.

13. The expression comes from Horgan 1993. Horgan credits Lycan with coining it.
14. See, e.g., Schröder 1998; J. Wilson 1999. Crane (2001) writes that the reliance on an absence of explanation marks emergentism's "epistemological attitude" rather than its "metaphysical content."

However, this clarification does not remove all grounds for grave concern. Stating outright that no such explanation exists may seem presumptuous. Isn't it premature for anyone to claim that he or she knows (or is certain) that this is so? Not only is it a negative existential, notoriously difficult to establish for any empirical subject, but this one seems particularly rash in light of the history of conceptual revolutions that have run roughshod over previous scientific certitudes. Any credible view should address this concern.

Of course, setting out thesis (2) as part of the definition no more implies that emergent aspects have been instantiated than a definition of 'dragon' implies that there are dragons. Still, to state that no explanation of a certain state of affairs is in the offing seems to impose a daunting requirement on any view. Moreover, bruteness, like unanalyzability, has not fared well historically. Nonetheless, emergentism requires no less *qua* ontological credo. My defense of it against the charge of its being a hasty and fragile thesis comes in two parts, one concerning fallibility and the other concerning rationality. The former is a minor matter; the latter gets us into more complicated issues of methodology. But before I set out this defense, allow me to emphasize that it is put forward not as an ultimate vindication of a claim that we know (2) with unshakeable certainty, but as a counterweight to the charge that (2) is a reckless speculation. Indeed, I believe that at the very least it places (2) on an equal footing with its physicalist counterpart.

Any such claim is certainly fallible in the generous sense that this term bears in philosophy. But some fallible claims are plainly warranted. Fallibility is a condition of most of what all of us, save the rare skeptic, regard as known. Setting aside a narrow band of propositions, it embraces just about everything to which each of us confidently subscribes—contingent and necessary truths alike. Admitting as much for the claim that there is no further explanation for E is no more venturesome than scrapping a Cartesian desideratum of metaphysical certainty.

As regards the plausibility of (2), the leading question ought to be not whether in fact we know there is no further explanation of emergent property E in terms of its base, but whether we are entitled to claim or believe that we know it. Knowledge that p requires that p be true, and with respect to the greatest share of what we know the actual truth of p falls outside a subject's introspective compass. However, that one's beliefs be well grounded is within the ken of the believer.[15] By 'well-groundedness' I intend a necessary condition for knowledge to which both epistemic internalists and externalists, despite their radically divergent approaches, might subscribe. In this liberal sense, it is not only a central condition for knowledge; it is the crucial ingredient for the plausibility of emergentism's claim to know that no further explanation of E in terms of its base is in the offing. If non-Gettierized, well-grounded belief is true, it is knowledge. The plausibility of claiming to know (2) rests on the well-groundedness of the claim that there are conscious properties that are not superdupervenient. So let us proceed to inquire whether this condition is satisfied in the present case.

The leading point is that for conscious mental states the possible moves have been fairly well plotted and the structure of the problem facing investigators seems clear. In addition, the methods are largely in place, though we can expect them to be enhanced by more sensitive instruments. In sum, the direction in which future inquiry will move is as thoroughly understood as we have any reason to expect in a mature science. The basic empirical research is what goes on in the so-called wet lab (or its computerized simulations). It will continue to uncover neural correlates of our conscious life as well as functional relationships that may be taken as evidence for a causal connection (e.g., alter neural state n and you alter conscious state c). This does not imply that such investigations are not open to astonishing results that only the wildest imagination would have anticipated. For example, Giacomo Rizzolatti's work on mirror neurons is an instance of an unexpected result that could be just such a major breakthrough. But mind-boggling as it is, it falls well within the parameters of the research programs alluded to here. Even for this standard research model the evidence demands some interpretation, but it will be firmly grounded in the research. That is both the current state of the science and its prospects for the future. This much can and should be accepted by all parties to the dispute.

Those sympathetic to physicalism have moved to a different level of theorizing about these matters, importing considerations more clearly external to ground-level research as just described. Those considerations seem to fall into one or more of three broad categories: (i) simplicity and coherence,

15. Although being well grounded or plausible does enhance the *likelihood* of truth in all but a few anomalous cases. See Vision 2005.

(ii) problems concerning the causal efficacy of the mental, and (iii) analogies with theoretical reductions elsewhere in science.[16] The first category is methodological, the second contains a large dose of conceptual argument, and the third depends on the strength of the analogy. No doubt each makes serious claims with which we will have to come to grips. However, even if we allow that such considerations are, speaking generously, empirical, they are supplements to, rather than ingredients of, the evidence on the ground and modest interpretations closely tied to the data gathered. That evidence provides the only direction in which continued research is currently imaginable, and by itself it doesn't establish physicalism. At this juncture I shall not examine in detail the issues raised by (i)–(iii). But if none of them were to hold sway, in the absence of a further external consideration we would be left with nothing more than the evidence mentioned earlier—that is, the evidence tethered to experimental practice. As a consequence, we would be without any reasonable inducement to proceed beyond the neural-mental correlations that neuroscience is capable of delivering. If we cannot expect to find anything more than this with controlled animal experiments and the diagnoses of mental deficits due to brain trauma or genetic mishaps in humans, then, in the absence of considerations on the order of (i)–(iii), we have good reason to claim to know that there is nothing more to be explained about the supervenience of the conscious on the neural.

Of course, a revolution in neuroscience could upset this picture. Let us then ask whether it is reasonable to withhold our firm belief about the direction of the current state of science in light of the possibility of a revolutionary breakthrough. Such an occurrence can never be definitively ruled out, but in the current case it would be an unimaginable cataclysm in an entrenched scheme of understanding. That it has occurred in some areas is slim evidence that one is in the works for any other particular field, and it grows slimmer the more the current science matures. It would be an act of faith rather than one of rationality to suppose that there must be, or is even likely to be, a change of this magnitude in the offing because some

16. Appeals to (i)–(iii) are usually taken as grounds for *identifying* the mental with the physical rather than *explaining* the former via the latter, and some philosophers have claimed that identities aren't explanations. However, these sum up the main and most promising routes I have found for venturing beyond the kind of empirical evidence obtainable by hands-on experimentation.

have occurred elsewhere in the past. Perhaps talk about such a prospect is no more than salubrious advice to be cautious in light of past events. But the more radical suggestion (the only one relevant to the objection under consideration) that we should withhold belief about our current carefully established results and methods would be the sort of advice we very reasonably reject for almost every other endeavor. Only an extreme skeptic would take the mere possibility of a conceptual overhaul to be a significant consideration when determining the plainly most reasonable attitude to adopt.

Indeed, taking agnosticism seriously on that basis suggests an intellectual disaster of even greater proportions. If a scientific revolution involving neuroscience, cognitive psychology, or a successor discipline occurs, and a new research program is established in its wake, the possibility of a yet further scientific revolution would cast just as large a shadow over it. If the prospect of an unforeseeable revolution were accepted as a reason to forgo confidence in thesis (2), we should also acknowledge that any new revelations about our conclusions or methods could themselves be undone by a succeeding revolution. If we were to take that prospect seriously enough to overturn knowledge claims about currently well-understood research, and given that such possibilities are always stamped "no expiration date," the lesson to be drawn would be to adopt a permanent suspension of belief. Should we wait that long, or should we read in the direction of our always-unfinished science an indication of what is achievable? Adopting universal skepticism gives no edge to any of the competing views, and certainly doesn't show that it is not eminently plausible to hold that the supervenience relation in our case is brute.

Of course, those who warn us of impending revolutions in a science rely on undercurrents in the present scene that seem to point toward imminent change. But when a case is made on those grounds, the argument can be over the estimate of the current inadequacies and need not rely on declamations regarding the history of science. Does the fact that the correlations themselves do not establish physicalism create the distance needed to make a warning about scientific revolution less than an airy gesture? My considered opinion is that it does not.

To sum up: Without importing considerations from outside the research, the sole current research trajectory is to examine and fiddle with neurological activity, both microscopically and through (no doubt enhanced) imaging techniques. And we have a good grasp that the sorts of things we shall find there are comparable to what has been found thus far—namely, causally suggestive correlations. Although this does not rule out unforeseeable conceptual revolutions, there seems no more reason to enter those into the equation here than one is inclined to do elsewhere. Such tolerance should also be extended to physicalism, which is a program rather than a *fait accompli*. But if I am even roughly right about the direction of the evidence we may expect, it is not merely a shot in the dark to deny emergent properties superdupervenience. Of course, the full justification for that declaration has yet to be played out. We must review what physicalists and representationalists have to say against it. For the present, however, I hope that what has been said thus far shows why an emergentist isn't defying the gods or the odds in claiming that there is no explanation of an emergent property's supervenience.

2.5   The Conceptual Gambit

In addition to the topic under discussion, a certain use of explanations in these discussions deserves special mention. I call this frequently adopted ploy The Conceptual Gambit. Basically, the move is that when a conscious property or capacity (call it Σ) appears to have features that elude the grasp of one's theory, Σ is construed as a *concept*, a mere device for explaining, rather than a property. A concept is a conventional perspective from which to view reality rather than a constituent of reality itself. The gambit has been a panacea for overcoming non-physicalist intuitions about cases, thereby allowing critics to reclassify unfavorable evidence. Its most obvious applications here are in section 3.6 (to classify Manhattan as a political invention rather than a land mass), in section 4.1 (to replace the threat of mental causation with mere causal explanation), in section 5.2 (to reduce the notion of the physical from the everyday to the scientifically serious), in sections 6.1–6.3 (to explain how we manage to conceive of the mental as distinct from the physical), and in section 6.6 (to explain how we can imagine sensations experienced by structurally diverse subjects). In some employments it works by showing first that its classification of Σs is merely conventional, thereby opening the path to regarding Σ as not carrying an ontological commitment. In others the gambit works by showing how explaining may cover both properties and the ontologically neutral concepts we construct for them.

The Conceptual Gambit is but a recent incarnation of one of the most ancient devices in philosophy: the practice of explaining why a vigorous appearance is not a reality. Such arguments have their legitimate deployments, The Conceptual Gambit no less. For example, the gambit may serve to bolster an independently strong argument denying the reality of a certain feature. However, in showing that the counter-evidence is deceptive it does presuppose that the view it bolsters is independently strong. Thus, the assessment of that view ultimately rests with the strength of the argument to which the gambit attaches. Or it may serve to test the limits of our ontological commitments. Still, as a way to reduce ontological commitments the gambit is quite general; applied consistantly across subject matters it could be used not only to eliminate the threat of mental causes but also to eliminate the material causes that its proponents use to co-opt the mental ones. (See, e.g., Quine 1966.)

However, my concern in this place is rather with The Conceptual Gambit's all-too-frequent misuse. As a self-standing argument it is no more than a bit of sophistry. Indeed, in some instances it is argued that there is a problem with Σ just because Σ can be treated as a concept rather than a property. To see that this stratagem when unsupported is sophistical, imagine that Σ represents your favorite example of any real property. It is possible to object to it by claiming that it is the mere appearance of Σ, its concept, rather than the property, that is the source of your conviction. Nothing appears to prevent this move once The Conceptual Gambit is legitimized as self-standing.

Naturally, whether it is a stand-alone ploy or whether it supplements an independent argument, The Conceptual Gambit plays an important role. By reclassifying a phenomenon or a datum, it removes what appears to be otherwise intractable evidence against a view. In each instance encountered in this work, it supplements an argument against an anti-physicalist view. However, in every case those arguments have weaknesses beyond their needs to appeal to the gambit. Thus, this stratagem must carry a heavy load in each instance, a load I am claiming it cannot bear.

Some—e.g., Hill (2009, pp. 48–56)—reject The Conceptual Gambit only because it can't be pulled off in every instance. However, whether or not it works for all cases, in every instance in which it is more than a mopping up of petty details in the shadow of powerful considerations, I claim that it should be considered a distracting ruse and withdrawn from circulation. Its easy availability encourages ready dismissal of data that warrant more careful and detailed investigation.

2.6   Some Alternative Formulations

There are versions of consciousness emergentism currently in play other than those mentioned thus far. It is beyond the scope of this essay to survey them all, but let's consider a few recent promising versions to better orient theses (1)–(3) with respect to its competition.

For Martina Nida-Rümelin what emerges is not a property but a substance, a subject of consciousness. Once an organism achieves a certain complexity, it becomes a new sort of subject, capable of taking on what she calls "consciousness properties." This new creature is no longer a body; it now has its body as a property. (It might be as primitive as a sea creature that senses comfort when it reaches warm water.) Although Nida-Rümelin's view of subjects and their place is elaborated in the works listed in the bibliography as 2007b and 2008, I shall concentrate on the work listed as 2007a, which bears directly on emergentism.

Nida-Rümelin's emergentism may be summed up in two propositions (2007a), p. 270):

It is nomologically necessary that new individuals (= subjects) emerge under certain physical conditions.

Nomologically all consciousness properties belong to the emergent subject.

The second proposition ensures the supervenience, with nomological necessity, of consciousness properties on its subject's physical properties.

Much of Nida-Rümelin's defense is contained in the further development of her notion of a subject of consciousness; it has volitional properties and operates on a principle of causation ("subject causation") altogether distinct from the event causation that marks the non-conscious world. But of more direct concern, she maintains that the only entrance to property emergence is through subject emergence. I am not sure I fully grasp her chain of reasoning, but perhaps it can be summed up as follows: There is no clear account of the distinction between emergent and non-emergent properties of, say, biological organisms. Thus, "any justification of the claim that a radical change has taken place when consciousness occurred must be based on the fact that the first instantiation of consciousness properties requires the coming into being of subjects of experience" (Nida-Rümelin 2007a, p. 274). The upshot is that we can sort out emergent properties only by citing them as properties of conscious subjects.

But what, more precisely, is Nida-Rümelin's objection to property emergence on the model of theses (1)–(3)?[17] Of course, she has her own positive account that brings in doings. But the most it could yield would be a sufficient condition for conscious propertyhood, not a necessary one. Moreover, we may well wonder how acknowledging conscious subjects allows one to make progress on the otherwise unprofitable task of singling out the emergent properties from the non-emergent ones. As she acknowledges, such subjects also have non-emergent properties (she cites shape, weight, and functional biological properties as examples on p. 274 of 2007a), so we would still have to perform a test to distinguish the two sorts of properties of conscious subjects. And how do we determine that such a subject exists? We can't determine it through its consciousness properties; having consciousness properties is supposedly explained by belonging to a conscious subject. Moreover, that such subjects are capable of "doings" and that they introduce a new mode of causation are equally futile here; whether a certain activity is a doing or whether a certain cause is the work of a subject rather than an event will be equally contentious issues unless we know that a conscious subject was involved.

Nida-Rümelin's ultimate appeal is that to deny the existence of such subjects implies that we are massively mistaken about the character of our world—a result to be avoided unless we have much stronger grounds for so pervasive a delusion. Not knowing her standards for strength of argument, I cannot comment further on this, other than to note that it has been a standard practice among philosophers who want to relegate what is ordinarily considered reality to mere appearance to explain why such appearances are not just bare delusions. Those hard-core metaphysicians couldn't be Nida-Rümelin's target here.

There is much in Nida-Rümelin's exposition that is insightful. But the charges brought against property emergentism are thin. Other than alluding to Beckermann in a note, she remarks that the common (viz., property) approach needs "a general theory of reduction" and a demonstration that consciousness properties are irreducible because they are "new and radically different from physical properties" (2007a, p. 274). Given the proliferation of reductionist concepts, I don't know that one or another general

---

17. "It is not a trivial task to account *in a precise manner* for the distinction between emergent properties of a whole and non-emergent properties of a whole (relative to certain microproperties and microrelations of microparts that make up the object)." (Nida-Rümelin 2007a, p. 274; emphasis added)

theory would be helpful. However, I agree that we need to explain just how emergent properties are irreducible. That has been the task of condition (2), while their "radical difference," their causal potential, is the work of chapters 4 and 5.

Other attempts at definitions have been made by writers who, though not themselves committed emergentists, have tried to give emergentism more than a dismissive characterization. Van Cleve (1990, pp. 222–223), attempting to formulate Broad's non-deducibility insight rigorously, affirms that a property is emergent if and only if it supervenes with nomological necessity, but not with "logical necessity," on the parts of its base. However, as McLaughlin (1997) notes, the additivity laws for weight and mass are contingent. Not only would including these features trivialize the notion of emergence; it would give precisely the result that we did not want for those properties. McLaughlin then amends this definition by appealing to what he cails "a fundamental law" (or "principle"): "A law L is a fundamental law if and only if it is not metaphysically necessitated by any other laws, even together with initial conditions." (p. 16) He then provides the following two-part definition of an emergent property. (I replace his numbering with (α) and (β).)

(M) If P is a property of w, then P is emergent if and only if (α) P supervenes with nomological necessity, but not with logical necessity, on properties the parts of w have taken separately or in other combinations; and (β) some of the supervenience principles linking properties of the parts of w with w's having P are fundamental laws. (p. 16)

Here (α) is, once again, Van Cleve's restriction. The fundamental laws of concern in (β) are relational; they connect a base to its property. On one reading this may amount to another way of putting what I attempted to convey by saying that there is no minimal explanation of the relation, that the relation is brute. But there are also some significant differences between McLaughlin's view and mine.

In a nomologically holistic world in which the body of laws hangs together, there are no individual laws unless a considerable number of other laws hold. In such a world, there are no fundamental laws in the relevant sense and so no emergent properties for McLaughlin's version. But there still could be emergent properties in my sense because there may be no further explanation of why the base should have that property supervenient on it. Of course, such holism could be demonstrably false. But it is difficult to know why its falsity should be a condition of emergentism.

Earlier I mentioned versions of emergentism that forgo supervenience altogether, others that are compatible with physicalism, and yet others that are epistemic rather than ontological theses. Also, emergentist claims have been entered on behalf of views that have denied a distinctive causal role of emergent aspects, in effect declaring such aspects epiphenomenal. With the exception of this last view, the others could be maintained side by side with theses (1)–(3). However, I hope I have provided ample reason for preferring my version. If I have, this review of alternatives, brief as it has been, should provide at least a glimpse of its comparative strengths.

2.7 Transition

We are now in a position to change our focus from supervenience to the more significant relation these sorts of properties would have to their base, *realization*. I have already noted that the realizer of an aspect is not identical per se with what it realizes. One might argue *from* the premise that B realizes A *to* the stronger conclusion that A and B are identical. But this does require an argument. To show that the claim of identity is a further step, consider the fact it would be at least odd to infer in the other direction— *from* A = B *to* the conclusion that A realizes B. Unlike identity, realization is asymmetric if not anti-symmetric, and suggests that the realizer has a kind of priority. These are not features found in identities.

While many philosophers agree that realization is not tantamount to identity, other equally thoughtful philosophers have not supported that view. It is important to get straight on this matter, not only because emergentism rejects the identity of its properties with those of its realizers, but also because a property's realizers are deeply involved in questions over the realized's causal status. Untangling that relationship may give us a leg up toward understanding the causal status of emergent properties stated in thesis (3).

All sorts of non-emergent tokens are realized physically. For example, actualized computational states and chess moves are realizations of something. For this reason, it would seem that our discussion of the relationship between causal powers of realizers and the realized is best conducted across a wide spectrum of cases rather than being focused on instances of emergent properties. However, any results we achieve will be directly transferable. The game's afoot! Let us turn our attention to those issues.

3 Coincidence: Realization and Identity

3.1 From Supervenience to Realization

Precision is an asset and formalization is its ally. But the price of devising rigorous specifications for supervenience has been to sacrifice a central feature of its initial attraction. As I noted in the preceding chapter, we lose the motivating idea that a supervenient token asymmetrically depends on its base. It has been maintained that it is harder to see how a conscious property is autonomous or even distinguishable from its base if we shift to the idiom of *realization*, which brings in its wake the idea of a grounding in the more fundamental. I also have noted that, although the notions differ, their extensions overlap so substantially in cases of present interest that it is allowable to speak interchangeably here of a conscious property's *supervening on* or *being realized by* (or *in*) a physical one. However, let us see how things fall out when we concentrate on what it is for a token to be realized in the physical.

For whatever reason, there has been less enthusiasm thus far for formal specifications of realization than for supervenience. Consequently, it carries along a fund of prior associations, and this has in turn created obstacles to framing strict formulations. Indeed, it is not easy to give a general account of realization without pressing into service near near-synonyms, such as 'embodiment', 'implementation', or 'constitution'. For starters, let's say that a property P's realization is a lawfully sufficient condition, other than P itself, in which the realizer belongs either to the same or a coincident individual that exhibits P. Multiple realization is then the condition under which a single type or instance of a property could be realized in more than one way. Thus, a move in chess of a white rook from h1 to h5 could be realized in ivory pieces, in plastic pieces, in pixels, in descriptions sent by surface mail, or even in an utterance.

Nothing realizes itself; as was noted in section 2.3, realization is neither reflexive nor symmetrical. If a neurological configuration realized a mental property, it would be problematic for the uses to which physicalists want to put it were it also possible that the mental property realized the neurological configuration. For example, whereas a slab of marble may realize a statue, the statue does not realize the slab of marble. As currently intended, a realizer must be more concrete, more grounding, or more basic than what it realizes. There is no good sense in which a statue is more concrete than its matter. There are also powerful reasons for holding that realization is *anti*-reflexive and *anti*-symmetrical, but in order to preserve an option (favored by some) of using realization as a step toward proving identity I shall claim only that they are *non*-reflexive and *a*symmetrical. Realization and identity are still distinguishable, but on this concession it is open to one to offer further reasons for showing that the realizer is identical with the property it realizes. (In some cases the additional reasoning has consisted in no more than citing spatial coincidence combined with a refutation of arguments against identity.) That view is not without baggage. Recall that if A is realized by B, and A = B, B is also realized by A, thereby losing the advantage of a grounding in the more fundamental. Informally, we come a bit closer to grasping realization by saying that when a property is "instantiated" (another near-synonym) it is instantiated by a physical feature that is in principle describable without invoking the character of the property instantiated.

In the sequel I shall argue for two theses: first, that there is a presumption that many properties, including conscious ones, are not identical with what realizes them, and, second, that once this relationship is better understood it opens the door to the prospect that both realizer and realized may serve as non-competitive causes of a single effect. If these results hold for realized properties generally, the case will be even stronger for the relation between supervenient properties and their subvenients. We lose nothing, and indeed we gain dialectical traction, by making that case in terms of realization.

For the sake of a clear contrast, let old-school physicalism—the view that conscious properties are identical with neurological aspects—represent the opposing view about their relation. I am not glossing over the fact that among physicalists and naturalists there is disagreement over the choice of realizers. Non-reductivists, representationalists, functionalists, and evolutionary teleologists may favor yet other candidates. Their views are considered in due course. But it will simplify without biasing our inquiry if we take an internal physical property, the neurological one, to represent the party of identifiers for the physical realizer. The chief question I want to raise is whether there is anything to be said on behalf of or against identity claims in light of the admission that conscious properties are realized in physical stuffs.

3.2   Realization and Identity

There is realization and then there is identity. A central condition for identity is the indiscernibility of identicals:

$$(\forall x)(\forall y)[(x = y) \rightarrow (\forall \Phi)(\Phi x \leftrightarrow \Phi y)].$$

That is to say: For any x and y, if x and y are identical, any property of the one is a property of the other. This implies

$$(\forall x)(\forall y)[(\exists \Phi)(\Phi x \ \& \ {\sim}\Phi y) \rightarrow x \neq y].$$

Or, for any x and y, if there is a property of the one that is not a property of the other, x and y must be different—two instead of one. (I shall have occasion to appeal to this later, but first I return to realization.)

In the present case, realizers are often seen as resolving otherwise intractable problems having to do with mental causation. Some even hold that the realizer having all the causal potency in the relation is realization's defining feature. However, even if realizers, or series of them, embody the causal powers of their realized properties, this seems the wrong place to locate that relation. More central is the fact that the thing or property (mental or otherwise) *comes into existence or gets instantiated* via being realized in something concrete. Whether a realizer or a series of them accounts for the realized's causal potential will be determined by additional considerations concerning what is involved for something to exist or to be instantiated. But at first glance a realizer's causal potential is a secondary matter—realized entities or properties could not be actualized without being realized.

Realization is a form of constitution, though not all constitution is realization. For example, whereas a state of affairs may constitute the truth of a proposition, it doesn't realize or embody that truth. Like realization, constitution in general is neither reflexive nor symmetrical.[1] However, once again to avoid begging the question, I don't foreclose on the possibility of further arguments aimed at establishing identities between constituters and their constituted. I emphasize only that an identity founded on constitution requires a further step.

Following in the traditions of a different set of taxonomists, there are lumpers and splitters. Lumpers opt for identity, splitters for difference. Let us introduce the subject with a classical case that has motivated philosophical splitters: a statue and a lump of clay. Splitters might call this realization-without-identity (RwI); lumpers maintain that the statue and the clay are identical. Cases of RwI have been a general strategy for combating physicalism, although in this instance both the statue and the lump of clay are physical. And a few other differences between the statue scenario and our topic warrant mention. First, the statue concerns individuals rather than properties. Second, mental properties, unlike statues, aren't artifacts. However, our immediate concern is only with constitutional realization. The lessons we can take from it will bear on the extent to which realization of any sort fares with respect to identity claims.

In what follows, I set out the reasons splitters offer for RwI, consider the main objections raised by lumpers, and, finally, argue that the lumpers' arguments have not dislodged the case for RwI. Let's begin with an instance of this sort of setup and the arguments for it.

Imagine a clay statue of Pericles. For convenience, I'll call the statue itself, not what it represents, 'Pericles', and the lump of clay out of which the statue is formed 'L'. Splitters contend that Pericles is one thing, L another. This is not altered by the fact that statues and their matter simultaneously occupy the same location and share a great many properties (e.g., weight, size, shape, color). For splitters, statues and their matter are merely coincidental objects. The case for this can be summarized in two points.

L's existing before and/or after Pericles. L may exist before the statue is molded. For simplicity, suppose that all and only an earlier ball of clay has gone into the formation of Pericles. If L existed before Pericles was created, it had properties the statue lacked, such as being round, which would

---

1. Shoemaker (2007, p. 23) seems to endorse the notion of a first-order property as one that is "self-constituted." He is entitled to introduce that convention, as well as conventions of being self-realized or self-caused. However, this innovation departs from the typical role that constitution is meant to play in these investigations.

differentiate the two. Furthermore, if while the clay is still wet we reshape it into a goat, thereby destroying Pericles, L continues to exist and to have properties that Pericles lacks. How could they be identical when one constitutes (or is) a statue of a goat at *t* and the other doesn't (or isn't)?

We needn't require that L *actually* exist before Pericles. Suppose I mold Pericles' bottom half with one lump of clay, its upper body with another lump, and then put them together to form my statue. Then L and Pericles come into existence simultaneously. The argument depends only on the supposition that Pericles *needn't* come into existence in this way for L to realize it.

Pericles' outlasting L. Be as liberal as you like, within reason of course, about conditions for re-identifying L. We don't take L to have disappeared if it loses a few atoms, or even if a tiny fraction of its mass is broken off. But *qua* lump of matter, L can't survive many of the indignities that might befall a persisting Pericles. The statue may lose a feature (e.g., Venus de Milo losing her arms, the Sphinx with a large gap where its nose once protruded) while remaining the same statue, but L will not be the same lump of clay after a considerable loss of its matter. Worse yet, some of the original clay may be replaced, just as the ceiling of the Sistine Chapel and Leonardo's *Last Supper* were retouched to restore their original brilliance. The lump could not continue being L after such considerable changes, but there may be the same statue. Such cases generalize easily. Compare a building, say, whose plumbing, electrical circuits, and porch have all been replaced, or a car, whose front fender and radiator hose have been replaced. The clay of the statue is one thing, the statue another. In spite of this, if I hit an intruder over the head with Pericles, I have also hit him over the head with L.

The claim being tracked here and through the polemics that follow is that an object falling under a sortal is not identical with the type of stuff constituting it.[2] Again, this doesn't depend on Pericles' actually continuing to exist after L. The statue may have exploded, destroying both it and L at once. The point is that L *could* go out of existence while Pericles did not.

2. Sortalhood is here a syntactic category, belonging to concepts or terms that take numerical qualifications (are countable), and definite and indefinite articles. There are no metaphysical requirements—say, occurring at a certain level of detail—for sortals in this sense. Even so bland a word as 'thing' passes the test as a sortal term as long as we can talk of one, two, or three things, or of *the* thing and *a* thing.

Although it simplifies our discussion to use a conventional object such as a statue for illustration, a multitude of natural objects are also composed of stuffs with which it appears they cannot be identical. Seas and lakes retain their identity while undergoing constant changes in the water composing them (see Heraclitus on rivers), dunes are composed of constantly shifting grains of sand, a sample of carbon remains stable with an exchange of neutrons in its atomic core, trees periodically add new rings and shed leaves, and so on. Conversely, if we were to take all the water from a pond in Minnesota and reconstitute it as a pond in the Gobi desert, it wouldn't be the same pond.[3] A set of persistence conditions, rather than artifactuality, is our quarry. More will be said about this in connection with my answer to the last (third) objection to RwI.

Next, L not only constitutes Pericles, it *composes* the latter. In the preceding chapter I contrasted the compositional and emission paradigms for emergent aspects. Ultimately, the relation of immediate concern is modeled on emission. More will be said in defense of this in chapter 8, but here is a brief preview. Whereas we can use the spatial co-location of L and Pericles as a premise in an argument for their identity, we cannot use the spatial co-location of pain and incidents in an organism's cortical stream *as a premise* from which to argue for their identity. If pains are spatially co-located with neural activity, this is but a consequence of their identity with the latter. Thus, some may view the example of a statue as an inappropriate model for the subject of interest. I maintain, to the contrary, that it supplies a direct and illuminating lesson for the brand of emergentism under discussion. If it is shown that L and Pericles are not identical, that serves well enough to illustrate the general principle currently on the table—the difference between being *different* and being *distinct* or *discrete*. The present point is only that the spatiotemporal coincidence of the statue and its matter, for at least part of the existence of each, shows that they aren't discrete (or distinct) entities. The arguments that have been mustered for RwI have purported to show that in spite of their non-distinctness they are different. It is the combination of non-discreteness and difference, despite

---

3. The same doesn't seem to be true of artifacts. Ships, furniture, paintings, and jewelry are certainly mobile. And artifacts that weren't designed for mobility may retain their identity after relocation because of their historical importance. For example, the Temple of Karnak is now in the Metropolitan Museum of Art, and a span once called London Bridge is now in Arizona.

any remaining dissimilarities between artifacts and natural objects, that I am emphasizing.

3.3   Objections

Lumpers have been quick to respond. I shall examine what I take to be their strongest, or at least salient, objections. However, in evaluating their remarks I largely, though not entirely, bypass a rarefied metaphysical hypothesis that blocks even homespun physical objects from a basic ontology. That is the view that quite purposefully rules out, along with artifacts, prototypical physical items such as islands, meteors, pelicans, electrical discharges, and mangos. I rule it out not because it isn't worthy of consideration, but because it would be out of place here. The type and token physicalists who line up against emergentism do not, by and large, rest their case on formulas that exclude widely recognized physical things, including neurons. Their physicalism would lose much of its attraction for them if it could be said that the situation of emergents is no worse off than that of neurons. Yet, whereas much of austere metaphysics concerns only an internecine squabble between competing physicalisms, and doesn't involve their disagreements with emergentism, some of their points bear on the place of emergent tokens in their scheme, and we must consider those metaphysical reasonings to the extent that they equip the lumpist arsenal.

The outcome of the splitter's argument is that Pericles and L are *different*, are two, not that they are *discrete*. Perhaps lumpers require discreteness for there to be two. Although that could be an underlying factor in their dissatisfaction with splitting, to the best of my knowledge it is not among the most clearly articulated lumpist reasons. Rather, the following appear to be the lumpists' most prominent objections to the conclusion that L and Pericles are different:

(I)   Claiming that the statue and its clay are different leads to paradox. However, if we are careful in describing their relationship, there is no difficulty in maintaining that the lump of clay became the statue when it was shaped with that intention: the statue is no more than a temporary stage in the history of that lump.

(II)   Persistence conditions, and the dispositions of which they form a proper subset, are subjunctive, and thereby the properties constituting them are modal. Modal properties of objects cannot differ unless the

categorical properties that underlie them differ. Because Pericles and L
share all their strictly categorical properties, they must be identical (that
is, if Pericles is even a genuine entity).

(III)   Artifacts are ontological second-raters. For some thinkers, there are
no such ontologically serious things; or, if there are any material artifacts,
we must cut away what makes them conventional so as to be able to identify them with their strictly physical constitution.

Let us look at these three objections and some of their offshoots.

3.4   Artifacts as Temporary Properties of Matter

It seems as if taking Pericles and L to be different things leads to a paradox.
Suppose that L weighs 10 pounds and Pericles weighs 10 pounds. If they
are different things, shouldn't the scale on which both are weighed read 20
pounds (Lewis 1986e, pp. 252–253)?

However, once again, to say that Pericles and L are different is not to say
that they are discrete (or distinct). I am not suggesting that identity and
difference don't form a dichotomy; this is not a prescription to revive the
notorious nineteenth-century Teutonic dodge "degrees of identity." When
considering features of different things, we typically think of things that
are also discrete. But the normal does not imply the necessary. Different
non-discrete phenomena can't be measured entirely by what is applicable to some different subjects that are also discrete; otherwise the simple
expedient of spatial overlap would sink the possibility of such differences.
10-pound Pericles and Pericles' 4-pound torso are certainly different. Then
shouldn't the scale read 14 pounds when Pericles and Pericles' torso are on
it? (Cf. Thomson 1998, p. 170, n. 5.) Even for those who hold that Pericles
is not a thing, L by itself can generate a similar conundrum. Suppose L
weighs 10 pounds and its upper half weighs 5 pounds. They are distinguishable, although not discrete. Extending the lumper's reasoning, the scale on
which we weigh L should read 15 pounds.

False paradoxes aside, the lumper raising this complaint may also claim
to be able to handle this identity in a smooth, non-paradoxical way by
maintaining that the statue is nothing more than a temporary property
of the clay. The clay becomes the statue at a certain time; thus, the statue
was there, though not *qua* statue, before the clay was so shaped. This
doesn't show that the identity thesis *must* be true, but by neutralizing the

distinction between sortals and their matter it undermines the argument that our ordinary way of individuating things *precludes* their identity. Still, this maneuver addresses only the first of our reasons for distinguishing Pericles from L—what I have called L's existing before and/or after the statue. Complications arise when we throw into the mix the second consideration: the statue's outlasting L. Consider a case in which parts have been replaced. Suppose, for example, that the sculptor doesn't like the attitude of one of Pericles' legs, takes that large chunk of clay off, and replaces it with another piece that she has first reshaped in a slightly different pose. Pericles survives the change, but L has been replaced by a different lump, L*. If we want to say that Pericles = L, we should also want to say that Pericles = L*. However, L ≠ L*—an inconsistency.

The lumper may use one of two strategies—splicing or slicing—to get around this difficulty. Each has a cost. I turn first to splicing.

Rather than taking L as our lump, suppose we take the union L ∪ L* to be the stuff composing Pericles. Accordingly, Pericles is still a property of the lumpish sum L ∪ L*. This method of individuating stuffs becomes truly nightmarish when extended quite generally, and naturally, to persistents. To take an extreme case, consider a thousand-year-old cathedral repaired with new materials and/or taking additions every few months. The formula for the stuff constituting it would be unmanageably long, and would require a reference to some materials that weren't discovered or invented when the building originally became a cathedral. And of course the list of such odd stuffs would grow without an end in sight. The kinds of stuffs we would then need would be flagrantly *ad hoc*. This method might be too bizarre to attract serious lumpers.

A more likely strategy for lumpers would be slicing. Divide Pericles into time slices, or at least transitory slabs: Pericles at t is identical with L at t, and Pericles* at t' is identical with L* at t'. While L at t ≠ L* at t', this is no longer problematic because there is no one thing that is identical with both of them; that is, Pericles at t ≠ Pericles* at t'. They are distinct segments in the history of the series that is Pericles. But why? Pericles is one series, L a different, if overlapping, series. What non-question-begging reason is there to consider the former no more than an extended segment of the latter? Only four-dimensionalism could save this and the previous move, and we shall see when examining objection III that just the same problems arise whether or not one adopts four-dimensionalism.

If the slicing maneuver is to succeed, it requires an independent reason to adopt a time-slice ontology. Aside from the fact that such ontologies have polemical burdens (e.g. for their accounts of causation, and other situations that have temporal continuity built into their specifications), this would immerse us in the wider discussion of revisionist ontologies that we forswore at the outset. Why do I insist that the reason to adopt this ontology must be independent of the current issue? To begin with, it is important to distinguish original arguments or justifications for adopting a view from what I shall call *alibis* in its defense. This isn't meant to denigrate that notion; some alibis are perfectly legitimate. But they are defenses—let us suppose effective ones—against objections, not initial grounds for adopting a position. A time-slice ontology appears to remove a potent objection to the identity of a property with its realizer. But it is not a reason for inaugurating the view that a property and its realizer are always or presumptively identical. Adopting the ontology *only* to neutralize an argument for RwI is desperate, a groundless extension of our current way of viewing the world. To remove the taint of the *ad hoc*, we need an independent set of reasons for favoring a time-slice ontology. It is understandable that such considerations don't intrude into the more localized issues concerning realizations that arise between lumpers and splitters.

Moreover, slicing no more ensures identity than it ensures persistence if a time slice of Pericles has different potentials for preceding and successive slices than one of L. That brings us to the second objection.

3.5 Identity and Persistence Conditions

A widely acknowledged starting point in these discussions is *the grounding principle*:

(GP) For all x and for all modal properties Φ, Φ is (or must be) grounded in x's non- modal (or categorical) properties.[4]

4. "There must," Heller writes, "be some nonmodal basis for the modal differences between the lump of clay and the statue." (1990, p. 31) And Dean Zimmerman asks, rhetorically, "Should not two physical objects constructed in precisely the same way out of qualitatively identical parts have the same capacities . . . [?]" (1995, p. 87) For versions explicitly tailored for dispositional properties, see Jackson and Pettit 1990a, p. 204, n. 17; Stoljar 2001.

Dispositional properties are modal. The dispositional properties of an F, taken broadly, include its abilities and inabilities (what F *can* or *cannot* do) and its capacities and incapacities (what F *can* and *cannot* undergo, what F *can* or *cannot* acquire). The persistence conditions of a thing's type are part and parcel of its sortal classification. They are essential to being a member of that sort, and in various cases being of that sort is a necessary condition of an individual's identity. The conditions may be loose, may be penumbrally indeterminate, and may allow for local variation, but if one hasn't the slightest notion of the sorts of changes in an F that entitles one to regard it as *the same F* then one certainly hasn't grasped what it is to be an F. For example, without a clue about F's persistence conditions one couldn't distinguish a single glance as the whole from F as a continuant. Persistence conditions comprise the changes something *can* or *cannot* undergo while preserving its identity, its *ability* or *inability* to withstand certain changes. Classification by sortal is thereby modal and calls for restriction by (GP). (The grounding principle, if true, is a necessary truth; assume for the sake of argument that this is nomological necessity.)

In our example, Pericles is classified sortally, and thus modally, as a statue; to classify L as a lump of clay is to supply its sortal property. (GP) tells us that such classifications must be grounded in categorical properties. On the most natural reading, we should infer that any difference in modal properties must be reflected by a difference in categorical properties. But there are no differences in the categorical properties of Pericles and L. It follows that they cannot differ in their sortal (= modal) properties.

Categorical properties may be relational; we must not conflate *categorical* with *intrinsic*. In addition to having the same shape, mass, height, density, and color, Pericles and L are the same distance from the prime meridian, are shaped by the same hand, are viewed by the same museum patrons, stand in front of the same wall, and so on. Properties in the second set are both categorical and relational (that is, extrinsic). The inclusion of relational properties is important to the plausibility of (GP). As Judith Thomson (1998, p. 171, n. 5) noted, if Honda A in my garage is intrinsically indistinguishable from Honda B in yours, it is possible for Honda A to undergo a replacement of parts without Honda B's doing so. Honda A's capacity for change is thereby independent of its *intrinsic* categorical properties, which are the same as Honda B's. However, adding Honda A's external properties—e.g., its relation to my garage—distinguishes it from Honda B categorically.

Nor is it clear that all the properties Pericles fails to share with L are modal in any way. Pericles sports a look of triumph, but does L? Moreover, recall that constitution and realization are non-reflexive; whereas Pericles is constituted by and realized in L, L isn't constituted or realized in L. According to Kit Fine (2008), a large number of non-modal properties are predicable of a statue but not of its matter. Those properties include being Romanesque, being admired, and being ugly. That seems plausible, but I won't press the point further. Instead let us assume that the relevant sortal properties are modal. I am construing the modality as *de re*—as the ascription of a modal property to a subject. Although Fine and I both hold that the lumper fails, our responses rest on different lumper arguments or on different interpretations of the same arguments. Fine reviews the prospects for having the lumper place modal properties inside an opaque context in order to show that they are not genuine properties. I do not deny that there may be lumper reasonings of that sort. If there are, there is no need to rehearse Fine's serious objections to them. But it seems clear that at least some lumper arguments are faithfully captured by regarding their relevant modal properties as *de re*, that is by (GP), as attested by the passages quoted in note 4.

Still, it is uncertain what lesson we are meant to draw from (GP). Is it that, despite appearances, L possesses all the elements of the persistence conditions for Pericles? That Pericles doesn't possess them? That non-categorical predicates don't express *genuine* properties? That whether or not they express properties, they are not relevant to indiscernibility tests? Lumpers sometimes omit from their discourses which of the many difficulties for realization without identity (GP) has for its target. Things might unravel if we were to probe more into any of those choices. However, there is no need to pursue the matter here. The grounding principle by itself is problematic enough to permit us to set aside further inquiries about its role in the larger argument.

The usual support for a principle in this family has been to cite paradigms and generalize from them. The brittleness of a pane of glass depends on the non-crystalline structure of its molecules, and the solubility of a sugar cube in water depends on its being a polar compound whose charged molecules break away from its crystal and are wrapped in water molecules. Underlying all these familiar examples of dispositional properties seem to be *states*. There are certainly asymmetric dependencies in these cases, and the sensible conclusion is that the objects' structural features account for their dispositional properties rather than vice versa. This relationship is then extended to that between all modal properties and the categorical properties of the objects possessing them.

However, this explanation—that dispositional properties must somehow have their foundation (or even their identity) in something's categorical properties—is questionable. None of the examples employed to show that dispositions always depend on underlying states result in states that do not themselves have further dispositional properties. Let us see how that plays out.

Either there are ultimate physical particles (call them proto-atoms) or there aren't. Of course, if we were to discover proto-atoms, being assured that we had indeed reached the ultimate level very likely would still remain unresolved. And if there are no proto-atoms, then, in principle, the physical analysis of particles leads to an infinite regress. This betokens the problem of "causal drainage," to be raised in chapter 4; it mounts a serious challenge to arguments against independent mental causation. For the present, however, I ignore this complication and assume here that there are proto-atoms—an assumption certainly favorable to (GP).

The notion of a proto-atom seems perfectly coherent. Proto-atoms could be superstrings, or quanta of one or another sort, or perhaps Higgs bosons. None of that matters here. Although they will have properties (e.g., location and motion), they will not have further structure. *Ex hypothesi*, there is nothing to count as components of their structures. Then is it reasonable to ascribe dispositions to proto-atoms? If we suppose them to lack all dispositions, nothing would happen to or for them under any conditions—a fatal consequence for any claim that everything else that happens can be traced to the interactions of fundamental particles. If two proto-atoms were to come into contact *without any dispositions*, they couldn't bounce off each other, explode, stick together, change into something else, move off with a new (or the same) velocity, give off signals, make a noise, or dance about. Any of those happenings would manifest a dispositional property—a tendency to do one thing or another upon contact. Those are no less dispositions than a sugar cube's habit of dissolving in water. Proto-atoms would be super-inert. Because everything physical supposedly depends on what happens at the micro level, if the world bottoms out in this way, how can anything happen at macro levels? Moreover, if there are basic laws about the activity of these entities, How is it possible that they do not involve dispositional traits, potentialities, of proto-atoms? An alternative might be that any of a multitude of things would happen, with no probability for any one of those eventualities. Proto-atom reactions would be random. But in those circumstances the disjunction of those happenings would still form a single disposition, or the disposition to react randomly.

Dispositions are relational, and some would say they are extrinsic. There is a view stating that a primitive something's essential characteristics must be intrinsic—perhaps a haecceity or a quiddity—because its relational features are all contingent. (See, e.g., Lewis 1986b and section 4.4 of the present work.) But in a possible world in which proto-atoms did not have equally primitive dispositions at least contingently—say, as a matter of natural law—we wouldn't have to worry about other modal properties, because there would be none. In such a world, the proto-atoms responsible for anything else would be supremely epiphenomenal.

I conclude that if there are proto-atoms they must have dispositions. These will be as primitive as a proto-atom's other properties. There is really no sense attaching to the supposition that they somehow depend on the object's categorical properties than there is to the supposition that the proto-atom's categorical properties depend on their dispositions. On this most natural interpretation of the sort of dependence envisioned, (GP) is simply false. Structural properties of macroscopic objects may have the advantage of being more useful in explanations of the object's dispositional properties than the dispositional properties are in explanations of its structural ones. However, that is not what a lumper needs to sustain the objection to the splitter claim that statues and their stuffs are distinguished by their divergent persistence conditions.

David Chalmers (1996, p. 153) flirts with this view, though concentrating on the relationality of the properties rather than on their dispositionality, when he writes that

physical theory only characterizes its basic entities relationally, in terms of their causal and other relations to other entities. Basic particles, for instance, are largely characterized in terms of their propensity to interact with other particles. . . . Reference to the proton is fixed as the thing that causes interactions of a certain kind, that combines in a certain ways with other entities, and so on. . . .

However, Chalmers ultimately comes to the conclusion that there are intrinsic properties *underlying* these relational ones (1996, p. 375, n. 29).

Still, the most that his completed argument is designed to show is that the basic particles cannot have relational (or dispositional) properties without also having intrinsic ones. Only pre-existing loyalty to a counterpart of (GP) for relational properties would get one from there to the conclusion that intrinsic properties must underlie relational ones.

In light of the foregoing, let us re-examine what was stated about the ordinary, macroscopic cases. Again, the states cited as responsible for the dispositions themselves have other dispositions. For example, certain atoms bond, so they must have a tendency to do so under given conditions. And within atoms, neutrons are disposed to attach to protons, but not to electrons. And aren't the positive and negative charges of subatomic particles themselves dispositional properties? In fact, I can't imagine any of the building blocks of the states cited as responsible for a disposition that do not themselves possess further dispositions. Whereas we are able to account for some specific dispositions in terms of states, the attempt to account for dispositionality in general by this method leads to a regress that the defender of (GP) is never in a position to close off. If proto-atoms can have ungrounded dispositions, there seems to be no reason why macro-objects can't have them. Take away the categorical property and you remove the disposition; but equally, take away the disposition and you remove the categorical property. Could a certain mass exist without its disposition to have certain physical effects? Thus, no matter what level of structural properties we arrive at, the alleged categorical base will not be dispositionless.

Lying behind this application of (GP) is a wider and more basic issue regarding dispositions. Many leading philosophers reject the bona fides of unanalyzed dispositional properties, those that can be elucidated at best in terms of subjunctive conditionals. On this battleground, *realism* for dispositional properties is the view that dispositions are nothing over-and-above the internally structured states that support their manifestations. Thus Kim (2006, p. 122) compares the two views by way of competing glosses of the sentence 'x is soluble in water':

[Irrealism] If x is immersed in water, x dissolves.

[Realism] x is in a certain internal state S . . . such that when x is immersed in water, S causes x to dissolve.

Unreduced subjunctive conditionals have been anathema in some philosophical circles. They are not amenable to popular types of regimentation.

It is inferred that without more tractable support, dispositional predicates are indicative of no more than *apparent* properties. But it is difficult to see how primitive dispositions can be averted. Without them primitive states would be wholly ineffectual. Rather than acquiescing in the orthodoxy illustrated by the above options, the arguments of this section recommend readjusting our standard of the real: being a conditional property needn't boil down to being a property only on a condition. Dispositions may be no less real or basic than what is taken for their underlying states, even if the possibility of further explication is out of reach.

3.6 Artifacts and Ontology

According to the third objection, there are no artifacts in a serious ontology; or, if there are any, they don't possess the features that enabled us to distinguish them from their material components. Artifacts are *non entia gratia* in a number of ontological schemes. Of course, on some ontologies all or most workaday physical objects disappear too. Among them some are based on the failure to obtain satisfactory re-identification, persistence, and individuation conditions for familiar three-dimensional objects. Defenders typically refine folk methods of identifying things with stricter principles of mereology. On some such ontologies (see, e.g., Heller 1990), the world consists of individual four-dimensional objects; on others (see, e.g., van Inwagen 1990), only a subclass of the material things recognized in folk metaphysics exist, perhaps only organisms, on yet others (see, e.g., Rosen and Dorr 2002), nothing exists save ultimate simples, because the principles of mereology don't support compounding. We needn't enter this thicket of competing primal schemes, because it isn't their objective to explain how the folk actually distinguish among the sorts of items that fall on the pretense side of their metaphysics. On the aforementioned ontologies, all such distinguishables may be consigned to the featureless porridge of conventionality. I turn first to the more specific reasons for rejecting artifacts.

For starters, to be an artifact it is required that a cognizer *intend it* to be that particular (sort of) thing. Perhaps the intentional activity amounts to no more than picking something up and displaying it, or, say, using it as a doorstop. Without at least this much mentality in its inauguration, every stone, every shrub, every ocean, every bird, and anything else on the planet would qualify as an artifact. But the demand for an intention covers a multitude of alleged sins. Is reading the origin of a thing into its current identity objectionable *per se*? Perhaps what is objectionable is not the inclusion of the origin, but the fact that this origin involves a mere mental state or property. Perhaps it is not an appeal to a certain type of origin that is objectionable, but that products requiring mental states in their identity conditions must be conventional rather than natural. Or perhaps the origins, mental states, and so on are themselves regarded as conventional. Or it might be a combination of these. Those are distinct strands emanating from an objection to the view that an entity's origins could be included among its identity conditions, and we shall eventually have to pull apart at least the more promising strands for closer examination. I begin with simple origins.

The sortal under which an artifact falls implies the persistence conditions that are key to distinguishing it from its stuff. The material itself—say, our lump of clay—would be the same no matter how it came about. Michael Rea voices a concern representative of many physicalists when he denies that the manner in which anything originates could have any bearing on its standing: "[W]hether members of a set S compose anything depends only on how they are arranged—it does not depend upon human intentions or attitudes toward the arrangement." (1998, p. 352) This claim may be developed in either of two directions. If we view artifacts as requiring originating intentions or attitudes, it implies that there are none. Or this might be the view that there are artifacts, but that human originating intentions or attitudes have nothing to do with their being so classified; only their arrangement matters. The latter appears to be Rea's considered view. Following up on the previous passage, he states that he "earlier reject[ed] this sort of conventionalism. . . . So if a *statue* is a genuine kind, then anything that is a statue must be so simply by virtue of how its parts are arranged, regardless of how it came into existence. . . . If *David* is a statue, any qualitative duplicate of *David* will be a statue as well." (p. 354) Because Rea is not denying outright that the *David qua* artifact exists, perhaps he is not denying outright the existence of artifacts. Let us examine that interpretation first.

On the same page as the first of our two quotes (p. 352), Rea offers the following condition, which, for handy cross-reference, I will call (RK): "For any kind K, arranging objects K-wise is both necessary and sufficient for bringing an object of kind K into existence." Artifactual kinds are indeed

kinds. Consider the implications of removing the requirement that an artifact be produced or originated by an intention or an attitude. The only
thing that matters is the arrangement of its parts; something is a statue
because, and only because, it has the shape of a statue.

Earlier I noted one difficulty associated with this condition: How are
we to prevent *everything* from belonging to an artifactual kind? Of course
not everything looks like the *David*. But if the sinuous forms produced by
Calder are sculptures, why isn't every tree branch a sculpture? Nor does
(RK) solve a certain problem raised by splitters: The statue of Pericles could
still go out of existence (viz., lose its shape) without L's ceasing to exist.
Thus, persistence conditions would still differentiate the two. In sum, (RK)
does not provide conditions for individuating kinds of things that overlap
spatially.

Problems for this view grow exponentially. Suppose that natural cata-
clysms and gradual erosion shape a bit of rock to look like an old arrowhead,
and an archeologist discovers the piece and declares it to be an arrowhead
of the type used by the Neolithic natives who once inhabited the valley in
which it was found. Have we any option other than to say that the archeologist is mistaken, even if the rock's shape is indistinguishable from that
of an arrowhead and her mistake is never discovered? But on (RK), that
"arrowhead" has the right arrangement and it is mandated that the archeologist is correct. Good grief!

It may be easier to see wherein the difficulty lies with the indifference-
to-origin view if we recognize that it is not confined to human intentions
or to artifacts. Sunburns, fish fossils, fingerprints, and many other natural phenomena must originate in a certain way. Intentions are beside the
point in those cases, origins are not. And origins are still distinguished from
K-wise arrangements. Of course, someone who agrees with (RK) might hold
his ground. But it would be difficult to deny that different sorts of artifacts
and sunburns are kinds. If that is so, what more could be expected to show
that origins are sometimes an indispensable aspect of a kind's identity?

More remains to be said about conventions, both in the process of creating something and in the product created. I shall return to that matter presently. But first consider the implications that this notion of composition
encounters for *individuals*—even for those, such as persons, which would
require a great deal of distortion to regard as artifacts. Two sorts of cases
come to mind.

First, there is the problem of the teletransporter in *Star Trek*, which takes the molecular structure of a "traveler's" body and re-assembles it in a corresponding teletransporter far away.[5] It makes sense to ask whether the reassembled individual is the same as the individual who entered the first teletransporter, and an affirmative answer cries out for a defense. It is far from self-evident that anything shaped in the right way emerging from the receiving teletransporter must be the same individual. (Would things be better if we somehow manage to collect the same token molecules for the reconstruction? What if a malfunction made the "transported" body show up in two distant places simultaneously?)

Second, consider the notorious Swampman: Two bolts of lightning strike a swamp in rapid succession. The first regrettably kills Tyler Burge. The second strikes nearby swampy material, producing a molecule-for-molecule duplicate of Burge. Swampman may erroneously "think" it (he?) is Burge, and may have a perfect replica of the complete Burgeian set of dispositions, preferences, values, and memory impressions; but, working from our commonplace standards of re-identification, we aren't likely to agree that it is Burge without its having the original's biological origin. It wouldn't even matter if, still more miraculously, the very atoms making up this concoction were all in Burge's makeup shortly before his untimely demise.

If origins cannot be peremptorily dismissed in these cases, what basis is there be for supposing that the origin of a statue is not a factor in determining that it is a statue? Unless you think ordinary persons are conventionally persons, it is no longer, as Rea mentions, just a case of whether or not one accepts conventionalism. Indeed, if the same atoms were to be re-assembled several centuries later, but from a different origin (say, having different parents), and the resulting individual were to be named Tyler Burge and to believe that it was identical with our contemporary Tyler Burge, under complete information would we say that it *is* the earlier Tyler Burge? It seems here that origins count enough to challenge any conclusion that relies exclusively on "arrangements of particles."

5. "My blueprint is beamed to Mars, where another machine makes an organic *Replica* of me. My Replica thinks he is me, and he seems to remember living my life up to the moment when I pressed the green button. . . . If we believe that my Replica is not me, it is natural to assume that my prospect, on the Branch Line, is almost as bad as ordinary death." (Parfit 1984, pp. 200–201)

Finally, objection (III) might be interpreted as maintaining that if *thing* is to have ontological import, artifacts aren't things. If they were things they would be material ones, but we can't bring a material thing into existence by an intention. That would be tantamount to introducing a material object by convention, and, as Mark Heller has stated, "the structure of the world is not a matter of convention" (1990, p. 40). Heller illustrates the point with the creation of Manhattan out of a land mass surrounded by water: "[T]he claim that we can somehow create a new physical object by passing legislation involves the absurd idea that without manipulating or creating any matter we can create a physical object." (p. 36) There is no room for an artifact in a serious ontology.

The point may be reinforced by the fact that the persistence conditions for artifacts are indeterminate, admitting things with indeterminate persistence conditions opens the door to undecidable cases. How then can artifacts be genuine? That line of argument also holds for many of the ordinary physical things that are not artifactual or conventional on a common understanding of those terms—pigs, mulberry bushes, hurricanes, comets, and so on. (More on that below.) This may not dissuade those who are attracted to an inventory of the cosmos more austere than our vernacular one, but it robs that consideration of a claim to be intuitively compelling. However, because having forsworn the scrutiny of objections that take off from such radical departures from bourgeois ontology, I will confine attention here to the earlier claim that mere intentions, much less their pronouncements, cannot create a new physical object.

Before coming directly to grips with that objection, it is worth keeping a few distinctions in mind.

First, it would be a mistake to lump together all the various things the objection is designed to cover. Whereas there may not have been "manipulating or creating matter" when Manhattan's physical boundaries were set, a considerable amount of physical manipulation was involved in the creation of Pericles. If that were sufficient to "create a physical object," Pericles would satisfy the condition.

Next, although Manhattan and Pericles may be conventional, that contrasts with their being natural but not with their being physical. They may require intentions in their initiation, but they have spatial locations and bulk. However, given their conventionality, how then can the former throw light on conscious mental properties (the subject of concern here) when the latter aren't at all conventional, at least not on those grounds? (See below for a further observation about the interplay of conscious properties with conventionality.) The only reason for bringing entities such as Pericles into this discussion was to explain how a divergence in persistence conditions could individuate two things that may overlap in their material embodiments. The objection under discussion makes it a requirement that ontically serious thinghood go beyond the ability to be individuated; it demands additional conditions. But nothing in that objection purports to show that statues and communities can't be individuated. Thus, whatever one thinks of the intentions involved in the origins of artifacts, in the absence of any reason to believe that it is impossible to individuate them, issues concerning, say, Pericles' status still provide a standing and convincing argument to make the point for which the example was introduced.

Returning to the core of the objection, the reference to creating "a physical object" runs together two subjects that are best kept separate: physical grounding and individuation. Pericles is a physical object: remove its matter and Pericles vanishes. Similarly, remove all matter from Manhattan and Manhattan is no more. But even physicalists who suppose that creation *via fiat* precludes these items from membership in serious ontology could scarcely avoid acknowledging methods (perhaps four-dimensional) for individuating any one physical thing from others. If they were to decline accepting that much, they wouldn't be merely materialists, they would be monists. Though monism is consistent with physicalism, it doesn't follow from physicalism, and it is not part of the current objection against including conventional beings in one's ontology.[6] Those who hold that conscious properties are identical to neurological ones will need a further argument if they want to show that neurological, atomic, or proto-atomic states aren't ontologically ultimate. That burden is an addition to a bare commitment to physicalism. There is no hint that those who raise the current objection are willing to shoulder it. Thus, I shall assume that the objector of concern acknowledges that particulars, even material ones, can be individuated. And individuation, rather than naturalism, is the crux here.

How, then, shall we view the intentions and/or manipulations that install conventional objects? Once more, consider Pericles. Of course, teleology comes along *gratis* with the sculptor's intentions, but that aspect can

6. For a defense of monism, see Schaffer 2010.

be ignored when our interest is only in *what* gets instituted, not *how* it is instituted. A sculptor's intentions and manipulations needn't be seen as an invention out of thin air; instead they can be seen as rearranging the physical in such a way that certain configurations of matter and their potential reconfigurations now count as constituting a single continuant. We needn't regard the material itself as having been created by the sculptor, though in the cases of present concern (i.e., artifacts) the *articulation* of the pre-existing matter is in fact new. However, from that angle the physical side of the creation consists not in the intention of the sculptor but in the molding of the clay, which is more than a verbal manipulation. The intention merely lays down conditions for changes that will and will not be countenanced for various configurations of this matter. Thus, let us allow that the statue can lose, say, the matter of its forearm, or that it can have lesions or disfigurements of a certain size in its clay replaced by new clay or some other substance. The intention does not lay down conditions for every contingency that can befall this new articulation, but that is no more a mark against its laying down the conditions it lays down than it is a mark against the conditions for being the same cat.

Similarly for the island of Manhattan. Before "becoming" a political entity, it was indeed a land mass. However, even for it to be considered a particular land mass, certain conditions for continued identity had to be in place. What if the Hudson River were to dry up, creating a land link from Manhattan to what is now New Jersey? Would Manhattan's earlier boundaries still count as the boundaries of Manhattan? Would Manhattan even exist anymore? What if Liberty Island were to be shifted so that the island would be connected to Manhattan? Would Liberty Island become a part of Manhattan, or would the result be an entirely new island? And what of every piece of silt that might belong to its current physical bulk, or every clod of dirt that might be lost to its bordering rivers? These questions arise independent of taking Manhattan to be a political entity. They concern only a clump of matter. Even if Manhattan is a four-dimensional object, if its actual past, present, and future properties are not *all* essential to it, must there not be definite answers for such counterfactual hypotheses? Could such answers be any less vulnerable to the charge of creating a material thing by manipulation than the political entity?

What instituting a political entity did was only to specify, in an open-ended way, the future configurations, including expansions, of land masses that could continue to be characterized along with, or could serve as replacements for, that land mass. In short, it carved out a category of perfectly physical things by declaring certain similarities and dissimilarities relevant and others irrelevant. This is no more creating a physical object than dividing things into ducks and swans. On the usual methods of re-identification that sort of provision of conditions is no more a deviation from the physical than the re-identification of the same lump of matter? Certainly philosophers have discussed a notion of strict identity on which the addition or subtraction of the tiniest particle extinguishes the original lump. On that principle, the continual gains and losses of atoms at the surfaces of any of our sensibilia would imply that nothing macroscopic exists longer than the blink of an eye. I am not sure why anyone believes that is purer than our ordinary methods: both are impositions of persistence conditions that do no more than divide the physical in a particular way. But if we loosen the strictest standard for re-identifying lumps of matter, however conservatively, it is easier to see that we admit that even *things* in one's favored ontology can change over time (say, in color, shape, and size), as do trees, valleys, and lakes. There is no reason why choosing one configuration over another should confound physicalism. The most important point to be made here is that this is accomplished without introducing considerations of artifactuality. Then why suppose that reconfiguring things so that different sorts of changes either allow or disallow persistence departs from the physical stuff any more so than those potential configurations permitted for retaining the same lump? Indeed, at this stage even to speak of *re*configurations is too concessive. What has been done is that the very same physical reality has been divided up in a different way. Nevertheless, it is the physical world that has been divided; no enigmatic mental stuff is a part of the potential changes, even if it plays a background role in realigning the physical changes that are to be allowed.

Notice that four-dimensionalism will not rescue the objection. Even if the actual changes in a thing's makeup determine its identity, they will branch out to different actual temporary states for different individuals under the same sortal, and moreover the actual changes will not be sufficient to disclose which unrealized possibilities would or would not preserve identity. Only if the future is fixed and the past is necessary can this be avoided. But that ambitious version of fatalism is wholly independent of four-dimensionalism. Not that things would be easier for four-dimensionalists if they stuck to their practice of using only examples of objects that have already exhausted their life-spans. It is possibility, not actuality, that presents the difficulty; and that difficulty infects past possibilities as much as future ones.

Manipulation aside, *intentionally* carving up the world in one way or another needn't be disparaged as inventing rather than discovering an item. It is no less (or more) natural to consider it a matter of arranging *via* classifying a pre-existing something. A notion with some currency in philosophy is that a categorization of any kind is conceptualization, and conceptualization is a subjective projection on an otherwise independent reality, not a part of what we find in the world. "Tis a common observation, that the mind has a great propensity to spread itself on external objects," wrote Hume (1739/1978, p. 167). And this consideration was an engine of anti-realism even before Hume's time. (Compare Locke's remarks on nominal essence in *An Essay concerning Human Understanding*.) I don't attribute this line of reasoning to the disputants now under consideration. But that assumption has contributed to a facile agreement with a conclusion shared with those anti-realists about the lightweight ontological status of our commonplace ways of carving up of the material world. According to that outlook, the only alternative would be a "God's-eye view" of the one non-disjunctive way to individuate things in physical reality, which of course is not attainable. So, this line of thought continues, all our conceptualizations are nothing more than convenient fictions. I believe, and hope, that this engine of anti-realism is decommisioned after it is exposed as a relic of an older and unpromising idealist philosophy. I see no good reason to give up our natural impulse to believe that we came upon the bounded land mass, and that by naming it we instantiated its continued identity with various strictly physical changes in the landscape. We did not bring those boundaries into physical existence; we simply acknowledged the extension and the limitations of their relevance to this continuing entity.

Finally, what of the objection that either the product of an intentional doing or the intentional state itself is conventional and is thereby precluded from a natural ontology? Without evaluating that claim, to make it stick the physicalist can't be a realist about these aspects but must become an eliminativist. Let us consider statues before turning our attention to emergent properties.

If a physicalist is a realist, there will be a particular dependence (either by way of an identity or a superdupervenient explanation) of both the originating intention of the statue and of the statue itself with something purely physical. For simplicity, suppose the dependence is a reductive identity. Its conventionality is thereby eliminated. But the very same issues raised about origins by intentions (now under their physical descriptions)—that is, origins informing the essences of their products or carving up (viz., individuating) those products according to their original intention[7]—would persist. When I look at the *David*, I am not looking at Michelangelo's intentions or his behavior, in whatever way those may be analyzed. Nevertheless, whatever led us to declare that the intentions of Michelangelo were essential to the *David*'s being a statue, rather than a natural formation, remain as relevant as they were before. Thus, what is at issue is whether certain hunks of matter have only the matter composing them for their conditions of identity, or whether this is inadequate for identifying the thing in question. Neither the statue's conventionality nor its mental origin is relevant to our current interest in the relation between the end product and its constitution or realization.

There may not be a pressing motive for a physicalist to be a realist about artifacts such as statues, cell phones, or counties. A physicalist may find it easier to live with eliminativism there. If this is the reformer metaphysician's view (as appears to be the case), those interests are only thinly related to the present dispute. In addition, for the purposes of this essay we have put eliminativism about conscious properties aside. Thus, suppose that emergent tokens turn out to have physical descriptions. Any of the previous issues concerning the distinction between an emergent token's physical base and the token itself could be restated in these terms. If the distinguishability of a realizer from its base survives the attacks we have vetted, this also applies to emergent tokens. The hypothesized conventionality of emergent tokens (or, more generally, mental tokens) raises no new issue for the realist. Eliminativists, on the other hand, believing that statues and emergent properties are really non-entities, disqualify themselves from being lumpists.

7. The set could in fact be a singleton, since reading the origin of a product into its essence and individuating a product according to its origin may come to the same thing.

3.7 Causation: Oppositions and Propinquities

One can never rule out the possibility that further objections have been overlooked. But in lieu of the production of one of those, the earlier reasons for differentiating a statue from its matter remain uncontroverted; they make a strong case for a *prima facie* distinction between a realizer and what it realizes. As we have seen, this dictates a distinction between being different (viz., non-identical) and being discrete (viz., non-overlapping). Pericles and L are different, though not discrete. A distinction in general between identity and overlap is widely acknowledged elsewhere. The torch in the right hand of Lady Liberty is not the Statue of Liberty. Similarly for a person and his or her torso. More to the point for us, although it has not been shown that *every* realizer is different from what it realizes, there are two reasons why conscious property instances and their neural realizers are prime candidates for RwI. The first is that the emission paradigm of a realizer is less susceptible to identity claims than a compositionality relation; the second is that aligning persistence conditions for conscious properties with those of their neural realizers is not promising.

To belabor an earlier point, this is not a scheme of degrees for identity. Things are either identical or not identical, period! Partial coincidence is not tantamount to partial identity. Absolute non-identity is compatible with any degree of spatial-temporal overlap—that is, with any degree of non-discreteness.[8]

It is generally agreed that physical realizers of the mental are causally efficacious, and that their causes operate at the same time and over roughly the same territory in which mental properties are commonly cited as causes. Consequently, whenever we cite a mental cause, there is a physical cause of "the same" effect. (Let's allow this mild overstatement to stand as a background against which to make the points to follow. It is re-examined below and in chapter 5.) The arguments against extensive causal overdetermination are compelling. If the only alternative to rejecting the identity of mental and realizer properties were this sort of overdetermination, it would be reasonable to conclude that mental properties couldn't be efficacious on their own; they would be epiphenomena. As was discussed in the first

---

8. Defending absolute identity is not part of the job description here. I merely point out that the foregoing view of realization is compatible with it. For a defense of non-absolute (that is, "relative") identity, see Geach 1967. For objections to relative identity, see Wiggins 1980; Perry 1970; Vision 1970, 1974.

chapter, that outcome is highly problematic. Thus, let's examine a bit more closely the threat posed by overdetermination. The issue won't be fully aired until the next chapter, but at this place we may begin to investigate some of the ways in which difference or non-identity without discreteness might bear on the causal role of that which is realized.

A pillar topples from high above the street and lands on a car. Both the pillar and its slab of marble toppling over might be cited as the sufficient cause of the dent in the car's hood. Assume that, as argued here, they are not identical. Does one cause preclude the other?

The notion of a *sufficient cause* that I have in mind can be loosely specified for present purposes. It comes to something less than that an effect must eventuate from its cause. It may even comport with a variety of probabilistic causation. Strict sufficiency would require citing the entirety of the universe's light cone immediately preceding its effect.[9] For the present, no stand need be taken on that precise notion of sufficiency. (That will change when we compare macro-causation with causation between fundamental particles.) Nomologically strict sufficiency would render germane every particular incident in the universe immediately preceding the effect; while metaphysically strict sufficiency would also include the body of natural laws as causes of everything. The closest I can come to an account of what I intend by 'sufficiency' in these discussions is a defeasible (= non-monotonic) notion in which $C \rightarrow E$ does not strictly imply $(C \ \& \ D) \rightarrow E$. This enables us to reject the argument that the neural property is only one part of the cause and must be supplemented by a conscious property. We may put this by saying that a cause C is sufficient for effect E if, for any B *in the same causal enterprise*,[10] neither 'C and B' nor 'C or B' is necessary to make it the cause of E. In fact, the non-necessary cause is superfluous. By this I do not mean that A is a *partial* cause, though that may be the case. But its partiality is not the role it is playing as defeasibly sufficient. (The notion of a partial cause will re-enter the deliberations, but only for the cases discussed in chapter 5.)

Defeasible sufficiency is meant to cover one of two sides of probabilistic causation. The other side concerns true chance. Suppose Quantum Electrodynamics is the last word. There is a chance that bombarding a radioactive particle will cause it to decay, but if it doesn't do so we may assume that

9. See, e.g., Field 2003; Loewer 2007.

10. That phrase is left unexplained in this quasi-formal specification. I trust the ensuing discussion will clarify it.

there is nothing further to say about its non-causation in this instance. In defeasible causation, there are identifiable reasons why the effect was altered or did not occur despite all the normal conditions for causation being present. It is the absence of the abnormal defeater that accounts for a cause's sufficiency. I use 'defeasibility' rather than 'probabilistic causation' here only because (a) pure chance is not an issue in the disputes now underway and (b) defeasibility emphasizes the fact that in the normal case we can reasonably expect the causation to occur. Otherwise, certain brands of probable causation would suffice for my purposes. However, (b) is essential here. It enables us to call something *the* cause rather than merely *a* cause. Syphilis may be *a* cause (or a causal condition) of the general paresis that infects 3 percent of syphilitic patients, and buying a lottery ticket may be *a* cause (or, again, a condition) of winning the lottery. But I wouldn't call either *the* cause of its outcome.

The question brought out by the example of the falling pillar and slab is whether different but non-discrete property instances (or events, or processes, or things) compete for their causal role. Obviously, not all different causes of a single effect compete: two or more distinct causes may be compatible, each being, in common parlance, *the* cause of the event. A trivial example would be a causal chain in which a proximal cause of E doesn't compete with E's distal causes. Another instance of non-competition among sufficient causes is that of determinables and their determinates. If a sudden drop in temperature below 0°C caused water to freeze, a drop in temperature of –15°C also caused it to freeze; if a berry's being red caused a bird to snatch it, the berry's being crimson caused the bird to snatch it. Stephen Yablo (1992a,b) has suggested that there is enough similarity between the more and less abstract, the determinable and determinate, and the mental and its physical base to save the first member of each pair from being sent off to the gulag of competing causes. I shall mention a few different considerations for non-competition compatible with, but not implying, Yablo's treatment. But, at the very least, both sorts of cases can spur one to reflect on non-identical causes of a single effect that aren't in competition, and the only remaining issue here is whether non-competition among distinct causes has a greater range.

Different but non-discrete properties or states present a problem that hasn't been as widely studied as this phenomenon deserves. RwI properties have been regarded as simply warranting the very same assessments we give to the case of discrete causes. Either that or it is supposed that if A and B overlap spatiotemporally they must be identical. The literature on causal overdetermination seldom contains distinctions more nuanced than those. The common understanding of that phenomenon, leading to the conclusion that it must be extremely rare, seems without exception to focus on cases in which the causes are independent existences. The conjunction of causes in these cases is not only contingent, but oftentimes happenstance. On the other hand, the relation of a realized to its realizer is as modal as constitution. Reverting to the jargon of supervenience, the base constitutes its supervening property. I have not seen an argument in the literature against frequent overdetermination that is inspired by cases in which the would-be culprits bear this sort of relationship.

Thus far this is merely symptomatic of a potential oversight. How might it be fleshed out to show plausible non-competition? Here is a clue.[11] I have in mind a recent *relevant alternatives* or *contextualist* theory of causation. It is really a family of views, but its varieties share enough similarities to allow it to be regarded as a single theory for these purposes. On that theory, the truth values and meanings of statements of the forms '*m* caused *p*' and '*m* didn't cause *p*' depend on the context in which they are uttered, which may include the intentions and the assumptions of the utterer and/or the audience. (For a general discussion, see Maslen et al. 2009.) Thus, on one popular account, a belief may be *a* cause of one's behavior if there is no alternative possible world in which the behavior that does not follow from the belief is as close to actuality as a possible world in which the behavior does follow from the belief. A distinctive feature of this view is that the proximity of possible worlds shifts with the context of utterance. Thus, the pillar's causing the dent may be contrasted with something wholly discrete from the pillar, such as a baseball bat or a falling piece of ice, causing the dent, but not with the marble slab's causing the dent. This may be spelled out in various ways—perhaps the context immediately delivers the possible worlds (see, e.g., Horgan 1989; Lewis 2004; Menzies 2003, 2004), or perhaps causal claims, which on their grammatical surface appear to be two-place relations, are really elliptical for three-place or four-place relations in which

11. Here and in chapter 4, I do not intend to defend a detailed theory of causation. That would combine the project of defending emergentism with another project that deserves its own extended treatment. However, the view outlined below has promise and gives us a hint of how the basing connections can clarify non-competition.

contextual or contrasting factors are the additional terms (see, e.g., Maslen 2004; Schaffer 2005). It is important to notice that the contextualization of truth values for judgments of causation does not render causation non-objective any more than the implicit contextuality of statements of the form 'x is flat' (which can be predicated of my kitchen table, of Holland, of a playing field, of a nose, of a wall, or of Galileo's frictionless plane) makes the flatness of an object non-objective.

Although this is not the place to mount a formal defense of contextualism (see note 11), observe that views in this family have the advantage of handling in intuitively satisfying ways the place of causal counterfactuals and causation-via-absences (Schaffer 2000). However, the primary point of introducing contextualism here is to put substance behind the suggestion that the modal connections between supervenient properties can disclose that they are not causally competitive. I do not rule out the prospect that other theories concerning causation will be equally adept at discerning the importance of these differences between types of cause.

An approach that leaves us only with a choice between identity of cause and overdetermination may fail to do proper justice to anything approaching the range of our folk concept. When embarrassed by the apparent overdetermination of cases such as that of the pillar and its marble slab, proponents of that common approach have tended to retreat to the safety of different representations (or descriptions) of a single event, thereby transforming the difference between pillar and slab from an ontological issue to a conceptual or linguistic one. (See The Conceptual Gambit in section 2.5.) But, whereas that distinction of issues may explain why we needn't complicate the original dichotomous choice, there may be little more to be said on behalf of its interjection than that it can relieve the orthodox adherent of a predicament of her own making. The expedient and the dichotomy feed off each other.

Isn't it only natural to expect further ontological fallout from the fact that the realized and its base are not discrete but instead constitutionally related? Perhaps this discovers no more than a unique form of cross-classification, in which one can include the realizer or the realized as the subject of a single thought, but not both. Shouldn't one expect an exceptional actual relationship to have further ontological implications, perhaps spilling over into the determination of the proper place of constitutionally related phenomena in the causal network?

4 The Menace of Non-Physical Causation

4.1 Arguments against Mental Causation

Once the emergentism of concern has been given an initially plausible explanation, we must turn our attention to its notorious problems. By far the gravest challenges to the view before us are arguments against the alleged causal role of conscious properties and against causation by the mental in general. Recall the last thesis of my version:

(3) Emergent properties can cause other properties (both mental and physical) in ways in which there is no sufficient cause in context at the levels of their non-emergent subvenients.

A familiar objection to any independent or separate mental causation is the Causal Exclusion Argument (CEA). (Except where specified otherwise, by *mental causes* I mean just these independent, unreduced ones.) CEA is the most popular vehicle for expressing dissatisfaction with mental causation. Shortly after encountering CEA, we consider the Redundancy Argument (RA). It is common to conflate the two, and they do share steps. However because each harbors commitments not found in the other, it will be clearer to treat RA as a separate objection. Whereas CEA rejects mental causation on the grounds that it would lead to massive overdetermination, RA proscribes mental causation as superfluous. Furthermore, while downward causation plays no official role in CEA, it is explicit in RA. After setting out preliminaries, I outline the arguments; the remainder of this chapter is then devoted to their critical examination.

Five assumptions are in force for the discussion to follow:

First, because the concern now covers all mental causation, of which emergent causation is but a special case, keep in mind that mental aspects across the board are supervenient (or realized).

Second, if a mental property causes anything at all, it must cause something physical, either directly or as a by-product. This follows from the fact that any mental effect of a mental property will supervene on something physical (thesis (1)). RA makes this explicit, but it is also important for CEA.

Third, I follow the standard assumption that the physical and mental exhaust non-abstract reality. If the mental is either eliminated or identified with the physical, physicalism for that reality is established.

Fourth, if there are any mental causes, there are lots of them. We are not interested in a mentalist defense stating that only the odd case can escape the objector's net.

Fifth, as in section 1.1, the discussion presupposes a conception of layered reality. It is important to preserve supervenience and realization relations. If that can be achieved without the layered conception, we can treat the latter as no more than an expository convenience. In lieu of that, we can represent reality as an ascending hierarchy in which the more fundamental is lower, supporting or determining the higher layers. 'Micro' and 'macro' are relative terms in this scheme, standing for specific lower-to-higher relationships. An instance of a micro property on one comparison may be a macro property on another. Both perceivable and sub-perceivable properties may be either micro or macro. Though others have used the distinction to mark off what is visible to the naked eye from what is not, my employment of it hangs on comparisons rather than sizes. For present purposes, at the top of layered reality we may find the psychological, while the bottom level will contain whatever unanalyzable fundamental particles nature affords. Following an earlier coinage, I use the cover term 'proto-atoms' for whatever the latter may be.

On the layered view, mental-to-physical or mental-to-behavioral causation is *downward*, from a higher to a more basic level. In common parlance and thought, acceptance of that type of causation is commonplace. For example, the following sorts of claims should be familiar (if I may be excused for some stilted prose):

Sam's thirst caused him to open the flask.

A sudden sharp pain caused Erin to massage her hand (or to take an aspirin).

An itch led him to scratch his elbow.

Believing that it was 8 o'clock, she turned on her radio (or joined a friend at a café).

He sat in the back of the room because he wanted to go unnoticed.

She left the clearing because she saw a bear approaching.

And so the list continues. Each claim identifies a mental cause for a physical effect.

Mental causation of this kind has seemed problematic to many. The two objections encapsulate those problems. I begin with a representative version of CEA, a staple for those queasy about mental causation. It has two steps, beginning with four propositions which form an inconsistent set. It is followed by an evaluation of the options for its resolution.

The propositions are the following:

(C1)   Mental properties are distinguishable from their physical bases.

(C2)   Mental properties are causally efficacious.

(C3)   *Sufficiency of physical causation.* Every physical effect has a sufficient physical cause.

(C4)   Overdetermination of causation is an extreme rarity (viz., there is no massive causal overdetermination).

Recall our second and fourth assumptions, that every mental cause has a physical effect and that if there are any such cases there are many of them. In conjunction with (C3), those assumptions lead to the conclusion that the overdetermination for mental causation will be massive, yielding an inconsistency with (C4).[1]

(C2) is a straightforward generalization of thesis (3) to mental causation as a whole. (C3) and (C4), though stated dogmatically, are initially plausible. To remove the ensuing inconsistency, we must discard at least one of (C1)–(C4).[2] The natural options are the following:

(a) Concede that all mental causation is overdetermined (i.e., scrap (C4)).

(b) Declare that mental properties are epiphenomenal (i.e., scrap (C2).

(c) Reject the sufficiency of physical causation (i.e., scrap (C3)).

1. Late pre-emption has also been taken as a type of overdetermination (Lewis 1986c, 2004; Paul 1998). I ignore it here because the pre-empting and the pre-empted causal candidates aren't superveniently related.

2. For the sake of argument, assume that our earlier assumptions are uncontroversial, although the second and fifth have been contested.

(d) Declare that mental property instances are identical *to* the physical property instances in which they are realized or on which they supervene (i.e., scrap (C1)).

Although both (a) and (b) have attracted minor support, *pro tem* let's concede that they are untenable. Indeed, not only is option (b) a direct threat to emergentist article (3) of present concern, it also runs counter to section 1.6's reasoning that epiphenomenalism of the mental is not a serious choice. Option (c), on the other hand, runs counter to the irresistible movement of scientific inquiry. Option (d)—scrapping (C1)—appears to be our only promising recourse. That trumps the argument of the preceding chapter for a difference between realizers and their realizeds, and not only in the area of immediate concern. On the surface, statues and their matter may not appear to violate (C3). But parallel considerations extend to them: their non-identity would be sufficiently representative of their class to imply massive causal overdetermination.

The problem cited in CEA, and in RA to follow, should be distinguished from that stemming from Descartes' insistence on mental-physical interaction. That problem was summed up in a famous exchange of letters between Descartes and Princess Elizabeth of Bohemia. She wrote to him (letter dated May 6, 1643; Descartes 1951, p. 287) asking how a mind, which lacks all material qualities, has the power to move a body. Dissatisfied with Descartes' reply, she responded (in a letter dated June 20, 1643): "[I]t would be easier for me to attribute matter and extension to the soul, than to attribute the capacity of an immaterial being to move a body . . . [which] has nothing in common with it." For Elizabeth, the peculiarity of a mental event or property with the power to affect something as different as a spatial feature may have been magnified by the deep ontological divide between Descartes' substances. But neither CEA nor RA relies on the very idea of mental causation being disturbing or magical. Rather, they find that there is no room left for it once physical causes are in play. Not only are mental causes superfluous, but they are always in tension with an admission that more likely claimants are available.

(C3) affirms that whenever there is a physical effect there is also a sufficient physical cause. Some have called this a closure principle for the physical. "The best evidence of contemporary science," Chalmers (1996, p. 125) writes, "tells us that the physical world is more or less causally closed; for every physical event [effect?], there is a physical sufficient cause." Kim

(2005, p. 43) refers to (C3) as "closure," or "the closure of the physical domain."[3] However, I reserve the term 'closure' for a different precept regarding physical causation:

(PCC)   The physical world is causally closed (no causes or effects of the physical from outside the physical realm).[4]

(PCC) implies, but is not implied by, (C3). Whereas (C3) requires the presence of a physical cause, (PCC) states that no other sort of cause will be present.

Although (PCC) has been touted as the causal closure of the physical, it would be a mistake to substitute it for (C3), *the sufficiency of physical causation*, in CEA. (PCC) *assumes* what the argument sets out to prove. It provides a double-whammy to ensure that (d) is the only acceptable alternative. First, since it covers effects as well as causes, we wouldn't be able to account for the physical world's even *causing* conscious states unless the latter were physical. Second, (PCC) states without argument that mental causes can never have physical effects. *Pace* a claim made by Jessica Wilson (1999), it renders overdetermination superfluous. The exclusion argument as written seeks to explain the difficulty through the use of devices such as (C4). (PCC) renders (C4) superfluous. Put unceremoniously, (PCC) merely affirms what the emergentist is thus far entitled to deny. Nida-Rümelin (2007a) and Van Gulick (1993) may have used this as a reason to reject (PCC).[5] (PCC) cries out for supporting argument, whereas (C3) has a cachet of intuition that makes it possible to bypass its formal defense at this stage.

This is not to say that (PCC) does not bear at all on our concerns. For one thing, it is implied by standard versions of physicalism. But it lacks polemical clout as an independent step in an objection to mental causation. Of

3. See also Antony 2007, p. 145. That title for (C3) is rife among discussants.

4. Kim, who has just labeled (C3) 'Closure', wrote some years earlier that the principle of physical causal closure can be stated as follows: "If you pick any physical event and trace its causal ancestry or posterity, that will never take you out of the physical domain. That is, no causal chain will ever cross the boundary between the physical and the nonphysical." (2000a, p. 40) (See also Kim 1993, p. 280.)

5. Nida-Rümelin accepts the principle that every *event* that is the cause of a physical event is physical (2007a, p. 284, n. 22). But because she believes that *subjects* (≠ events) are the sole causes of some physical events, the limitation on this outcome is more readily construed as a counterexample to any closure that might interest the physicalist.

course, physicalism, as I am construing it, is incompatible with separate mental causation; but replacing one ontological view with another is not the same as mounting a separate objection against the competing doctrine. Put otherwise, arguing *from* physicalism to the non-existence of mental causation is not tantamount to arguing against mental causation in order to support physicalism. If physicalism could be established on its intrinsic merits, there would be no need for CEA or RA. Thus, an examination of (PCC) is better suited to the examination of physicalism in chapters 6 and 8.

Note that although physicalism implies (PCC), the latter does not strictly imply physicalism. If mental causation could proceed without physical effects, it could co-exist peacefully with (PCC). For many, such mental causation would demand a bizarre medium (say, an ectoplasm) in which it could take place; but its possibility does point up differences between (PCC) and physicalism.

Whereas (PCC) claims too much, (C3) claims too little. If one assumes that sufficiency of causation is at least partially transitive (modulo context), physical property P may be causally sufficient for physical result R, and there may be an intermediate emergent cause E on the chain:

$P \rightarrow E \rightarrow R.$

Causes on a single chain are not overdeterminers. At first one may be tempted to try patching up (C3). E. J. Lowe surveys the likeliest candidates, arguing that none of them work. The underlying difficulty with attempted reformulations is quite general: the fix-ups move in the direction of making the sufficiency principle more like (PCC), causal closure. That seems the only direction in which to eliminate the potential for intervening mental causes. We have seen that this is something the emergentist is entitled, indeed poised, to reject. It is far from clear that a formula which is truly intermediate between (C3) and (PCC), but which doesn't beg the disputed question, can be found. But I set aside that question; finding the right reformulation will not matter if the problems raised in sections 4.3–4.6 can't be resolved.

A variant sometimes conflated with CEA is framed in terms of explanation rather than causation. That causation and causal explanation are not sharply distinguished certainly contributes to the conflation. Kim, who is aware of the difference, nevertheless consistently states the problem exposed by the foregoing argument as stemming from "causal or explanatory exclusion," and even non-physicalists have adopted that phrasing. Causation and causal explanation are intimately related, but, as we saw in chapter 2, it is a tangled relationship. It is worthwhile to lay out at least one difference between the two versions. On an explanatory exclusion argument, (C1) would remain unchanged; the rest of the argument would continue as follows:

(X2)   Mental properties are (causally) explanatory.

(X3)   *Sufficiency of physical explanation.*   Every physical aspect that has an explanation has a physical explanation.

(X4)   Overdetermination of explanation is an extreme rarity.

I set this variant aside, in part because the prohibition in (X4) is highly controversial and certainly not as striking as the problematic character of massive causal overdetermination in (C4). Even on the ontological view of explanation set forth in section 2.4, a host of complementary explanations of a single explanandum are possible because objective reality can be carved up in numerous ways. However, observe that the explanatory exclusion argument has a peculiar twist in light of earlier discussion. Suppose we ask how one accounts for the widespread but mistaken belief that there are independent mental causes. Such exculpatory stories are typically integral to accounts given by defenders of CEA. A natural temptation would be to use The Conceptual Gambit—that is, champions of independent mental causation mistake (causal) explanation for causation. However, explanatory exclusion is an argument against mental causal explanation; it bars use of the gambit. And it is hard to see where another account of this sort might be sought. In any event, the explanatory-exclusion argument is problematic enough on its face so that I give it no further play in these deliberations.

Turning to the second objection, the redundancy argument (RA), it too can be divided into stages. In its first stage, the argument makes explicit use of article (1) of emergentism (generalized for all mental properties) to show that mental-to-physical causation is a precondition of mental-to-mental causation. The result is that downward causation is a desideratum of mental causation. From there the emergentist's plight comes into view. A second stage gives an additional reason for the superannuation, and elimination, of a separate mental causation.

The first stage starts with the tentative hypothesis that mental property (or event) M is the cause of mental property (or event) M*. Whereas M supervenes on physical base P, M* supervenes on physical base P*. This yields the mapping shown in figure 4.1.

Because M* supervenes on P*, producing M* requires instantiating its supervenience base, P*: M can cause M* only by way of causing its base, P*, a case of downward causation. That would be an arrow running diagonally downward from left to right (figure 4.2(a)). The argument's second stage contends that this scenario precludes a causal role for the mental.

The second stage of RA focuses on M's base, P. According to (C3) of the earlier argument, P* has a sufficient physical cause. At first glance that need not interfere with the fact that we have already identified M as a cause of P*. But if P is sufficient for M, it is hard to resist taking it as the physical cause needed for P*. P* can then bring in its wake the supervenient property M*. Moreover, since P* is necessary for M*, M would have to guarantee P* to produce M*. How could it do that without causing P*? What place is left for M to be the cause of M*? At best M is an intermediate cause. The resulting chain might look like the N-shaped one in figure 4.2(b).

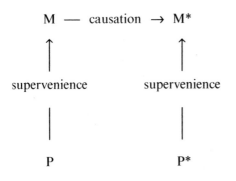

Figure 4.1

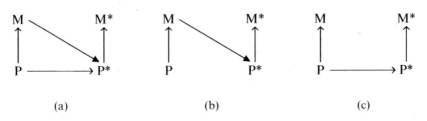

(a)   (b)   (c)

Figure 4.2

4.2(b)'s chain is not strictly causal. Rather, the relations of P to M and of P* to M* are constitutional. It is, nevertheless, a chain of dependencies. What is the role of M in this dependency chain? P is a sufficient cause of P*, which "appears to make emergent property M otiose and dispensable as a cause of [P*]" (Kim 2000b, p. 319). Thus, the final edition now looks like that of the two distinct chains emanating from P in figure 4.2(c). If M's place, instituted by P, were removed, the remainder of the chain would have sufficed. Even if there is no overdetermination here, M is superfluous, its claim to causal efficacy is baseless. Thus, stage two.

Let us turn to a consideration of what more precisely we are supposed to take away from the two arguments. What difficulties in mental causation do they reveal?

4.2   The Lessons of the Criticisms

Wading through the various difficulties implied in our arguments, they seem to boil down to the absurdity of massive overdetermination and the superfluity of mental causation once physical causation of the same effect is in the mix. This may be summed up in the following charge:

(i)   *Too many causes*—the extreme unlikelihood of massive causal overde-termination or the superfluity of mental causes.

But CEA and RA also bring to the surface two underlying misgivings about mental causation:

(ii)   Absurdities attending downward causation

(iii)   *All causation ultimately residing in the interaction between fundamental particles.*   Any supervenience relations we trace can end only where there is no further underlying causation.

I shall also refer to (iii) as the thesis of *descending support*. That label empha-sizes the fact that higher-level causation is but a surface manifestation of the real causal work taking place in God's boiler room. Common-sense and special-science causation "must somehow reflect or derive from features of causal thinking (or true causal claims) that can be found in fundamental physics" (stated though not endorsed by Woodward 2007, p. 66).

Although (ii) is the most frequently cited objection, it invariably col-lapses into either (i) or (iii). On the one hand, downward causation is perplexed by a competing cause, which overrides it and whose resolution sends us to (i). On the other hand, the downward progress continues until we arrive at a fundamental level, (iii), which again elbows out (ii) as the explanation of the failure. Nonetheless, downward causation is the difficulty most often highlighted in these discussions, and thus shouldn't be ignored when discussing attacks on thesis (3). It is discussed in section 4.5. The topic of too many causes, first broached in chapter 3, is taken up again in section 4.3, and the issue of descending support is the featured topic of section 4.6. Interspersed with these considerations section 4.4 introduces a potent argument for the non-identity of mental properties and their bases, ruling out the solution CEA's supporters propose: option (d).

4.3   Too Many Causes

My discussion of (i) covers three points, the first two of which were first mooted in the preceding chapter: the distinctive character of the gap between supervenient mental properties and their bases, the limits of that difference, and the core of the realization relation.

First, even if supervenient or realized properties are *different* from their enabling bases, the two are nevertheless not *discrete* or *distinct*. When we have different properties, events, processes, or particulars (*tokens* for short), normally they are wholly distinct. But that is not always so, as a human body and its torso illustrate (see Sider 2003). The familiar examples of overdetermination, which have led us to the conclusion that it must be an extreme rarity, all involve causes that are not only differentiated but also discrete. However, the situations now under consideration are unlike that of two bullets entering a victim's heart simultaneously, or the content of a visual experience prompted by the scene before the subject's eyes and by a concurrent experimental probe of the subject's brain. The threat of massive overdetermination wasn't designed for situations like those envisioned in CEA and RA. It is not clear what lessons we are to take away from this very dissimilar kind of case.

Second, problematic cases of overdetermination from which objectors draw its chief lesson are always coincidental. In the present case, a property and its base have a tight modal relation. Just as identity changes the causal landscape, shouldn't so quintessential a dependence have implications for a different relationship between distinguishable causes? Pursuing this point, let us consider once again the dependency chain recoverable from figure 4.2(a):

$$P \to M \to P^* \to M^*.$$

It would be premature to assume that the rules hold generically across different species of dependence, especially when two or more kinds occur on a single chain, as above. Kim's way of formulating his Principle of Determinative/Generative Exclusion (2001, p. 277) indirectly acknowledges this complication, suggesting a need to qualify (C4):

> If the existence of an event e, or an instantiation of a property P, is determined/generated by an event c—causally or otherwise—then e's occurrence is not determined/generated by any event wholly distinct from or independent of c (unless this a genuine case of overdetermination).

Because M is not "wholly distinct from and independent of" its realizer, the chain in question doesn't violate Kim's principle. That qualification countenances limits on provisos to restrict multiple generators such as (C4). Indeed, these sorts of modally related causes open the prospect of generally overturning one's maxims about elements of causal chains. It needn't be claimed that they do so in every case or even in this case. Nevertheless, it is incumbent on those who place reliance on the threat of massive and systematic overdetermination to show that (C4) has its intended force when the overdeterminer is this brand of mental-to-physical causation.

The upshot is that the causes may be non-competitive, and non-competitive causes do not engender overdeterminations of single events, or at least not overdeterminations of a threatening kind. Of course, more must be said before we can put the menace of (C4) behind us. In the past, critics deploying The Conceptual Gambit have maintained that what is non-competitive about correlative mental and physical causes involves concepts rather than objects, causal explanation rather than causation. But this very method for defusing the non-competition by relocating it in concepts could itself be justified only by the perceived need to avoid the consequence of overdetermination. If the competition of causes is eliminated by their modal kinship, it deprives the critic of the rationale behind that move.

If only to illustrate how some recently defended views about causation can accommodate these cases, the contextualist account of causation outlined in section 3.7 shows how a theory can readily accept the view that modal companions need not issue in competing causes. It would explain why it is that citing a particular mental or physical cause can, on occasion, be regarded as a complementary way of noting the same facts about the objective world.

Finally, there is some reason to believe that realizers account mainly for the *existence* rather than the *causation* of that which they realize. These aspects can come apart. It is at least debatable that whatever constitutes my existence (my body, my genetic makeup) is also the factor responsible for each of my causes. This is not to claim that my action is free in a sense relevant to squabbles over free will. The present scenario does not foreclose on the possibility that all my behavior is determined by factors beyond my capacity, perhaps antedating my birth. But that determination would be causal, and causation isn't constitution. Supervenience and realization are constitutive relations.

A pertinent illustration of the last point concerns the relation between proto-atoms and higher-level dependents. In a possible scenario (developed in greater detail in section 4.6), a chasm between existence and causation may be opened up by a certain, albeit highly speculative, interpretation about the current state of particle physics. On that interpretation, physicists engaged in the study of fundamental particles have been exclusively targeting the interplay of different sorts of particle. As dictated by the relevant equations those functional relations are neither asymmetrical nor temporal, and, as Russell (1912) noted, they do not satisfy our conception of causation. Nevertheless, if these particles, or their yet-to-be-discovered parent stock, are truly fundamental, then everything else physical is constituted by them. Combined, those theses would mean that even non-contextualized causation would be a by-product of constitutional dependence, not its engine; the fundamental particles themselves would yield no information about causation occurring at their level.[6] It would be rash to place great weight on so controversial a portrait in a volatile area of research, but it illustrates how dependence can be preserved without a causal connection to animate it.

4.4   A Distinction between Mental and Neurological Properties

Before investigating the challenges of downward causation and descending support, (ii) and (iii) respectively, let's pause to consider a view that could mark a serious drawback to the identity of mental and physical causes: that is, to a resolution by means of option (d). (Combined with the view,

6. Thanks to Eleanor Knox for bringing this to my attention.

advanced in section 4.3, that mental causes and their bases are not in competition, this is a further boost to that way of relieving (i).) To get the view off the ground, suppose that the realizers in question are neural properties or configurations—*neural tokens* for short.

Consider afresh the question of what makes something a mental property. One view is that these properties are identical with their causal powers. This is not a recent innovation. Kim (1993e, p. 348) cites approvingly what he calls "Alexander's Dictum:" "To be real is to have causal powers." And generally properties do have causal powers. Sydney Shoemaker (2003b, 2007) develops this thesis in detail, regarding these as forward-looking causal features of properties—what they can cause in combination with other properties and in certain circumstances (say, C). They also have backward-looking causal features, that which can cause them in C^*.[7] Call this combination of a property's affinities its *causal profile*. It might be surmised that a property's identity consists in its causal profile. The view derives some credibility from the fact that there appear to be so few substantive alternatives. In sum, mental properties and their neurological bases will have different profiles, thereby making them different properties.

Not all is well with this as a theory of property identity. For one thing, on most accounts mathematical properties aren't capable of causal relations. For another, functionally defined properties may be defective. Suppose that being an artery is defined in terms of its function of conducting blood from the heart to other organs. Although a clogged artery doesn't have a causal potential to permit blood to flow, a clogged artery is an artery. Despite this, I can find no way to say what makes it an artery without mentioning that forward-looking potential of arteries in the abstract, perhaps in terms of an evolutionary function. Also, consider once again the case of fundamental particles. The prospect of proto-atoms lacking causal profiles (contemplated in section 4.3) provides a further reason against regarding property identity as identity of causal profile.

Some of these difficulties may be overcome by regarding causal profiles not as *identifying* properties, but only as sufficient conditions for their *individuation*. Principles of individuation and identity may be distinguished. Suppose C( ) is a function taking properties as arguments and yielding causal profiles as values. Then

7. For our limited purposes we may ignore backward-looking powers.

$(\forall F)(\forall G)[(F = G) \leftrightarrow (C(F) \equiv C(G))]$

states the identity of properties with the same causal profile. On it, all mathematical properties, because they have no causal profiles, would be identical. However, if that view is rejected, it may still be case that if properties lack identical causal profiles they *must* be different. Omitting the modal operator, that comes to

$(\forall F)(\forall G)\{[C(F) \neq C(G)] \rightarrow (F \neq G)].$

We require but a sufficient condition for individuating properties, for saying that they are two rather than one, thereby enforcing non-identity.

The latter view is compatible with virtually any theory of property identity. For example, consider the theory that properties are defined by their haecceities (Lewis 1986b),[8] or quiddities (Hawthorne 2001), which are not qualitatively distinguishable from the properties themselves. That view may encounter its own problems. We needn't detail them here. The only relevant point is that this condition for individuation is compatible with a haecceitist theory of property identity. Suppose we accept, with the aforementioned haecceitists, that all of a property's second-order properties are contingent, and thus that it is possible for me to be a poached egg. Still, if F and G have different contingent properties in actuality, they must be different properties!

But we haven't quite nailed down the case for a separate individuation. We must show that the causal profiles in question may apply to particulars—e.g., property instances—as well as to types. If they applied only to types, or if changing possible worlds changed the identity of the token, one might still maintain that particular instantiations had, as a matter of fact, the same causal profile as their neurological bases. Here is a case that may serve us.

Returning once more to the splitters of chapter 3. the distinguishability of a sortal from its matter has an analogue for property instances. Consider my belief that there will be a frost tonight, and suppose it is realized by neurological configuration N. If we accept the common view that beliefs can last over time, the very same belief may be hesitant at one time and firm at another, certain at one time and diffident at another, vivid at one time and faded at another, obsessive at one time and dispassionate at another.

8. In Lewis' sense in which they don't span possible worlds (or counterparts).

Shouldn't the members of each pair indicate a difference at the level of their cortical support? If beliefs are continuants, to combat this view one must deny that the differences are reflected in the belief's neural base, or one must suppose that neural configurations can be individuated *only* in terms of the beliefs that they subserve (which would defeat the point of the exercise). Neither seems plausible.

Yet another way to make the same point would be as follows (cf. Pereboom and Kornblith 1991; Yablo 1992b): A radio report leads me to believe that there will be a frost tonight, causing me, in turn, to cover my tomato plants. It is *caused* audiologically, but it is reinforced by my later reading a similar forecast in the local newspaper. Now imagine that in a different possible world things changed only by whatever is required by the fact that the belief was initially caused by reading the forecast in the paper (visually) and reinforced by later hearing it on the radio. It is all a matter of which I did first, pick up the paper or turn on the radio. It is not implausible to suppose that scenarios with such different etiologies will differ (by how much I dare not venture) in the way the neurons subserving them are configured. The question I want to raise is whether this fact alone—that the belief's base is embedded differently in the cerebral cortex as a result of those differences in etiology—would make them different beliefs. *Ex hypothesi* they are different neurological configurations. But to make them different beliefs one would have to hold that this difference in etiologies was sufficient to do so.

These points rest on nothing more elaborate than the platitude that continuants can change their non-essential properties. For example, consider an island (chosen arbitrarily from a list of things that resist functional definition). It can remain the same despite losses or accretions of clods of earth and slight dislocations prompted by slight shifts in the planet's tectonic plates. Similarly, changes caused by the neurons' forward-looking causal powers (assuming an independent means for re-identifying neural configurations) will not be matched by the belief's forward-looking causal powers. Put otherwise, the belief's ability to remain the same will outdistance the neural configuration's capacity to remain the same. The pattern is a clear one: for any realized individual, the counterfactual that it can remain the very same individual (or that its counterpart is close enough to be the same individual) with a different realizer shows that the causal profile of the individual deviates from that of its realizer.

Let us then turn to (ii), the perils of downward causation.

4.5 Downward Causation

Can something at one level have a consequence at a lower level? Our second assumption makes it a part of the package for mental causation; the very logic of RA extends that prohibition to every supervenient cause of a supervenient effect. Cases of interest are those in which mental properties cause properties of physical behavior. If there is downward causation, it would appear that the action of an eddy relocating its water droplets, a turning wheel or a bird in flight carrying along its molecules and their structural configurations (Sperry 1969, 1976), or a vase or a typewriter scattering molecules as it falls from an upper-story window and hits the ground (Kim 1999, 2000b) would be instances of it. None of these causes is an emergent property; each is physical and is constituted molecularly. But the first issue before us is downward causation, which by RA covers non-mental ground as well as the mental.

Before getting down to assessments, it should be noted that not all downward causation fits a single recipe. Distinctions between varieties of it are in order; they make a difference to the strength of the arguments against it.

First, there is a distinction between *diachronic* and *synchronic* forms. Synchronically a realized (or supervenient) property must alter a lower-level property at the very instant it is realized. Ordinarily what it alters is its realizer, but, as further distinctions show, it might be any property at a level below that at which the realized occurs. Those who hold that emergent properties do not supervene on base properties *because* at the moment of emergence they thereby transform the base properties from which they emerged would be committed to a different form of synchronic downward dependence. Whether that dependence was causal would hang on the further details of one's conception of causation. But anyone bothered about synchronic downward causation might find any type of synchronic downward dependence troublesome, regardless of its exclusion from a more narrowly circumscribed notion of causation.

On the other hand, if the view that after being instituted an emergent property can have a causal influence on properties and events at a lower level—say, at that of its base—permits *diachronic* downward causation. The earlier examples of the eddy, the wheel, the bird, and the falling typewriter are specimens of it.

Next, we distinguish *reflexive* from *non-reflexive* downward causation. On reflexivity, a higher-order property causes a change in its own base. On non-reflexivity, the effect might be a property at any lower level, but it must not be a constituent of the cause's base. The level of the effect may be one at which a base is found, but the higher-order property's influence will be on elements not involved in the cause's supervenience or realization. The effects in the cases of the eddy, the wheel, the bird, and the scattering of the *constituent* molecules of the typewriter and vase when they hit the ground are all reflexive. The typewriter and vase scattering surrounding air molecules as they fall are non-reflexive downward causes.

We may thus distinguish four types of downward causation: synchronically reflexive, synchronically non-reflexive, diachronically reflexive, and diachronically non-reflexive. If neither supervenience nor realization were transitive, further distinctions would be appropriate. But those before us suffice for the purpose at hand.

Kim claims Sperry holds that emergent properties require synchronic, reflexive downward causation, a view that makes no sense according to Kim. His chief complaint seems to be that synchronic reflexive downward causation violates the condition that until a supervenient property has been instantiated it is incapable of being a cause.[9] However, enlarging the scope of our concern from causation to physical dependence appears to avert those absurdities. A property or a conjunction of properties can transform a base from which the property or property complex arose. That is the view, mentioned earlier, of those who hold that instances of emergent properties do not supervene on a base because the moment they are instantiated the previous base morphs into something else.[10] The Neo-Lockean view of persons, which states that a person is distinguishable from its biological self, can be read in this way. This is a downward consequence, although not a case of efficient causation as currently understood. I do not claim that any of those views are invulnerable, but they are not prey to this sort of an attack on their intelligibility. In addition, the passages in Sperry on which

9. Kim also notes that if causation (or dependence) were transitive it would create a cycle in which the emergent property would be self-caused, yet another absurdity. Kim's complaint in the main text addresses the synchronicity element, this one addresses the reflexivity element. Broadening the character of the dependence resolves both problems.

10. See, e.g., O'Connor 1994; Humphreys 1997; Nida-Rümelin 2007a.

Kim appears to be relying are, at a minimum, ambiguous between claims of synchronic and diachronic causation, and between claims of reflexive and non-reflexive causation.[11] Despite some unguarded prose, I do not find a clear reading on which Sperry is unequivocally committed to synchronic reflexive downward causation.

However, in the long run it doesn't matter whether Kim's interpretation of Sperry is correct; defenders of mental causation needn't be committed to it. Diachronic non-reflexive causation will suffice quite nicely for the advocate of mental causation. At the risk of belaboring the point, the problem now under review arose as a result of the commitment of mental causation to downward causation; that causal direction was unqualifiedly ruled out by the structure exposed in RA. The reasons for that prohibition were various, but distinctions were not drawn between the forms of downward causation listed. Kim's earlier objection attacks only one form: the synchronic reflexive. Removing it leaves a number of forms of downward causation still available to the emergentist, and that remainder covers the overwhelming majority of ordinary ascriptions of mental causes for mundane behavior: I take an aspirin for a headache, I reach for a pen to sign a form, I agree to join others for an outing, or I decide to work late to finish a project. Nothing in objections to synchronic or reflexive downward causation touches this multitude. At one place (2000b, p. 312), Kim seems to admit as much. He writes that the simple typewriter example "suffices to show that there can be nothing strange or incoherent in the idea of downward causation as such—the idea that complex systems, in virtue of their macro-level properties, can cause changes at lower levels." We see below that his compliance is short-lived; but thus far it is difficult to see wherein the objection could lie.

Kim observes that Sperry's examples, "taken as cases of diachronic reflexive causation, from properties of a whole to properties of its constituent parts at a later time, . . . appear to be free of metaphysical difficulties" (2000b, p. 317). It is likely that he is thinking primarily of those sorts of examples. The key phrase in this passage for us is "from properties of a whole to properties of its constituent parts." Conscious properties should not be assumed to fit this pattern; the emergentist certainly will want to deny that they are collections of activated neurons, and causation by conscious properties is

11. As far as synchronism goes, Sperry writes (just to take one of a number of examples) "I see the brain as a generator of emergent novel phenomena that *then* exerts supercedant control over lower-level activities." (1980, p. 200, emphasis added)

Sperry's real target. Eddies and turning wheels are used only to soften up readers by showing that downward causation with less embattled examples is commonplace; they are not intended to pinpoint the exact relation of a conscious property to its neurological base. What, then, might Kim have in mind when he suggests (2000b, p. 319, n. 15) that those cases are not the sort that the emergentist needs? If he means that emergentism requires synchronic reflexive causation, that has already been ruled out, and we have provided a sense in which synchronic reflexive *dependence* evades his attack. On the other hand, this might be another instance of the traditional objection that, when the cause is a conscious property, downward causation involves the exceptional difficulty of trying to understand how the mental can cause something physical. There is no defense against this charge other than to ask the objector to be more specific. But if this is the complaint, a prohibition against downward causation or some of its forms no longer figures in it. Perhaps neither of these is what Kim intends; however, this is the only other likely construal that occurs to me.

Thus far, we haven't seen a sustainable objection to downward causation. The phenomenon doesn't even look very remarkable. Whatever the problems for which it is blamed, they seem to be attributable either to downward causation's inevitably exposing a lower-level cause that overrides the supervenient one and leading to senseless overdetermination, or to the fact that once the descent has started there is no way to stop it short of causation at the fundamental level, which then trumps everything above it. These are objections (i) and (iii), respectively.

In various writings, Kim raises some further issues that start from downward causation but whose resolution ultimately rests with objection (iii). A quick review of a few of those issues provides a useful transition to the discussion of descending support.

First, another of Kim's objections is framed as a response to a counter-objection raised earlier against the redundancy argument's prohibition of downward causation. That counter-objection, known as *the generalization argument*, states that the form of argumentation in RA would disqualify all supervenient tokens from having a causal role. It would prevent a causal role not only for the mental, but would also prevent one for the characteristic properties and events of the special sciences. Biological, geological, chemical, and other aspects are supervenient on structural relations between the micro-particles of the physical world, the subject matter of particle physics.

That a special science has for its subject matter only things that are, broadly speaking, physical is irrelevant. They would still require downward causation if they had any causal role. The generalization argument is set out as a *reductio* of RA and its exclusion of all downward causation.

Kim has responded to the generalization argument in several ways. First, he has hypothesized (1997b, 2000a) that mental causation isn't genuinely downward, because the relevant properties are properties of the same individuals. The causes occur at the level of their bases. This has puzzled various critics (e.g., Antony (2007)). Why, for instance, is a hierarchy of properties not comparable to a hierarchy of substances or a hierarchy of sciences? In fact, it is difficult to see why, with a bit of tweaking, we couldn't say the same thing about every instance of realization. Is a leaf more than a physical entity with biological properties? Is a layer of rock more than a collection of particles belonging to a geological stratum? Then why aren't *being a red maple leaf* and *being a Devonian stratum* nothing more than properties of physical particles? In addition, what seems to matter to the argument is only the supervenience of the would-be causes. If that relation doesn't generate a distinction of levels, differences in level are irrelevant. And it is obvious that both mental properties and special-science constructs supervene on physical somethings other than themselves. It appears that the difference Kim envisages between emergents and the special sciences doesn't remove the sting of the generalization argument.

More recently, Kim emphasizes a different tack, in which he appears to bite the bullet (if only for the sake of argument). In 2005 he declares that even if we accept the generalization argument, it leaves us with the same options: epiphenomenalism or reductive identity. To this he adds that the obviousness of higher-level causation doesn't suffice: "what has to be shown is that these kinds of 'higher-level' causation are irreducible to basic physical causation. . . ." (p. 54) Not everyone will be persuaded by this declaration. As is now platitudinous in our racket, one philosopher's modus ponens is another's modus tollens, and in the present case the clear appearance of causal laws, or at least causation, in physical sciences other than basic physics may be plain enough to support that premise-conclusion inversion. Whether this is so depends on its comparative strength when weighed against the reasons for determination by "basic physical causation." And it seems clear that we needn't rest content with the mere fact that higher-level causation strikes us as evident. The argument of the preceding chapter showing that realizations shouldn't be identified *en masse* with their realizers and that the causal powers of the two don't coincide, supplies a substantive reason for holding that the powers of a realizer do not always suffice for those of its realized. Moreover, if a property can be delineated by means of its causal profile, as argued in section 4.4, then realized properties, on the basis of no more than their realization, have distinct causal profiles, which counts against collapsing the causation of the realized into that of its realizer. The realized will have causal conditions and partners in its causal transactions not present in those of its base. That challenges the epiphenomenalism-or-identity dilemma with which CEA and RA are meant to confront mental causation.

Recently I mentioned that Kim seemed comfortable with certain sorts of downward causation, although not the sort he believed necessary for emergentism. However, in passages that seem to reflect his bedrock convictions, Kim expresses doubt about any form of downward causation (2000b, p. 318). Descending support ultimately triumphs over downward causation. For example, consider Kim's summary of a baseball that shatters a window: ". . . the baseball = this composite structure of microparticies. Presumably, the causal powers of the baseball are *determined* by its microstructural features and perhaps also *explainable* in terms of them." (2005, p. 56)

To bring this into line with Sperry's illustrations (the eddy, the wheel, a bird in flight), one would say that it is the motion of the changing location of the baseball's micro-particles, not the baseball itself, that scatters the micro-particles of the window. There is an indication in this and the previous passage quoted from Kim that he believes, along with a host of others, that it is at least *prima facie* the case that *all* causal efficacy resides ultimately in fundamental physical particles. If so, that would create for all supervenient causation, including that of *physical* supervenient properties and events in the special sciences, the same predicament outlined for mental causation. Let us then look more closely at the objection in (iii), that all causation is vested in the interaction between proto-atoms.

4.6 Ultimate Particles and Descending Support

I take it as abundantly clear that causation occurs in the natural world. Although this is highly plausible, not every serious thinker agrees (e.g., Russell 1912, Norton 2007). Some regard causation as nothing more than a folk concept, useful but not an item on the list of reality's mind-independent ingredients. Although contemporary critics who repudiate thick natural causation have done so under the banner of an unflinching naturalism, they are the heirs of a tradition whose disciples thought that at most one needs to account for causation's appearance. The views of Leibniz and Malebranche on the subject are, at best, equivocal. Kim reports that Jonathan Edwards held that the appearance of natural causation was illusory. Edwards regarded natural causation as analogous to a succession of images in a mirror. It may seem as if a succeeding image was the result of the one immediately preceding it, but we know that this is not the case.[12] Views such as these require supernatural intervention to bring about change, a result warmly received by virtually all of those peddling or purchasing it. However, the appearance of natural causation is sufficiently robust to allow us to agree here that it actually occurs, and to ask what follows from that. (In order to see how descending support fares on its own turf, I put aside the contextualism put forward at the end of chapter 3.)

As we trace causation yet deeper, it is only natural to surmise that proto-atoms must be responsible for all the causal relations cited at supervenient levels. As Strevens put it, "there simply are no causal relations of which we are aware that cannot be attributed to lower level interaction and, ultimately, to the causal influence of fundamental particle on fundamental particle" (2008, p. 82). As was noted earlier, this may not conform to what working physicists seek as their fundamental particles, the ones that fit their equations. One view is that causation, or even a mechanism for causation at a higher level, does not appear at a very low order, where the relations are functional but not causal. I have more to say about that shortly. But let's provisionally sidestep that issue, as it concerns potentially fugitive features of current scientific practice, and treat the thesis of descending support not as the holy grail of an idealized physics but as a plausible

12. Edwards declared that causation was always God's constant recreation of the world. Kim cites a passage from a 1758 work. Earlier Descartes had expressed a similar view in elaborating a "causal" argument for God's existence: "For it is quite clear to anyone who attentively considers the nature of time that the same power and action are needed to preserve anything at each individual moment of its duration as would be required to create that thing anew if it were not yet in existence. Hence the distinction between preservation and creation is only a conceptual one. . . ." (1641, p. 33)

generalization based on past successes of the direction in which discoveries having been driving us. Things at level n have regularly been discovered to have underlying mechanisms operating at level $n - 1$, those at $n - 1$ to operate on mechanisms discoverable at $n - 2$, and so on. Thus, mental tokens are subserved by neurological ones, and neurological tokens are brought about by chemical ones (e.g., DNA molecules). Proceeding on that assumption, what are we to make of causation in biology, geology, chemistry, and in ordinary macroscopic events—say, changing a ball's trajectory by hitting it with a bat, opening a tap to make water flow, flipping a switch to turn on a light, or bringing the blades of a scissors together to cut paper? Those who refuse to accept downward causation generally advocate descending support—causation that bottoms out only with proto-atoms. Tracing all efficacy to proto-atoms leaves us with the following options for non-basic causation.

First, efficacy might be liberally bestowed on properties at any level appropriately related to (say, constituted by) proto-atoms. We might think of fundamental causation as a licensing bureau for other causation, or perhaps as nature's ichor, infusing whatever partakes of it with its assets. Past a now insignificant distinction between original and derived efficacy there is no further metaphysical ordering.

Next, properties above the level of proto-atoms might have a causal role, but with qualifications. On some accounts, macroscopic and microscopic causation each have causal *relevance*, but only the latter has *efficacy* (Jackson and Pettit 1990a). Ordinary causal talk is legitimate, but candor compels us to acknowledge that this is at most a practically useful way to talk rather than a guide to causal reality. It is possible to invert this picture; perhaps proto-atomic causation is so foreign to our everyday notion that macroscopic causal relevance is of prime importance. Still, if other venues get their relevance only because of the causal work of proto-atoms, it is difficult to resist the view that mere causal relevance possesses but a steerage-class ticket. This two-tiered scheme provides yet another opening for the view that macroscopic causation gains its prominence for contexts of explanation rather than for unvarnished causation (Jackson and Petit 1990b).

Finally, one might refuse causal powers of any sort to aspects above the proto-atomic level. The passage from Kim quoted in section 4.5 hinted at this *if* it should turn out that there is nothing left to claims for higher-level causation other than that they strike us as obvious. Higher-level causation may suffer the fate that Jonathan Edwards proclaimed for all natural causation.

Returning to the Causal Exclusion Argument, even on the first (liberal) construal of macroscopic causation, the causal role of the mental is preserved only through that role's identity with its physical realizer. The mental's realizer is determinative of its causal powers. But we don't stop there; its realizer—say, a configuration of neurological properties—will have a further realization, down to proto-atoms. Nothing in this line of reasoning presupposes that all macro-physical and mental aspects are supervenient on, or realized by, their determiners in precisely the same way, or even that there is a unified hierarchy of levels. Differences among types of dependency are no solution to objection (iii). The only supposition needed is that the fates of mental and macroscopically physical causation are sealed by something belonging to a more basic class.

But what if there are no proto-atoms? Suppose the potential physical decomposition of particles continues without end. That has been called *causal drainage*. Though not an orthodox view, it has not been dismissed out of hand. Ned Block (2003a) and Jonathan Schaffer (2003) have examined its implications. Let us track some important consequences.

Under causal drainage structure descends infinitely. According to the argument for (iii), the reason macroscopic items have causal roles only derivatively, or not at all, is that there is a level below them at which the real causal muscle is exerted. Under drainage, however, any level one chooses will be derivative. There will always be something beneath it whose causal work accounts for its causation or the appearance of its causation. Nothing will have an original efficacy by means of which it can categorically authenticate anything else's causation, although on descending support everything requires just such authentication. What then are we to make of causation?

I hope we can dismiss without further ado the view that because of causal drainage there is no causation anywhere. Even those who write off causation as no more than a convenient folk concept don't do so because there is no fundamental level. That conclusion based on drainage alone is unlikely to tempt anyone. What falls under censure is the demand that (iii) places on causes rather than the whole edifice of natural causation.

If there were causal drainage, we would need to seek other grounds for attributions of causation. There seems no firmer starting point than the robust appearance of causation in the special sciences and in our everyday, observable world. This doesn't mean that we can't find specific reasons for exposing one or another pretender. We may be able to discover that the apparent work of certain properties in a particular venue owe their potency to properties elsewhere. If so, this will occur on a case-by-case basis, and for reasons related to the details of the concerned subject matter. It will not be a causation fire sale. The Causal Exclusion Argument and the Redundancy Argument are not of that ilk. RA places mental causation in a quandary besetting *any* higher-order property. If there are other reasons for attributing causal efficacy, the mere fact that there is an aspect P_{n-1} on which P_n supervenes, and which has causal credentials, will be insufficient to show that a mental cause could be efficacious only through its identity with that aspect. In consequence, the reasons (iii) provides for rejecting separable mental causation have been undermined. And the causal exclusion and redundancy arguments, insofar as they are interpreted as locating the source for all causal efficacy at the proto-atomic level, are equally endangered by a failure to frame an acceptable response to the threat of causal drainage.

Kim's most developed response to "drainage" (in 2003) is that once we reach the physical level, the same reasoning that led us to support the identity water = H_2O will apply to the identity of water with whatever is one level below H_2O, one level below that, the next level below that, and so on. We thereby stanch the seepage with a single multiple-identity formula:

$$P_L = P_{L-1} = P_{L-2} = P_{L-3}. \ldots$$

However, this is too hasty. For one thing, mereological supervenience does not guarantee identity. Various types of particles, even those below the level of observation, supervene mereologically on others. But in the case of a statue and its clay and that of a statue and its replaceable parts, we have seen that mereological supervenience doesn't amount to identity. It couldn't. Constitution is, at a minimum, asymmetrical and non-reflexive; identity is neither. Mereological composition is not sufficient to promote a relation from constitution to identity. Nevertheless, Kim has stated that the reasoning leading to his identity claim is "the same reasoning" (2005, p. 69) that led us to identify water with H_2O and to adopt other similar theoretical reductions. However, the comparison is moot. The identity of water and H_2O is a passage from water's manifest image to its scientific image (to borrow a striking turn of phrase from Wilfrid Sellars). That is a significant step in declaring not only that water is made up of H-O-H but also that we end up with the very same substance despite the variation in idiom. The reason for identifying H_2O with water is the supposition that nothing has changed other than the dialect. It isn't clear what sense there is to the claim that H_2O *constitutes* water—it *is* water. The circumstances may be otherwise for the subatomic strata in the subsequent identity claims. If the descending levels of properties are already firmly within the scientific image, that distinction will not help us to get past mereological supervenience. We need something beyond such a constitutional relationship to warrant identities as we descend farther.

A second reason the response fails is that the identity of P_{L-n} with P_{L-2n} requires that P_{L-n} not be multiply constituted (or realizable). There is no warrant for supposing that the descending levels meet this requirement. A possible rebuttal to this point is that differences of realization imply a difference of kind.

If the realizing kinds do genuinely differ in their causally relevant properties, . . . they are different kinds. But if they are different kinds, then they are not the same kind, and so we do not have a case in which a single kind has multiple realizations. (Shapiro 2000, p. 647)

A standard illustration of the foregoing claim is the case of jade, which can be either jadeite or nephrite. Jade is not a single mineral because it is not projectible—that is, not a kind supporting causal laws. By parity of reason, one might argue that, if an apparent particle at level n has the constitution 'A or B or . . .', it is really different particles for each disjunct, not a unitary type. Laws governing one of these embodiments need not cover the remainder. However, it is doubtful that the analogy with jade succeeds. Jade is a disjunctive property, but not a multiply realizable one. Following Fodor (1997), it is as necessary that jade is either nephrite or jadeite as it is that water is H_2O. If I create something superficially indistinguishable from jade with my chemistry set, it will not be jade any more than a zircon is a diamond. Jade doesn't exhibit the sort of open disjunctivity that one associates with multiple realizability. However, if there is a kind of stuff constituting creatures on a planet in the Pelican Nebula, but that stuff is not present in the Milky Way, metaphysically speaking those creatures might feel genuine pain, much as a silicon gadget I concocted in my basement laboratory might feel pain. But the issue here is projectibility, not metaphysics, so let's see if the objection can survive that challenge.

Following Block (1997), scientifically respectable causal generalizations do not invariably carve reality at the pre-selected joints. For example, although eyes and their neurological support structures have evolved along different physiological channels, some robust perceptual generalizations seem to hold across a broad spectrum for differently constituted creatures. (See, e.g., Shepard 1987.) Indeed, it is a commonplace that lawlike generalizations can apply across different incarnations of a multiply constituted phenomenon (e.g., heat or ice). For example, there are hydrochloric acids, sulphuric acids, amino acids, nitric acids, phosphoric acids, carbonic acids, and others, but all of them turn blue litmus paper red, corrode metals, and burn the skin when topically applied. In light of the glut of such cases, even if we grant that there is a tight relationship between causal connections and laws, the division between laws that support causation and those that don't threatens to make the cutoff point arbitrary. I will treat these matters in greater detail in chapter 6. For present purposes, it suffices to note that this method for arresting the drainage encounters serious difficulties.

But what if The Standard Model is correct; there are proto-atoms? Does my response to (iii) collapse if there is a bottom level? For starters, there are problems with relying heavily on the standard view once the conceivability of causal drainage is on the table. Shouldn't the mere yet to be controverted conceivability of drainage dissipate any confidence we might have that the bottom level is the engine of all causation? Don't some earlier problems— e.g., the generalization argument—still threaten descending support? And could a concern about whether there are in fact proto-atoms really have this central a place in an analysis of causation *per se*? On its surface, descending support deals only with the *extension* of causation. Could an issue about the extension of causal relations make that much difference to the intrinsic nature of the property? I believe all these issues are still in play for those who rely on there being proto-atoms. But there is a more direct problem involving the ultimate causes view, to which I now turn.

As was mentioned earlier in the preceding and present chapter, fundamental-level causation, if it exists, will behave radically differently from familiar, bourgeois causation. Differences in the conditions under which the two operate are so marked that some have been skeptical about causation at lower levels (Russell 1912; Field 2003; Norton 2007); others (Hitchcock 2007; Woodward 2007) maintain that it can be salvaged in spite of these discrepancies. But both sides acknowledge significant differences between what counts as causation at the fundamental level and what counts as causation at higher levels. Equations distinctive of our knowledge of fundamental particles do not preserve intrinsic features of macroscopic causation, such as asymmetry and temporal priority. Rather, they fold some features into others, sometimes symmetrically. Anything said about this is likely to be subject to conflicting interpretations, but consider the Pauli Exclusion Principle. It tells us that no two fermions in a single system can exist in the same state at the same time, but, to the best of our knowledge, it gives no direction to those correlative states, and any changes in the states would have to be simultaneous. Nevertheless, this fact is responsible for many of the features of ordinary matter. Whether this is sufficient to allow us to declare that what happens at that level is non-causal may be largely a terminological matter, but at a minimum it indicates a radical difference with commonplace instances of causation.

However, for present purposes the more interesting feature of what might count as causation at the fundamental level is the absence of *defeasibility*. Any causation at a proto-atomic level must be invariant, providing a nomologically sufficient condition for its supposed effects. There is no room for something else to intervene or interfere to defeat those causal connections. This contrasts with the defeasible sufficiency I emphasized in the preceding chapter. The appeal of descending support has been the expectation that fundamental-level causation merely complements, by fleshing out, macro-causation. Its role was supposedly to fill in the details of derivative causal connections, to specify a more fine-grained account of the work of what we take to be causation at observable levels. Even though it may not replicate or make recoverable all the descriptions in upper-level causal explanations, presumably it is taken as a self-sufficient account of apparent causation at those levels. But, as Woodward emphasizes, far from filling out the finer details of macro-causation, it subverts them.

In addition to the ability to trace ordinary causation to the work of fundamental particles, fundamental particle interactions, it has been assumed, resolve issues in a way that threatens realism about ordinary causation. For example, although much has been written about the differences between causes and mere conditions, it has been difficult to pin down a distinction that isn't deemed to be interest-driven and therefore merely pragmatic. Thus, whereas the plague may be cited as the cause of Bartholomew's death, while Bartholomew's being born is a mere condition of his death, it has been pointed out that even the latter can be the cause of death for sufficiently bizarre contexts. (See, e.g., Lewis 2004, p. 101.) However, as mentioned in the preceding chapter, even without descending to the causal boiler room, the price of a physical causation more resistant to this sort of charge is to cite as the cause of an event the light-cone structure in the entire universe immediately preceding it. (See, e.g., Field 2003; Loewer 2007.) Nor is that the end of the matter. Everything falling within that light cone will be the effect of the preceding light cone, and so on *ad infinitum*: a distal cause is as much a cause as a proximal one. (And for standard and presumably observable causation, we seldom pinpoint the absolutely proximal cause.) Only if we apply that method will macro-causes line up with fundamental-level determiners. But that entitles everything preceding the effect, including omissions, to be equally efficacious. This may be prefigured in the widespread notion that the cause *necessitates* its effect (though, as a warning against putting too much weight on that usage, I note that 'necessitation' sometimes is thrown out merely as a loose synonym for 'cause'). This is not the isolated cause that serves us so well in the special sciences and in everyday life. In contrast to the plague-birth case, the nomologically sufficient account suggested by causation for fundamental particles avoids at least that particular support for skepticism about the objectivity of causation.

But now consider a typical case of ordinary causation.

Smithers has an infection, for which he receives a shot of penicillin, and he recovers the next day. We think the penicillin cured the infection, not Smithers' praying that the infection would disappear, his opening a car door to leave the clinic, his going thence to his daughter's soccer match, or his snoring loudly that night. But we may assume that all these are parts of the successive light cones preceding Smithers' recovery. Indeed, if we import the light-cone-structure view into this case, the outbreak of the Crimean War is as much a cause of Smithers' recovery as that dose of penicillin. We require this much if we are to preserve the necessity or non-defeasibility present at the fundamental level. Thus, if our demand is that causation well up from the bottom, it not only replaces the coarse-grained notion with a more fine-grained one, which by itself could be an advance in precision; it renders nugatory any more particular selection we may make of the cause of a particular episode. If non-defeasibility attaches to causation at the lowest level, ordinary causation, if countenanced, is yet another emergent phenomenon.

This doesn't rule out *all* dependence of the upper levels on the (now assumed) bottom level. However, the dependence seems to reside in the ontology of things rather than in their causal potentials, a point introduced briefly in section 4.3. Although causation is also an ontological matter, the two concerns are distinct ontological matters and may be treated separately.

In light of this result deeply committed physicalists may make another move. For them, the foregoing argument shows only that commonplace causation has no independent metaphysical standing. The commonplace use of causal vocabulary is purely pragmatic, lacking a foundation at the level in which all reality is grounded. Though this may appeal to certain dead-enders, I find it difficult to countenance. That the scissors really is cutting the paper and that the bat really did change the trajectory of the ball are robust data that must be overcome by more than an allegiance to an incompatible top-down outlook, and causation in general seems indispensable rather than merely useful (cf. Woodward). But that needn't be argued here, for if causation is a secondary quality or a useful fiction, that doesn't place the causal role of conscious properties at a disadvantage; it restores their footing with macroscopic physical properties. The unfavorable comparison of mental causation with that in the physical world, other than the most basic, dissolves.

4.7 A Causal Nexus

Nothing in the most general theories of causation (say, regularity or counterfactual theories) prohibits mental causes. However, what is sometimes labeled "productivity theory" (see Anscombe 1971; Hall 2004) introduces another scenario that Kim (2007) finds troublesome for mental causation.

Elusive though its precise statement may be, one generally intends by 'productivity' the sort of connection that Hume (1739/1978, p. 157) sought in vain under titles such as 'necessary connection', 'power', 'force', and 'efficacy'. Because of his lack of success, Hume replaced that notion with his pioneering regularity theory. On a productivity view, the actual *bringing about* of a particular effect by a particular cause is the essence of causation. Kim allows that the account may work well only at the level of fundamental particles. Nevertheless, he tries it on. The problem for mental causation, then, is a causal desideratum, which Kim takes from Hume, that the cause and its effect must be *contiguous*. This rules out an independent mental cause of anything physical, because a mental cause cannot be physically contiguous with its effect.

By 'contiguous' Kim means "in space *and* time," whereas Hume evidently meant "in space *or* time." In fact, Hume's first and most prominent example of a causal relation displaying contiguity is just such mental causation:

The motion of our body follows upon the command of our will. Of this we are every moment conscious. But the means, by which this is effected; the energy, by which the will performs so extraordinary an operation; of this we are so far from being immediately conscious, that it must forever escape our most diligent enquiry. (1748, p. 65)

The point of Hume's contiguity condition is that where it makes sense to speak of a gap in space or time, its existence *sans* intervening links defeats causality: no action at a distance. Nothing intrinsically non-spatial can fail for that reason alone. It is in the very nature of a gap to be capable of being of various sizes—in rough terms, large, small, moderate. If there had been a spatial gap between Hume's act of will and its bodily motion, we could sensibly ask how wide it was. But there is no sense to be made of such a question. Kim's version fails radically if omissions can be causes. (See, e.g., Schaffer 2000; Horgan 1989; Maslen 2004; Menzies 2003.) Whereas a very loose temporal contiguity may be relevant (e.g., Alice's plants died because she didn't water them), the requirement of spatiotemporal contiguity has no place here. Kim (2007) rejects omissions as causes on the grounds that we are unable to distinguish any of them from the vast multitude of others whose non-interference is required for the effect. However, this difficulty is no more severe than selecting Kim's own "productive" cause from among the many other things in the effect's immediately preceding light cone. If we can isolate one feature as the productive cause (e.g., the aspirin cured the headache rather than the bourbon), we can select Alice's not watering the plants yesterday (rather than President Obama's not watering them) as the cause of their death.

A satisfactory contiguity requirement would need to be Hume's rather than Kim's. The productivity theory stands a chance of surviving if it demands no more than that the cause and the effect be contiguous in any dimension in which both can be found, ruling out actual gaps between cause and effect. However, as Kim interprets the requirement, not only does it beg the question against mental-to-physical causation; it replaces the perhaps plausible motto "No action at a distance" with the controversial "No causation at a distance." (See Lewis 2004.) Running together causation and action has a long and checkered history. For example, Berkeley (1710, part I, §25), following the lead of Descartes and Locke, wrote: "All our ideas . . . are visibly inactive—there is nothing of power or agency included in them. So one idea or object thought cannot produce or make any alteration in another." To assume that causation is always an action not only leaves no room for the role of absences but requires patches to the roles of the most prominent accounts—viz., regularity and counterfactual theories—as sufficient conditions. No doubt one can salvage the sufficient conditions for the major theories through The Conceptual Gambit; one admits the non-action cases as explanations rather than causes. But whatever the prominent theories to which I just alluded may accomplish, they are strengthened when we don't proscribe so much of what they could handily incorporate. The contextualism sketched in section 3.7, and even fact-based causation (Mellor 2000), whatever their ultimate bona fides, accommodate those theories with a dexterity that is lost when it is necessary to appeal to extraneous contrivances.

5   Belief, Desire, and the Physical

5.1   Access Consciousness Revisited

Thus far, phenomenal properties, pains in particular, have been emergentism's shock troops. However, in chapter 1 I issued a promissory note that my emergentism would also cover access-conscious properties. It has come due. Access consciousness's natural contrasts would not be a lack of unmediated inner recognition and transparency, but it would contrast with features of sentient life such as Freudian unconsciousness or blindsight. Some maintain that phenomenal awareness is not a distinct category of items but an ingredient of access-conscious properties. We needn't choose sides. Of prime importance here is only that this emergentist theory cover the whole spectrum of cases—including belief, expectation, fear, anxiety, hope, and the like—in which the mental episode is directly available to its subject for behavior and reasoning.

In this chapter I argue that certain effects, instances of behavior, are not possible without access-conscious causes. However, before turning directly to that task, let us look at some preliminary distinctions surrounding the conception of physicality that are found in philosophy. It is my (perhaps quixotic) hope that this will aid us in more clearly discerning what is at stake.

5.2   Two Standards of Physicality

In section 1.9, I gingerly avoided the question of what counts as physical. I now propose to re-open it by way of a meta-issue. The question of concern is not "Which things are physical?" but "What tests are used to decide whether something is physical?" Of course, knowing the answer to that question will contribute significantly toward deciding the question at the object level, but that is not my focal concern. Rather, I want eventually to compare two standards for calling something physical. They have proved largely complementary, but, as we shall see, their differences can make a difference to an issue.

The first standard, which I shall call *rigorous physicality*, can be explored through a combination of (PCC) and descending support. This pair does not add up to physicalism, but the present task is to describe the bases for something to count as physical, which is a different issue. Earlier it was noted that property dualism is compatible with (PCC) because it is conceivable for a mental causal chain to operate wholly independently of any physical causes. Also, *pace* descending support, a version of physicalism would survive the view that there are higher-level physical laws irreducible to any lower-level physical laws. (See Laughlin and Pines 2000; Kitcher 1984.) Nevertheless, both would be central if one went on to defend a rigorous version of physicalism. (PCC) is implied by physicalism, while descending support not only has been a powerful incentive to physicalism but is often regarded as its core. For example, in a passage already quoted in chapter 1 Shoemaker (2007, p. 3) has written: "if physicalism is true, all of the facts are determined, constitutively, by the microphysical facts—by how fundamental micro-entities are distributed in the world."[1] Although descending support is not tied to the ultimate truth of any particular stage of a science, on The Standard Model suppose these are currently collections of quarks, leptons, bosons, and their anti-matter counterparts, along with the four fundamental forces.

Returning to (PCC), and gauging its role in physicalism, notice that it is a rather odd representative of a closure principle. A standard closure principle for a deductive system states that anything logically implied by a theorem is a theorem. Similar principles have been tried out for other subjects. For knowledge, if S knows that p and knows that p implies q, S knows (that is, has the resources for knowing) q; for epistemic justification, if p is justified and p implies q, q is justified; for obligation, if Φ is obligatory, and Φ mandates Ψ, Ψ is obligatory. These principles, whether or not they pass close scrutiny, display a common pattern. Each is a principle for enabling

1. Earlier, in a related passage, Shoemaker wrote about "states" and "properties." In this one he mentions only "facts." But he gives no indication that what he says about facts is not equally applicable to states and properties.

something with a certain feature to extend that feature to something obtainable from it via a rule of detachment. Notice that in each it is not required that the bearer of the feature in the antecedent of the conditional acquire its status—viz., as a theorem, as knowledge, as a justified belief, or as an obligation—through a similar derivation. However, (PCC)'s role is not primarily to infuse *being physical* into what it causes or what caused it. On it something doesn't *become* physical by being caused by something physical; that is determined independently and prior to the application of the principle. Rather, (PCC)'s role is to exclude all causes or effects from the outside. It is physicalism's immigration officer.

I call the second standard of the physical *vernacular physicality*. In contrast to the previous standard, it is the notion under which we confidently subsume objects and properties in our workaday environment. Some authors (e.g., Endicott (1989), Sturgeon (1998, 2002), Pereboom (2002), and Stoljar (2001) have called into question bringing the loosely physical within the ambit of the rigorously physical. I share their suspicion, and the rest of this section is devoted to spelling out my reasons. Moreover, much if not all of the underlying source for a lack of fit can be traced to an exhaustive physical-mental dichotomy. That is not to say the classification is itself defective. The problem I shall be emphasizing arises only because of the lumping together of disparate things that fall on the physical side of the distinction. Once a subject is classified as physical (the only option that makes sense on this dichotomy), there is a tendency, which even the wary find difficult to resist, to refit the humdrum physical to the demands of definitions deriving from assumptions about fundamental particles. Were the physical a monolith, all might go well. But as things stand, differences within that class must be acknowledged to avoid distortions in the metaphysics of mind.

In everyday discourse, spatially distributed action and other mammalian behavior are indeed physical. Some instances may provide material over which philosophers can quibble, such as thinking out a mathematical problem without writing implements. But we certainly believe that hailing a cab, dialing a telephone, opening a door, and pouring a drink are all physical activities, possible only with the cooperation of commonplace physical objects.

On the other hand, when devising conservation, closure, or isolation principles for the physical, descending support has invariably been in the forefront; as we have seen, a frequently exploited paradigm for physical causation has been the interactions between the most fundamental set of physical items known or conceived. One way to appreciate the drawing power of this outlook is to imagine an argument against mental causation in which physical closure was a component, but in which, say, the neural causes of behavior did not owe their own efficacy to the power of lower-level constituents of the neurological. This is (PCC) minus descending support. Thus, imagine that tracing the mechanisms of causation ends abruptly at neurons. Of course, we should be impressed by the fact that whenever there is a supposed mental cause there is a neural counterpart, and by the fact that we seem capable of bringing forth or suppressing mental results by fiddling with neurons.[2] But in another respect we now lack the picture of a unified physical world that has sustained contemporary physicalism. Tracking of causes now stops at an arbitrary node. If we must choose an arbitrary point, why not stop with mental causes? A physical world divided into discrete stopping points, with no further unifying mechanisms, takes away a pillar on which the attraction of physicalism rests. Although the revealing correlation of neural and conscious episodes remains, wouldn't this reinvigorate the suspicion that their interaction might sometimes go in either direction?

To elaborate, physicalism as a systematic philosophical outlook is driven not by the fact that large boulders are never moved by telekinesis but by the commonly accepted outlook that scientific progress has enabled us to uncover with ever-increasing specificity the more basic physical mechanisms behind relatively accessible causal relations. This mindset has proved prophetic. Further fuel has been added by a series of successively sharpened principles of conservation via redistribution (of, say, matter, motion, momentum, or energy) to offset the appearance of the loss or gain of something material in causal transactions. Those sorts of considerations lend significant support to the supposition that causation *of* the physical is adequately and exclusively brought off *by* the physical. Although there is a consensus among physicalists that the ordinary macroscopic activities sampled two paragraphs ago are as physical as the objects they require for their

2. I do not claim that the unified picture is the only support for this customary physicalism (see, for example, Kim's requirement of spatial contiguity, discussed in section 4.7), but other support does appear to be subsidiary to the assumption that the physical is a comprehensive and unified causal system.

completion, instances of that type are of secondary importance for physical science, and their standing as physical, as well as that of their objects, could be brought into question if they were discovered not to conform to the working principles of fundamental particles. This seems to have inspired some to restrict our options either to conforming to reductive causation at a much lower level or being eliminated altogether from our ontology. The possibility that an item which didn't find a place in this order might still be physical is not contemplated. (And for the non-physical there is no option that it might still be an objective part of nature.)

The physical supports a grounding in the fundamental by this route. It will simplify our discussion if we set aside the questions raised in section 4.6 and assume that the grounding is causal at every level. However, we must be careful in how we understand the distinction between these standards. The crucial difference between the rigorously physical and the vernacular physical isn't one of size. Routine physical things and their properties can be as tiny as one likes. We think of big things as made up of smaller things, and it would be difficult to find a cutoff point for the vernacular in terms of size alone. It is certainly within the realm of ordinary causation to hold that mental phenomena are caused by neurological aspects, and that neurons and the qualities issuing from them are not detectable through unaided human perception. The differences between our two conceptions lie, rather, in the disparate bases for their classifications as physical. Size enters our deliberations only insofar as it might figure into one of our two standards.

In salient cases, vernacular physical things are perceived as such, although we regularly *extend* membership to whatever we believe proximately grounds them. On the other hand, certain things are initially discovered and identified only, or primarily, as mechanisms underlying the causal interactions of those large or tiny ordinary things, and it is at that hazy juncture that a different perspective on physicality begins to dominate. It would be hard to deny physicality of the first sort to the publicly perceivable, and equally hard to deny it to the nearby causal mechanisms of what is has already been granted that status. Nor does the difference cited here imply that the two sorts of physicality cannot mesh; overwhelmingly they do. However, the subtle shift in our conception of physicality no longer guarantees that causal principles which operate smoothly within one of these nuanced conceptions will continue to do so when we hitch elements of the ordinary conception to the rigorous one. We must look more carefully at cases to see where, if at all, conceptions conceived on these divergent paradigms begin to clash. The suggestion I am pressing is that we shouldn't be complacent about top-down schemes, such as the one imposed by rigorous physicality, to warrant that all causal mechanisms can be grounded in interactions between collections of fundamental particles.

If we merely agglomerate everything generally taken to be physical, then, no matter how we originally came to classify homespun perceivable objects as physical, their persevering in this class will depend on their continued integration with the particles that figure in our most advanced theoretical physics. This is never an official pronouncement. There is no point in formulating the policy until we are pressured to do so by recalcitrant data, and it has been generally presumed that everything will eventually fit together. Unfortunately, past instances are not clear enough to rest my case on. The fortunes of phlogiston and caloric will not serve. Not only have they been ostracized for non-conformity to those principles; they have disappeared altogether from the roster of reality, and they were never paradigms of vernacular physicality in the first place. The theory of secondary qualities—such as color, sound, and taste—is a better example. Passing over the ancient atomists, the Aristotelian scientists of the middle ages seldom questioned color's physical credentials. But with the ascendancy of modern physics its status became, and remains, precarious. However, the clearest case I can think of comes not from physics but from chemistry.

By the everyday tests of sight and touch, glass appears to be a solid. However, a group of chemists contend that glass is a liquid, aligning it with water and vodka rather than wood and stone. I don't know how extensive or powerful this faction is; it is sufficient for my purposes that their view can't be off-handedly dismissed. What stands out for this revision is not the place of glass in the world of ordinary physical interaction or among the vulgate-tongued, but its molecular bonding. For those theorists the everyday criterion of solidity is abandoned in favor of our most up-to-date chemistry.

Similarly, if something once seemed to be a perfectly respectable instance of the physical that embraces both our types, but was discovered not to conform to the notion of physicality in an impressively developed physics, it would inevitably raise the question for some whether it was in fact physical. I am not relying on the likelihood of this happening, only on the substitution of one standard of physicality for another should they come into conflict. Were that to happen, the clout of fundamental particles would surely outweigh the folk notion. Although there may be divisions within the scientific and philosophical communities as to whether this is a legitimate reason for ostracizing the vernacular physical (and, if it is, there is a further issue about where to draw the line), there is now a live option of giving up the familiar rather than qualifying or scrapping the theory.[3] Indeed, this is only the other side of the coin from the historical fact that material existence has greatly expanded in the course of the development of modern physics. (Recall the quotation from Chomsky on pages 29 and 30.) If we are able to increase physicality's membership for theoretical ends, why shouldn't the possibility of its contraction in the light of theoretical discovery be an option? That is some indication that the physicality prin-ciples for the accepted fundamental mechanisms can decommission even our most deeply entrenched common notions.

This very natural progression operates on the assumption that every-thing physical will interact smoothly. The distinction between the rig-orously physical and the vernacularly physical gives us a glimmer of a diversity in this class that may block bringing the former into line with the latter. I intend this as a cautionary tale, designed only to warn us against dismissing distinctions within the physical itself. But the discussion thus far has only been a prelude to a further distinction within the vernacular, namely, that certain behavior is physical should not lead us to suppose that its etiology, indeed its very character, is exhausted when we have tracked it to the collection of elementary particles preceding it. However, before going directly to a defense of that view, we may note another fact that could throw a wrench into this line of physicalist reasoning (although I shall not press it further here).

Even if we ignore the distinctions between our types, descending support runs smoothly from the ordinarily physical to fundamental particles when the former is conceived as a mereological sum of the latter. Everyday physi-cal things depend on fundamental particles because they are compositional

3. A smidgen of apocryphal evidence: A theoretical physicist once told me that he didn't (officially) believe in "things" such as the train station in which we were standing, but only in series of eigenstates. Presumably the station was nothing more than the brainchild of our macro-sensitivities.

wholes of those particles. Although phenomenal properties or states may *depend on* neural ones, claims that the former are *composed of* clusters or activities of neurons already presupposes the truth of physicalism and the falsity of mental emergentism. However, we are examining arguments for physicalism, and, although it is a ground rule accepted by all the parties to our limited discussion that the phenomenal depends on the physical, it would be inappropriate at this stage to assume that the phenomenal is composed of something physical. Initial appearances do not support the view that a phenomenal state is nothing but a configuration of neural ones, and, as I argue in the next section, the same is true for access-conscious tokens. Recall the distinction first encountered in section 2.3 between compositional and emission versions of emergentism. It is important to decide whether it is dependence that matters, however spelled out, or whether it is the compositional character of the dependence that is propelling descending support. If the latter, we have even less of a reason to employ principles such as (PCC) to overturn mental causation. I don't know if compositionality is a root attraction of descending support, but the supposition of compositionality from top to bottom certainly makes descending support more palatable.

5.3 Access-Conscious Properties and Behavior

Once conflations between physicalities in this heteromorphous class are removed, we should be able to see with renewed clarity how emergentism may be extended to access-conscious tokens. My claim is that some of those tokens are indispensable causal elements for an otherwise elusive collection of behavioral events and properties. The further reduction of those tokens to their physical bases would make it impossible to capture the ontological standing of this important group of behaviors.

Consider ordinary specimens of human actions, such as frying an egg, jumping into the river, or going to a football game. They are not the only sorts of behavior at which the remarks below are aimed, and those remarks will not cover all such activities, but they are model instances of a class to which I want to draw attention. They are no less physical than the motions of the celestial spheres, and their movements are composed of the stuff on which they supervene; they couldn't occur in the absence of physical mechanisms of causation. It would be absurd to describe my frying an egg or my going to a football game as mental.

However, stopping at the dichotomy between the physical and the mental encourages philosophical moves that would lose much of their vigor if we weren't forced into making that stark choice. I am not suggesting that we adopt an expanded list of options. Rather, I recommend that we resist a tendency to dismiss anything about those activities that they don't share with more vanilla physical events, such as the interaction between groups of neurons. This is because, as I shall argue, certain behaviors couldn't occur without intentionality in their causal histories.

This is not to say that all intentional states are access conscious. For example, I may be said to believe that 2^2 is greater than 3 while thinking of my next move in a chess match or even when asleep. If one is non-conscious while asleep, it would be needless, not to say paradoxical, to suppose that there is a sense in which one is consciously non-conscious, or even that one has immediate cognitive access to that belief. But there are other circumstances in which that belief is available to the believer for action or reasoning, and those dispositions are candidates for being ineliminable causes.

Again, suppose that I go to a football game. I could have gone to the game in many ways—by train, bicycle, on foot, borne on a litter, and so on. There are also ways I could have been *taken* to the game without it being correct to say that I *went* to it. To go the game, I had to be in an intentional state to go somewhere, though perhaps not to the football game. I might have arrived there by mistake, thinking I was going somewhere else. (We must make room for the notion of going someplace by mistake or by accident—as, say, when someone absent-mindedly walks into a loo of the wrong sex.) But if I was bound up and forcibly carried by miscreants to the game, or I was swept there by a tornado, it would be a mistake to say that I went to the game (as distinct from simply ending up there). There are borderline cases (e.g., sleepwalking), but, absent special pleading, the intention is a *sine qua non* of *going* somewhere. Thus, when the chair of my department accuses me of having gone to the game when I should have been in class, I can honestly reply I didn't *go* to the game but rather was forcibly taken there, or taken there against my will. In light of this, for the chair to continue insisting that I nevertheless went to the game could be construed only as semantic ignorance, as ribbing, or as a lame excuse to fire me, but not as a serious, well-formed commentary.

There is a vague, and non-accidental, resemblance between this view and one advocated by Anscombe (1957) and Peters (1958) that actions are explicable only by reasons. Its proponents may have been on to something; however, they crucially miscalculated when they proceeded to require that intentional explanations be non-causal and insisted that the intentional token was both necessary and sufficient to distinguish human actions from mere "happenings to." No doubt those additions contributed to the subsequent neglect of their view. But nothing in the present thesis is committed to those further developments. My claim is simply that in some cases access-conscious causes are indispensable to the ontological status of a certain class of behaviors, although the class is not sharply defined.

The issue calls for finer-grained discriminations. The lesson of the foregoing examples needn't hold for everything that falls under the category of action,[4] and, as we shall see, it may extend to some mere reactions. After all, robots, dogs, and dolphins can be said to *do* things (say, on command), and this is compatible with denying that they are capable of forming the requisite thoughts that distinguish some human *doings* from *happenings to.* Also, certain bland descriptions that in some contexts may refer to actions can in other contexts describe reflexes (e.g., my lower leg rapidly rising when I kick a football or when the doctor's rubber-tipped hammer strikes just below my patella). Conversely, we all regularly *do* things automatically, apparently without a scintilla of forethought. We shouldn't deny that these are actions or that we need intentionality in their account as actions even if those intentional states lack all phenomenality. The point to be emphasized is rather that a host of human actions in specified though broad contexts can be described via our vocabulary of actions only if their etiologies include access-conscious elements. The difference between my raising my arm and my arm's going up (or its being raised) illustrates the point. Of course, there are many ways to capture this sort of difference in general terms, but it can be best appreciated if we aren't mesmerized by a sharp and exclusive distinction between the physical and the mental. Some behavior is such that, when it reaches a certain threshold, stopping at its material incarnation is at a minimum misleading, not because the behavior isn't physical, but because stopping there encourages an assimilation to occurrences that may trace their sufficient causes, without compromising their ontic standing, down to a level at which volcanic eruptions, meteoric collisions, and rainstorms can be understood. The assimilation glosses over

---

4. Of course, I am ignoring a number of irrelevant senses of 'action'—say, the action of a solvent in removing paint.

information about *causes* of certain physical events—not (I emphasize) just about their *explanation*, or even about their *causal* explanation.

To illustrate the danger, consider a case in which mental causation is actually being defended. Ernest Sosa offers the following example: "I extend my hand because of a certain neurological event. That event is my sudden desire to quench my thirst." (1984, p. 277) Shortly thereafter, Sosa notes that the potency of a causal event is due to certain of its properties, while other of its properties are causally inert. So far, so good. But then he remarks of this distinction that "the being a desire of my desire has no causal relevance to my extending my hand (if the mental is indeed anomalous): if the event that is in fact my desire had not been my desire but had remained a neurological event of a certain sort, then it would have caused [my] extending my hand just the same." (p. 278) Presumably Sosa is drawing out what he takes to be a consequence of regarding the mental as anomalous. But whether he is talking in his own voice or exploring the commitments of a view he rejects, I am more interested in the line of reasoning itself, which violates the distinction that I have been belaboring here.[5] The claim in the quoted passage is that (a) my desire (to drink) and (b) a similar neurological event *sans* any desire could each issue in an event describable as (c) *my extending my hand*. Certainly if (b) obtained there would have been an event, which would still be a physical event in the fullest sense, of (d) my hand being extended. But if there were no thirst or other affect that we could cite as responsible for the event, wouldn't (c) be an erroneous way to describe what (b) brought about? Extending one's hand, when used of a conscious agent (not a robot,[6] a sleepwalker, or someone with an uncontrollable tic) requires an intentional cause. It could have been done without any deliberation or forethought, as it were automatically. But it could not have been done by activity in my brain without my affective token (e.g., desire) or that of some individual controlling me.

This is not to say that we always rely on descriptions to classify instances. In a case brought up in conversation by Elizabeth Anscombe, suppose a

5. Chalmers (1996, p. 379, n. 41) appears to defend that line when he writes: "Nothing in the story about emergent causation requires us to invoke *phenomenal* properties anywhere. The entire causal story can be told in terms of links between configurations of physical properties." Despite Chalmers' qualification ('phenomenal'), his discussion makes clear his intention to include what I have been calling access-conscious properties as among those dispensable to the causal talk.

6. At least, one not under the direction of a conscious agent.

butler drops a tray of hors d'oeuvres. The description *dropping the tray* does not tell us whether this is an action, or even whether it is a "doing" in a broader but still in the agentive sense proposed by Nida-Rümelin (2007a,b). If the butler dropped the tray to startle a burglar in the garden, its causal antecedent requires the inclusion of an intentional state. If the butler dropped the tray because of his arthritis, or because he was startled by the burglar, intentional content needn't enter in this way. We can't tell from the bare description 'he dropped the tray' which of these is the case. And the same is true of many of the things that, under the right conditions, fall into the class of human actions. Of course, without the cooperation of bodily motions I could not go to a football game, extend an arm, drop a tray, or jump (rather than fall) into a river. My contention is only that the physiology that must cooperate if these events are to occur also does not reveal what events they are (viz., actions), but introduces factors that differentiate them only from other sparsely depicted physical motions (e.g., my arm's going up rather than down).

5.4   Elaborating and Augmenting

This has been intended as no more than a bare outline of a defense, but it is incomplete even on that generous standard. One question that cries out for an answer is "How fine-grained or coarse-grained are distinguishable causal sequences in this area?" For example, do we need different causes for the strictly physical at different levels, such as for my arm's going up and its underlying molecular activity? Or for two actions comprised in a single physical event, such my playing the piano and my playing the piano loudly?

In 1970 Alvin Goldman proposed a view of human action on which the commonest distinct levels of act-descriptions denote different actions. We begin by distinguishing causes from level-generations, one level of which is causal-generation. Distinct level-generations give rise to distinct actions. Thus an act might be generated causally, conventionally, simply, or augmentationally, each issuing in different acts. For a condensed description of one of Goldman's examples, consider 'Lisa's moving her hand', which may generate (simply and conventionally) 'her moving her queen', which may in turn augmentationally generate 'her moving her queen with deliberation', which may in turn conventionally generate 'her checkmating her opponent', which may in turn causally generate 'flustering her opponent'.

Goldman's scheme created a stir, critics claiming that the data could be handled by regarding these variations as identical acts under different descriptions. The proposal I have put forth about the indispensability of access-conscious properties for some behaviors commits me to going part of the way with Goldman, but for different reasons and not all the way to his fine-grained theory of actions. Goldman's reasons have to do with the identity conditions for the action sub-class of events; mine have to do with the need to have an intentional ingredient for certain behavior. Thus, I require only that when we reach the juncture of behavior at which events are not happily describable as physical without qualification, the grounds for physicality no longer automatically support the view that its causes can be traced without remainder to the interaction of lower-level particles. However, for all that, my reasons do not require us to distinguish neurological activity from proto-atomic activity, or my playing the piano from my playing the piano loudly (or Lisa's moving her hand from her moving her queen).

Of course, neither do I require that the above pairs are identical property instances or events. I take no stand on these matters here; identities between pairs of behaviors described either at the intentional level or at sub-intentional levels are orthogonal to the vague boundaries I have been at pains to delineate. Thus, although the differentiation of effects may be more finely grained than is generally acknowledged, from the claims defended here it *need not* be as fine-grained as Goldman's. I draw a distinction only between (some) actions and component motions of them that do not qualify as such. That distinction is an antidote to a cheap victory for option (d) on page 96, the identity of mental with physical causation. If intentions (and thus beliefs and desires) are needed for the event caused being a raising of one's arm (and not merely one's arm going up), then to that extent it will not suffice to describe the behaviors in terms of their causes' austerely physical realizers.

There may be ways to extend a mental cause requirement to a small collection of cases in which the conscious cause is not intentional and the effect not an action. Consider a case of wincing in pain. I am assuming that, *pace* representationalism (examined in chapter 7) pain is not an intentional state, although that is less important here than that the effect, the wincing, is a visceral reaction rather than an action. Some wincing is voluntary. I exclude those cases from this illustration. Figure 4.1 (in section 4.1) can be applied to wincing in pain as follows: M = the particular pain, P* = the wincing, and P = the neural state that is M's supervenience base. (M* may be omitted here unless one wishes to classify the wincing itself as mental, and therefore as M* rather than P*, which then becomes the physical motion needed to wince. Either choice suits the illustration.) The question I want to consider is whether it would count as wincing—rather than as, say, a tic—if P without M were sufficient for P*'s occurrence. My firm intuition is that because the wince is a particular kind of behavior, without a certain mental etiology we would be hard pressed to consider it wincing. The case is not as clear as one might hope. Still, I find it hard to shake the belief that there is something untoward in calling the movement 'wincing' on the basis of the strict physical motions alone, and I suspect readers will generally agree. If that is so, then even a proper subset of behaviors that are no more than automatic reactions couldn't be accurately described as those behaviors if they lacked a conscious cause.

Returning to actions, it only exacerbates the objector's predicament to hold that the intentional states causing the relevant behavior are themselves more sparsely physical than I have allowed. For starters, if we suppose that the intentional states are describable in the vocabulary of exiguous physical tokens, let us then ask what it is about that particular subset of physical causes, and not others, that allows the former to ratchet up their effects to the ranks of actions without mentioning their identity with the intentional. And there is worse to come. This view opens itself to a line of argument similar to one designed to show that mental properties are epiphenomenal. It was raised earlier by Broad (see section 1.6) and revived by McLaughlin (1993) as "type epiphenomenalism." It is also known as "the Qua Problem" (Maslen et al.(2009)).

The identity of a mental with a physical aspect was thought to be one way to avoid epiphenomenality for mental aspects. However, as was noted by the authors just cited, mental aspects are nevertheless *type* epiphenomenal if they cause something only by virtue of their identity with a physical cause. Their causal status is completely borne by that of their physical incarnations. *Qua* mental they are causally inert. This is not wholly analogous to the present situation: the physical isn't similarly inert with respect to the cases of behavior I have highlighted. Its implementation is necessary to the behavior insofar as that behavior involves physical motion. However, if the foregoing shows that the mental *qua* mental would be causally inert, by parity of reasoning it shows that the physical *qua* physical is caus-ally *inadequate*. It is by dint of the intentional cause that the subsequent motion counts as a particular case of action. It is not by virtue of its physical side as such that it enters the etiology of those actions, but by its depen-dence on its intentional aspect. Electrical activity in one's nervous system is not enough for a motion to count as one's extending one's arm, even if it captures the vehicle implementing it. Unless the motions are caused by certain access-conscious intentional states, they aren't actions.

To avoid a result that most would consider calamitous, one might claim that actions are not ontologically distinct items but merely ways of describ-ing the physical events with which they are identical. But the causal short-coming just highlighted is grounds for disputing that claim.

As a last resort, critics may turn once again to The Conceptual Gambit. Explaining intentional actions via intentional origins is no guarantee that the effects described are more than plain physical effects, just as *the dam's breaking* could explain a flood whereas the same event described as *the big-gest news in the county* does not. To further strengthen the objection, it may be suggested that the link between going someplace (say, to a football sta-dium) and intending to go someplace is conceptual and thus cannot be the sort of contingency required of a cause's relation to its effect.

However, this use of the gambit is gratuitous. Its role in removing the dialectical advantage of a dogged appearance by classifying it as an explana-tion requires that it serve as the mere addendum to an otherwise unencum-bered clear snapshot of the real. But I have been at pains to show that no such case exists. Although some philosophies have subscribed to the adage that if something can be explained away it should be, without a plausible further reason to do so this is mere hand-waving.

As for the comment that the conceptual connection between intentions and actions strengthens this objection, the short answer, as we saw ear-lier, is that the conceptual character of a connection does not preclude its being causal. Numerous instances of such quasi-logical relationships are also causal. It is logically the case that a person's identity is tied to the sperm and the ovum that caused her, and it is conceptually the case that a sunstroke is caused by the sun, that a moonbeam is caused by the moon, and that an earthquake is caused by the earth. In short, this is no barrier to an action's being caused by a intentional state the canonical description of whose content overlaps with that of its action.

Interlude

Here is a summary of the emergentism explored and defended in part I.

The goal was to argue for emergentism's plausibility for instantiations of conscious properties. Beginning from an acknowledgement that conscious properties are grounded superveniently in the physical and have physical realizations, the view's next thesis is that its dependence on the physical is brute, or, as I also put it, nothing available minimally *explains why* the emergent properties are grounded in those bases. Consciousness emerges from a certain complexity in its base.

The common view that a thing's constitution—say, its realization—is identical with what it constitutes is emergentism's first big challenge. I set out to show that it is neither invariably nor even presumptively the case for items sharing this relation that they be identical, or even that their causal powers coincide. Realization and identity differ sharply, though it is conceded for the sake of argument that they are compatible. The best illustrations of this are differences between the persistence conditions of a realizer and those of what it realizes (for example, a portion of matter and a building constructed from it or a sea and its water droplets). Lumpers respond that a realized's subsistence conditions are modal, and modal properties are no more than reflections of their categorical property bases. This negates any mileage a splitter might get from differences between a subject's matter and its subsistence conditions. The most effective splitter reply is a direct denial: the principle that necessarily modal properties, when they include dispositions and abilities, are reflected in the nonmodal is either false or vacuous.

It was noted that there are two patterns for emergentist theses, the compositional and the emissive. For the emergence of causal laws in the sciences, the compositional pattern may suffice. That form of emergentism is fully compatible with some standard forms of physicalism, even if not the most favored variety. However, when considering the emergence of conscious properties, the compositional pattern is a misfit. If emergentism for a conscious property were regarded as the mereological sum of neural properties, states, or activities, the conscious property would be no more than a giant neurological complex. That would nullify the very feature that emergentists and other dual aspect theorists emphasize. Thus, the only option for emergentism is to consider conscious properties not as composed of elements whose parts are recoverable, but as *emitted* or produced by physical aspects in their bases once those bases achieve a certain complexity and arrangement. Our closest approaches to describing this relationship must rely on metaphors, but if I may appeal to a causal analogy, the emergent product stands to its base much the way the product on a production line stands to the robots that produced it. They are distinct existents, though the product may be wholly dependent on the robots that produce them.

The monumental challenge for emergentism is to explain how any mental property, much less an emergent one, can *cause* anything, especially a physical something. Doesn't everything that has a cause have a physical cause? Two intertwined arguments, Causal Exclusion and Redundancy (CEA and RA, respectively), flesh out those concerns. They can be boiled down to three points: (i) since a supposed mental cause must always be in competition with a physical one, the physical cause elbows out the mental candidate (no massive causal overdetermination or superfluous causes); (ii) mental causation must be downward, and downward causation violates commonsense; (iii) all causation is ultimately dependent on, and must be understood in terms of, causation that occurs at the level of the most fundamental physical particles.

In reply to (i), I argue that the necessary (viz., modal) connection between physical and mental causes undermines the claim that they must be viewed as competing causes. They appear to be more akin to complementary ways of dividing complicated configurations of reality. (ii) is answered by isolating the few problematic from the nontoxic versions of downward causation, and noting that the latter are common and impeccable features of our world. Any misgivings on this count must have their source in (i) or (iii). My response to (iii) is divided into two parts. First, we may ask rhetorically what the situation would be for causation if, as is conceivable, there is no level of fundamental particles—that is, if particles were analyzable into an

unending string of ever more basic particles. Suppose this is at least a possibility. It is then difficult to see how issues concerning the very nature of
causation could rest on its not actually being the case. Next, if there is a bottom level, serious questions arise over whether anything at that level can be
the sort of causal base that can refine or specify our macro-causal notions.

Two additional points were raised. First, the critic's favorite solution,
identifying conscious and physical properties, is troubled by the need to
individuate the general run of empirical properties by means of their causal
profiles, which differ for mental properties and their bases. Second, significant ambiguities have plagued the uses to which emergentism's critics have
put principles of the closure of physical causation.

Finally, it was urged that some of what we want to include in the ontology of action indicates that this (vaguely bounded) class is distinct from
the motions which the actions embody. The subclass of action involved
requires an intentional origin, including beliefs, and desires. Nothing less
will suffice in a host of cases to ratchet up a mere motion to the level of an
action.

With that in the archives, it remains to consider more closely the chief
realist alternatives to this version of emergentism. The views to be reviewed
include the following. First is the heir to central state materialism, which I
denominate old-school physicalism. Two varieties, chauvinism and pluralism, are examined. Chauvinism requires a single material identity for all
conscious properties or states of a single kind; pluralism permits different
material identities for different type embodiments of what would otherwise be regarded as a single type of conscious property or state. Next, I
investigate representationalism, which identifies conscious states not with
a neural complex but, omitting qualifications, with features of intentional
contents of mental sates. Here also we examine two varieties, one which
makes use of teleological, primarily evolutionary, notions and another that
emphasizes a semantics grounded in causation. Finally, I examine nonreductive or token physicalism, in a form that states that there are token
identities of conscious and physical properties/states and in a form that
states only that individual physical properties/states explain or necessitate
their correlative conscious properties. Psychofunctionalism, another favorite alternative to emergentism, enters these deliberations to the extent that
it interacts with the other physicalisms.

Let us then proceed to our first physicalist view.

II Orthodox Alternatives

6 Physicalism: Chauvinism and Pluralism

6.1 The Physicalist Landscape

Old-school type physicalism was encountered in section 1.9, its two main
varieties labeled as 'chauvinism' and 'pluralism'. Behaviorism was once a
significant physicalist option, but nowadays it is rarely defended in the literature; the fragments of it that show up at present are likely to be incorpo-
rated into its successor functionalisms. I defer consideration of physicalist
representationalism to chapter 7, and of physicalisms that reject type-to-
type identities, basing their position instead on token identities or explanations, to chapter 8. In this chapter, I will take up theories that identify
conscious properties and physical types.

The main difference between our remaining camps is that chauvinists
regard having a constitution approximating that of humans as the exclusive
basis for having or ascribing phenomenal consciousness, whereas pluralists
countenance radically differently constituted creatures as potential possessors of different kinds of phenomenal consciousness. Although distinctions
between the two camps are not always sharp, I shall concentrate on representative versions—McLaughlin's for chauvinism, Kim's for pluralism—in
which the distinction is clearly marked. That one's conspecifics have such
experiences is not in question. For example, for chauvinists it is assumed
that humans share whatever degree of phenomenality is generally ascribed,
and that other members of the animal kingdom can be sentient creatures
to the extent that they approximate a human neurological constitution.

Sections 6.1–6.5 are devoted primarily to chauvinism. For convenience, I
suppose that our representative physicalist holds that the property of being
in pain, at least for familiar creatures, is identical with a neural property.
Also for convenience, I adopt the popular over-simplification that pain is

identical with C-fiber firing, at least in a creature fully equipped with further cortical and mid-brain activity, and whatever else is required for pain in a normal human. Let's also suppose that this discharges current physicalism's explanatory debt.[1]

The chauvinists of this tale are phenomenal realists. They agree with philosophers such as Nagel (1974), McGinn (2001), and Kripke (1980) that there is a "what it is like" in undergoing a conscious experience. This is not the consciousness *that* we have the experience (which might be called *epistemic* consciousness), but the experience itself (*phenomenal* consciousness). Christopher Hill (1997, p. 79) writes: "When we are aware of pain from this perspective [viz., introspection], we are aware of it as in itself. We are presented with the intrinsic nature of pain." Brian McLaughlin (2001, p. 322) adds that "we can introspectively recognize when we are in a sensory state simply by focusing our attention directly on the state." Brian Loar (1997, p. 607) goes so far as to say that it is natural to suppose that "we have direct grasp of [a sensation's] essence." Although these comments are in the first instance about second-order awareness, not the experiences of the pain, they disclose that when we have latched directly on to the subjective character of pain we have revealed something about its true nature. This needn't be a *complete* grasp of the sensation. Nevertheless, the felt quality is as important to those who advocate physicalist identity theories as it is to emergentists or to dualists.

Stating that this information is direct or transparent is not to imply that its subject is infallible. Someone may be too distracted to realize that she is in pain. Cases are rife in which people cavalierly dismiss an observer's suggestion that they are in pain but, after further reflection, make remarks on the order of "I must have been too engrossed to realize then that it really did hurt."

Physicalism's lively model for reductive identities is of the sort of case in which folk phenomena have been explained in terms of their scientific counterparts, or in which one scientific theory is subsumed under another. However, each of these illustrations began from something describable from an objective third-person standpoint and ended up with something else describable from that same perspective. On the other hand, pain, as

1. For present purposes we may ignore the objection, found in Kim 2006, in Block 2003b, and elsewhere, that identity is not explanatory. The debt in question needn't be discharged only by an explanation.

chauvinists acknowledge, is captured in its feeling; it should be puzzling how that can be the very same thing as a third-person detectable token in which being felt has no place in an ability to discern it. Below we shall see how physicalists believe such differences can be overcome.

6.2 Multiple Realizability

The chief obstacle to completing the chauvinist project is the multiple realizability (henceforth MR) of mental properties. I shall give a brief outline of that notion, explore attempts to meet the challenges it poses to physicalism in sections 6.3 and 6.4, and argue there and in section 6.5 that those challenges withstand physicalist counterattacks.

In section 3.1 a *realizer* of a property was tentatively characterized as a set of lawfully sufficient conditions for an aspect other than itself; not a wholly adequate account, but accurate as far as it goes. MR may then be described as the view that *many, if not all, mental aspects can be realized in various (actual and potential) differently constituted creatures (even in artifacts)— creatures that do not share enough of a constitution to identify a single type of material realizer for a single type of mental property.* For example, if the same kinds of conscious properties that humans experience could be reproduced hydraulically or in silicon, there would be no physical *types* with which to identify their types. Less *outré*, if we humans share conscious properties with, say, reptiles or mollusks, whose nervous systems differ markedly from ours, the physical types subserving those mental properties are too diverse to form any non-vacuous physical class with which to identify them.

Like statues and houses, we suppose that the instantiated mental properties require an embodiment, a realizer, of some sort, even though rich descriptions of statues, houses, and mental properties are possible without identifying their embodying stuffs. Different embodiments are possible in all such cases. Indeed, many phenomena other than conscious properties exhibit MR. For example, probabilistic automata (Putnam 1973), Gresham's Law (Fodor 1997), chess games, and even sentences (oral, written, or signed) are multiply realizable. Our focus is on MR's application to at least some of the mental.

The absence of a rigorous method for individuating realizations may disappoint some. How, it may be asked, are we to evaluate a multiplicity of realizations if we don't know what counts as one rather than two of them?

However, if any camp requires such a method, it is old-school physicalism. If we cannot tell when we have different realizations, we cannot tell when two realizations are similar enough to count as of the same type. I shall simply assume the same loose and informal standard for individuating realizations to which chauvinists at a minimum must be committed. In the present case, I cannot see a demand for greater rigor from either camp; indeed, too precise a formulation could be an obstacle to covering slightly divergent conceptions. Although we can expect indeterminacies, clear cases on different sides of the divide will suffice. For example, it is obvious that a spoken sentence and a written one will be different types of realization of "the same" sentence even if we puzzle over whether a printed and a handwritten sentence constitute distinct types. The challenge with which MR confronts chauvinism is that potential realizations of consciousness don't seem as fine-grained as the assortment of their underlying material bases.

How do matter and structure rank in determining similarity of a realization? Both count, but matter must definitely predominate. We do not deny that there is a role for structure in chauvinism, and radical deviations from it can lead to negative judgments about cases. (I am not sure whether this is only an epistemological point for physicalists or it is intended to have ontological implications.) However, structure in isolation—tantamount here to functional isomorphism—would result in a more basic failure. It would allow neurological, hydraulic, and silicon realizers to be of "the same kind." Chauvinists maintain not only that creatures so constructed lack *the right kind* of conscious states, but deny that they have any consciousness at all. This insufficiency of similar structure by itself is not only important to McLaughlin's (2003) grounds for rejecting claims of robotic consciousness; it is also instrumental in Hill's (1991) strategy for refuting the argument for consciousness for non-neural but functionally equivalent aliens. Thus, whereas a chauvinist may hold that S's pain is necessarily correlated with spiking activity in S's peripheral and central neurons, and that S's sensation of blue is necessarily correlated with activity transmitted from S's temporal lobes or loops between V1 and MT+V5 (see, e.g., Pascual-Leone and Walsh 2001), thereby rejecting any other way of individuating the pain or experiences of blue, he or she will reject, say, a silicon process for replicating these phenomenal states. Sameness of structure by itself is indifferent to material; it would be powerless to prevent neurological, hydraulic, or silicon realizers from satisfying similarity of kind.

MR doesn't threaten every brand of physicalism. Not only can pluralism and token physicalism accept it with equanimity; it has been a major inspiration to them. It is also compatible with various forms of representationalism and functionalism. However, our present concern is with chauvinism, on which pain simpliciter is modeled on human pain. Ontologically, to be capable of feeling pain is to have a supporting anatomy and histology close enough to that of humans; epistemically, it is for it to be reasonable to make judgments about others' pain on the basis of this similarity. Different chauvinists may locate the limits of similarity differently, but nothing clearly falling outside whatever boundary is drawn can feel pain. Once again, our highlighted chauvinists—Hill (1997, 2009), McLaughlin (2001), Hill and McLaughlin (1999), and Loar (1997)—pursue broadly similar paths in reaching this conclusion. I shall use them to represent chauvinists as a class. Others, including David Lewis (1983c), are perhaps phenomenal realists more in letter than spirit; but, although Lewis is closer to pluralism than chauvinism, he shares important dialectical moves with the chauvinists.

We may take note of other matters of detail as they become relevant. But the characterization given thus far already covers enough of realization's leading features to allow us to proceed with summarizing the state of play.

To elaborate the challenge, it appears that dogs, squids, frogs, and other creatures experience pain, though their nervous systems differ widely from ours and from each other. (For example, frogs lack cerebral cortices.) If one is willing to continue descending the phylogenetic scale, even worms and fish, yet more divergent, feel pain. Perhaps some chauvinists will concede this: they might profess to discover enough similarities between all such creatures to identify a single kind of material property that realizes pain in each of these species. But then consider potential intelligent extraterrestrials—'Martians' for convenience. They may have radically different physical constitutions, but aren't we in as favorable a position as we are with our conspecifics to gather reliable evidence that they experience pain, the kind of evidence that normally satisfies us? Is there a principled barrier to the hypothesis that computers won't have phenomenal experiences some day? Why should the conduction properties of silicon be any less capable of underwriting sensations than those of organically constituted electrical connectors? I investigate typical old-school responses to these cases presently, but first I want to make a preliminary remark about a different path for dismissing these examples.

If chauvinists confined their claims to what is *nomologically* possible, would that bolster their position? They might hold that it is all that reason entitles us to. And our knowledge of natural laws gives us grounds for believing that such creatures or artifactual concoctions in fact are not conscious. I return to that strategy later in this chapter. However, notice that it does not remove MR's threat, but locates it elsewhere. The new threat is that the chauvinist is being parochial about the boundaries of nomological possibility.

6.3   The Rudiments of Chauvinism

In section 2.4, I mentioned that physicalism has been advanced by supplementing ground-level neurological investigation in at least one of three ways: (i) by appealing to simplicity and coherence, (ii) as a way to avoid conundrums over mental causation, and (iii) by arguing from analogous cases of theoretical reduction in science. I dealt with the second of these in chapters 4 and 5. In this chapter, I address the first and the third. In addition, Chauvinism employs The Conceptual Gambit (section 2.5) to evade MR. Before addressing (i) and (iii), and setting aside the earlier limitations I placed on the gambit, let's track the way it plays out against MR.

Functionalization is a typical first step. Functional analysis discovers in its subject a second-order property, a property of properties—in brief, a concept. A concept is a property's *mode of presentation*. The first-order property is the physical realizer of that functionally characterized concept. Chauvinists such as McLaughlin, Hill, Loar, and Lewis invoke just such a concept/property distinction. One route to it might be to construct a Ramsey sentence, and to identify mental property M as whatever unitary physical property realizes that role.[2] If there is a physical realizer for each instance that doesn't require quantifying over too many diverse properties, chauvinism is triumphant. If the physical realizers don't form a unified whole, token physicalism or pluralism takes the palm. However, MR has been used to claim that the realizers are too diverse for chauvinism. In fact, multiple realizability and functional theories were originally interjected to explain why central-state materialism fails. (See, e.g., Nagel 1965; Putnam 1973.)

2. Constructing a Ramsey sentence for M: (1) Create a lengthy conjunction of all the platitudes about M. (2) Replace occurrences of names of M with the variable *x*. (3) Existentially quantify over that conjunction.

On the other hand, chauvinists may bypass MR via another application of the gambit, using functionalization to argue directly for their view. They may claim that the inference *from* the conceivability (or imaginability) of a distinction between sensations and neural processes *to* their ontic difference is fallacious. Conceivability may encourage the thought that the content of our conceiving is possible, but it shouldn't be confused with the possibility of that content itself. This particular inference from the strictly epistemic to the metaphysical is illegitimate. To see this, note that it is (or at least was) *conceivable* that commonly experienced heat is not molecular motion, or that Hesperus is not Phosphorus. But in fact neither is possible; their identity statements are necessary truths. Suppose we ask what enables us to imagine that a distinction is metaphysically possible when in fact it is not—for example, what enables us to conceive of water as other than H_2O. The likely answer is that we think of water as a colorless, tasteless, potable liquid found in our streams, lakes, seas, and public fountains and flowing from our taps. If that is water, knowledge of its natural composition has only the slightest relevance to our quotidian success with its instances. We can understand Shakespeare's and Locke's remarks as about water even though Shakespeare and Locke lacked knowledge of its true nature.

Turning back to phenomenally conscious properties, we must discover something about them that, according to the physicalist, enables us to conceive of such properties as distinct from any physical property. The way they consciously strike us, their "self-presenting" character, is the key. A critic relying on MR will maintain that creatures with very different physical properties could nevertheless experience relevantly similar phenomenal qualities. The old-schooler needn't reject the appearance but may respond that a phenomenal property, as experienced, is a special brand of *concept*, a property of classes of (probably heterogeneous) properties rather than of a single property. Functionalization suits this outlook by delineating functional properties entirely in terms of their extrinsic features. Of course, if first-order properties could be multiply realized, this line of defense would crumble. *Pro tem*, I set that unwelcome suggestion aside. It is reconsidered in section 6.4.

Once the flaw of a complacent inference from concept to property has been exposed, there is no barrier to contemplating that neural process N delivers the intrinsic character of phenomenally conscious property E. At the next stage, it is discovered that pain and N are constantly correlated. McLaughlin observes:

The correlation thesis, together with physicalism, gives rational grounds for the conclusion that "a being is conscious if and only if it is relevantly like us in physical respects." (2003, p. 182) (See also Hill 2009, p. 31.)

What are we to make of the qualifier "together with physicalism"? For McLaughlin, its inspiration is the methodological virtues of coherence and theoretical simplicity. Together they dictate that the best explanation of the correlation is the identity of the conscious and the physical. A word about each is in order. I begin with theoretical simplicity.

Take the qualifier 'theoretical' seriously. It acknowledges that simplicity's current application is tagged to theories rather than to their relatively observable instances. In our case it prescribes that we do not require an extra set of psychophysical laws that would have been demanded by a non-physical realm. That is indeed a form of simplification. But the uses of simplicity in philosophy have disguised significant ambiguities. According to Alan Baker, simplicity can be glossed either as *elegance* (syntactic simplicity, or the number and/or complexity of one's most general claims) or as *parsimony* (the number of [types of] things postulated). Although the distinction is often overlooked, claims for each occasionally work at cross-purposes. Philosophers usually focus on parsimony; their notorious preference for desert landscapes is a desire for fewer entities, not fewer laws. Parsimony might have as a consequence that fewer laws are needed; but if it does, that is a by-product, not parsimony's office. However it is equally possible that more laws would be needed to relate the more parsimonious basic ontology to its richer upper levels. Starting at the other end, although elegance may reduce the need for some entities, it is farther from having implications for a philosophically interesting parsimony. Peano's frugality in requiring only five axioms with which to generate the truths of arithmetic does not appear to have eliminated any arithmetical entities, nor was it intended to do so, though it could have demoted some of them from undefined to derived. And even when a streamlining of a scientific law reduces the need for certain entities (relative to a given level of working), the reduction is seldom in terms of the broad categories that interest ontologists. Furthermore, it has yet to be explained how the work of active scientists, as distinct from metaphysicians, is burdened by claiming that neural states *subserve* mental ones rather than regarding the former as identical with the latter. That is, it isn't obvious why causal laws are less elegant, even if they are less parsimonious, than statements of typal identity.

Next, consider coherence. Suppose we notice that it rained last night and that the grass is wet this morning. We bring these incidents together by noting that the wet grass was caused by the rain (McLaughlin 2003, pp. 189–190). Or we might explain the constant correlation of lightning and electrical discharge by supposing that they are the same thing, just as Lois Lane might explain Clark Kent's sudden disappearance just before Superman's entrance by hypothesizing that they are one and the same. McLaughlin admits that the illustrations aren't perfect parallels, but he insists that, despite the "striking dissimilarities between our case of interest and the case of water, . . . the relevant similarity holds: there would be mutual support through explanatory coherence" (2003, p. 190). Identity is inferred as "the best explanation" of so intimate and regular a correlation between conscious and neural states. However, if that were the whole of the story, the correlation would be equally explained (and thereby made coherent) by the fact that the one causes, or is dependent in some other way on, the other, the direction of the dependence being granted. In fact, that is precisely the explanation in the example of the wet grass: the grass is wet *because* it rained. Of course, the water content of the grass overlaps with that of the rain, but the identity of the water droplets is not the focus of the explanation. On certain accounts, a cause transfers some aspect from itself to another thing (e.g., energy, motion), but the identities of those transferred elements is not at work in causal explanation. For all that matters, the rain droplets might have become transformed chemically when they became the wetness of grass. An analogous application of coherence would to be food getting cold in a freezer. The frigidity of the food concerns its slowing molecular movement, which is not identical with the molecular motion of the ambient air in the freezer. Coherence allows a causal hypothesis; any identity of the coldness properties of the food and the ambient air is beside the point. In our target case, the neural token's "bringing forth" the mental one satisfies coherence as such. And that explanation is compatible with forms of property dualism and emergentism.

Let's compare the explanatory coherence of the mental-physical correlation to that of the correlation between water and H_2O. Presumably water is a natural kind. I do not know whether pain is a natural kind; but if it's a kind at all, it is certainly not supernatural. To settle the question whether something is a natural kind we must first know what is expected to follow from being one in the preferred sense, which can't be divined by a close reading of the analogy that McLaughlin admits is strikingly dissimilar to the cases of interest. However, because water is a natural kind, any liquids that have all the appearances and macroscopic influences of water (that are *qualitatively similar* to water),but have a radically different chemistry, are not water. That accounts not only for why mistaking another liquid for water needn't be a simple blunder but it also accounts for why water's not being H_2O is conceivable even if not possible and why there is no flourishing science of armchair chemistry. How would that explanation work for pain? Can we suppose that something has a *qualitative* appearance, the pain-like feeling or self-presentation, but it isn't pain because it isn't neurological activity of the right sort? Wouldn't that be tantamount to a dogmatic declaration that multiple realizability couldn't occur, whatever the phenomenological outcome?

Notice also that identity, whether or not brought off by coherence and simplicity, would be as consistent with pluralism as it is with chauvinism. Even if the conscious tokens of humans are generally paired with similar neural tokens, this would not show that Martian conscious states weren't identical with a specific kind of Martian stuff. Put otherwise, and ignoring the objections just lodged, the most coherence yields would be the conditional 'If a being is like us in physical respects, it is conscious'; but chauvinism declares 'If a being is conscious, it is like us in physical respects'. We are confronted not by one issue but by two: identity and similarity. Let us turn first to similarity. All sides currently engaged in the debate are entitled, at least on this issue, to assume that similarity of physical and neural makeup is sufficient to allow us to ascribe phenomenal states broadly within our own species and in closely related species. The issue is whether, as chauvinists claim, such similarity is also necessary. Chauvinists hold that if we were to replace the human neuronal system with one of silicon, or with a hydraulic system, or with some yet-unknown extraterrestrial stuff, we would lack any reason to suppose that the resultant beings would have phenomenal states similar to those of humans. (See, e.g., Hill 2009, p. 31.) In place of the problem of other minds, we then have the problem of other kinds.

That issue was brought to a head (if I may use that term) by a disagreement between Ned Block (2003b) and Brian McLaughlin (2003) over a scenario involving a character in the television series *Star Trek: The Next Generation*. Commander Data is an extremely well-designed robot, so much so that he (?) is regarded by other crew members of his starship as a compatriot. He even had intimate relations with a female (non-robotic) member of the crew.[3] However, Commander Data was created by a since-deceased cyberscientific genius who left no record of his craft. A young cyberscientist, in the interests of advancing his science, wants to take Data apart to see how he is constructed, though he has no confidence that he will be able to reconstruct Data. Thus, the crucial issue: Is Commander Data a sentient creature, so that such an act might be tantamount to killing Data? Block claims we not only lack an answer, but that we lack even a clue to a procedure for how to go about finding one. (Block doesn't rule out that a future scientific revolution might fill in this epistemic lacuna, but maintains that just such a scientific revolution would be required.) McLaughlin, consistent with his chauvinism, holds that we have no reason to believe that Data is sentient, but that simplicity and coherence give us enough evidence to allow us to conclude that Data is not sentient. Any other decision would commit us to holding that our toasters, radios, and iPods might have inner lives. Although the issue is superficially epistemological (viz., what it is reasonable to believe), the ultimate quarry is a question of fact. Is Commander Data sentient? (My fellow non-Trekkies may be relieved to know that Data was spared.)

6.4 Levels, Functions, and Forms

Before returning to Commander Data's predicament, I raise a further question concerning multiple realizability (= MR). A common assumption, which I take to be a semantic illusion, has been used to convert certain first-order properties into concepts—for our purposes, second-order properties. The culprit is the functionalizing of first-order properties by converting *having* a function into *being* a function. Because the tokens in question do not fit my earlier characterization of realization (for example, the would-be realizers are not sufficient conditions for tokens different from themselves), clarity seems to suggest that we designate them as *multiform* rather than multiply realized. (The conflation of the two notions may account for the odd practice of referring to features as self-realizations.) But even if we extend talk of realization to the multiform, MR will not serve as the basis for exposing an ostensible property as no more than a concept.

3. I rely for details on Block 2003b, note 18.

Biological eyes and wings are multiform. Each has independent evolutionary strains. The wings of an insect and those of a sparrow are homologous, but that is a structural similarity, which, as we saw, isn't enough for chauvinism. Are eyes and wings, *qua* eye and wing, not properties of their subjects? Isn't each biological eye paradigmatically physical? What is functional here is our calling them 'eyes' and 'wings'. But eyes and wings would operate just as they do however we might classify them. Whether they are natural kinds on a more refined understanding is beside the point if they are concretely physical rather than abstract properties. A further question, which I defer to my discussion of pluralism, is whether such properties can enter into lawlike generalizations. Here I confine my attention to the bearing of these examples on The Conceptual Gambit.

A familiar sentiment in old-school circles is that "to say something is a wing is to say that it has the function of enabling its possessor to fly" (Brooks 1994, p. 813). Only a functional description, and nothing else, can be used to support its consignment to a second order. To maintain that wings and eyes can't be first-order properties on the grounds that they are multiform and shared by different kinds of things would commit a consistent reasoner to hold that size, shape, and color were also second-order properties. Nor is it plausible to relegate wings and eyes to the conceptual by virtue of the fact that they mereologically supervene on parts that are not wings or eyes. That argument would demand a similar fate for any macroscopic property. Thus, it is only description via function that matters here. Can anything be said in its favor?

Notice first that many wingless things—blimps, helicopters, rockets, spores, jet packs—have features that enable their possessors to fly under their own power. Biological wings are particular anatomical structures, and their intrinsicality is not obliterated by citing them as wings. Moreover, some winged creatures—e.g., penguins and emus—don't or can't fly. A natural response is that their wings are counted as (vestigial) wings only because they were developed to enable those birds' evolutionary ancestors to fly. I do not really know if this is true for flightless birds; the bland assumption that anatomical wings must be connected to the ability to fly is the sort of pub-night biology to which it is easy to become habituated, but it would need further support to be a serious proposal. Natural, as distinct from artificial, wings are anatomical formations that have intrinsic characteristics. It is possible that evolutionarily they were enlisted as much for insulation as for flight, or perhaps they were exaptations. X's having an ability to fly is not enough to say that X has wings if those are not limbs or extensions protruding to each side. Nevertheless, wings, or a creature's being winged, is multiply formed in insects, birds, and reptiles (if indeed birds and reptiles are sufficiently distinguishable on the evolutionary bush).

Eyes, too, have evolved along distinct strains, three in fact. Any photo-sensitive surface structure connected appropriately to an internal neurolog-ical transducer may count as a (biological) eye. And a transducer may not even be essential if the photosensitive cells are sufficiently developed. Thus, V. B. Smocovitis (1996) notes that some jellyfish, in particular cubomedu-san, have image-forming eyes, but lack a nervous system, which is needed to process a visual image. In fact, Robert Reid (2007 has called into question whether the trait has evolved as an adaptive mechanism of any sort.

Both features have internal structures that one would be wrong to overlook when trying to understand their constitution *qua* wing or eye. A human eye, being nothing more than a physical structure, would do all the things it does now if we never considered it under the form of an eye. Swampman's eye—it is an eye—is as physical as yours or mine. It is our classification of it as an eye, not the purely physical routine it would undergo in any event, that leads us to regard it as an abstraction. I cannot tell whether we are misled by popular examples, but specimens of artifacts are often used to introduce the notion of realization. And there we have a distinction between the drawing-board idea and its concrete realizations, say in steel, plastic, or wood. It is then easy to think of the drawing-board version as conceptual, and the building of it as making it concrete. Perhaps we subconsciously regard the idea of an eye or a wing as something on nature's drawing-board.

Again, let's distinguish sharply between the reasons members of our spe-cies initially had for naming and paying special heed to eyes and what is picked out by those features. It doesn't follow that if the function of the eye initiated our usage of the term and our interest in eyes, then an eye is defin-able by means of this function. That is the distinction I insisted on earlier between *having* and *being* a function. Emeralds may be a natural kind, and are probably not multiply realized. Still, their function as precious com-modities illustrates the point. If emeralds had not been valued by members of our species, we might never have devised a common name to designate them. But in the case of emeralds there is little temptation to confuse min-eralogists with jewelers.

If we choose to consider multiformity in creatures as a form of MR, we should guard against the possibility that in calling something a wing or an eye—or a pain—we have thereby categorized it as a second-order property of its possessor.

6.5   Dora and Commander Data

Sad to report, a portion of Dora's nervous system, connected to her pain centers, must be replaced. Her nervous system has dangerously deteriorated, the symptoms of which include severe headaches. The replacements are nano-manufactured silicon chips, perhaps including synthetic C-fibers and nocioceptors in Dora's peripheral system and parts of the postcentral gyrus of her parietal lobe (more specifically, in her somatosensory cortex). For starters, allow the portions of Dora's prefrontal cortex, hippocampus, and amygdala (even her inferior temporal lobe) dedicated to long, short-term episodic (or declarative) and recognitional memory storage, including skill (or procedural) memory, to remain intact. As we shall see, this is but the first of a long series of replacements of Dora's defective central-system neurons and/or peripheral C-fibers. After the operation, Dora awakens in her room surrounded by her close friends. Other than the expected post-operative complaints, she appears to be the same old Dora. She seems to remember whatever she is likely to have remembered had she just awoken from a night's sleep, seems to express annoyance at the scratchiness of her blanket, seems to have her thirst slaked by a cool drink, and complains about her roommate's inane chatter. However, she also claims to suffer from a headache like the one she had previously, although her doctors assure her it is no longer a symptom of neural deterioration. Should we be any more skeptical about Dora's claim to have a headache than we would have been before the operation? Shouldn't we agree with her doctors that she should take an aspirin? Could her intact memory be deluding her about what counts as a headache? The only plausible answers I can muster are No, Yes, and No.

Now imagine that Dora has undergone a series of operations in each of which small clusters of neurons were replaced by micro-micro-chips, and she has similar post-operative reactions to various qualia—e.g., feeling hot, thirsty, itchy, or annoyed. Her memories of past qualia must be massively delusional if she is wrong about comparing them with her current mental state. We may suppose that her central nervous system, aside from blood vessels and glial cells, is eventually more than 50 percent Intel. At what point do we declare that she cannot experience a headache, or, for that matter, anything else previously subserved by the replaced areas?

No doubt, on our laws Dora might not retain sentience, although a comparison of replacements with other major organs makes it difficult to suppose that it is anything but plausible that she is veridical about her own condition. The appeal of MR is not that we know that this will happen, but that there is little reason to believe otherwise. Indeed, should Dora lose phenomenality as a result of any of the operations, the most likely outcome would be for her to "know" it, and, assuming that she is sincere, to report just that. (Compare individuals recovering from severe depression, who are often quite articulate in describing the loss of ordinary experiential reactions.) Taking Dora's utterances any other way is not a good presumption, and it is neither simpler nor more coherent. However, the real question is "If Dora isn't out to deceive us, are we in a position to reliably judge that a creature now differently constituted has phenomenal states?"[4]

Of course, Dora is the exception, so while the problem of other minds is off the table, the problem of other kinds remains. But now let's thicken the fiction. Imagine that it is discovered that silicon replacements have important salubrious effects on brain health, and that an advanced technology makes transplantation so elementary, safe, and cheap that pediatric surgeons routinely perform it on newborns. (The transplant acquires the status that vaccinations against tetanus have today.) Or perhaps changes in the atmosphere weaken people's central nervous systems, so it is a pressing preventive measure to replace original neurons with artificial ones early in infancy. Suppose some people will not have undergone the replacement. What will members of each group be entitled to think about the appearance of pains, itches, hot flashes, and so on in members of the other group? It is hard to believe that, if the only changes are replacements of some natural parts, our reactions to similar behavioral patterns in others would, or should, change. And if our reactions do change, can we avoid extending that change in attitude to everyone, thereby reinvigorating the problem of other minds?

4. Block suggests a companion scenario of genetically engineering a virus to replace DNA cells with no effect on consciousness. He expresses no doubt that the outcome will be the preservation of sentience.

In this connection, consider the current status of perceptual experience. Eyeglasses and hearing aids are artificial devices that we might compare to the material makeup of Commander Data. It may be said that they do no more than boost a signal, but that the processing is still done in the same physiological way in which unaided humans would receive it. But now consider cataract surgery and cochlear implants. After cataract surgery, a person's biological lens is replaced with a plastic one. Patients regularly claim to see better after the surgery. Unless something goes badly awry, how can it be claimed that what they now have is a different kind of thing from their pre-operative visual experiences? Are they delusional? Does it matter that this is only a certain small portion of the entire visual process? But medical technology is rapidly advancing to a point where we can imagine wholly artificial corneas and other larger prostheses. Where do the old-schoolers propose we draw the line? Of course, it is possible to put one's foot down and refuse to be moved on the grounds that doing so would open the floodgates to absurdities. But that doesn't make the vast potential for prosthetics any less compelling. Why, then, should a neural transplant rob a person of phenomenality rather than preserve or enhance it?

Might we not treat this, particularly in its later development, as a sorites puzzle? The hirsute man becomes bald by a gradual loss of hair, the mountain becomes a molehill by gradual loss of clots of dirt. But to those cases it is objected that, although we are never in an epistemically favorable position to determine at what point the crucial change occurs, it does occur at a specific point in the progression. Of course, not everyone holds that sorites can be dispatched so handily. But we needn't broach the issue. Aside from the fact that at each stage we have the addition of Dora's vocalizations (a bit of evidence for which there is nothing comparable in the baldness or molehill scenario), her case is more like the ship of Theseus than a sorites. It is reasonable to suppose that the ship of Theseus is the same ship after the gradual replacement of all of its planks, so that none of the original planks is now a part of the ship. Given that the ship is a continuant, it still deserves to be called the same ship, even if its original planks had been hoarded and are later re-assembled into a ship. The second ship, call it 'Scrapyard Theseus', would be a different ship. Dora's neurons have not undergone a simple decremental loss; rather, they have been replaced by devices that fulfill their strictly mechanical task without a discernible loss of a step.

Consider now a further tweaking of Dora's case. Researchers have learned to trick stem cells into growing new neurons, and a surgeon now replaces Dora's faulty neurons with neurons grown from her own stem cells. This overcomes the more obvious reasons chauvinists might have had for denying that the silicon-filled Dora has the headache in question. Is there anything in the offing like a grounds for rejecting her headache claims after the stem-cell replacements? I can find nothing that would not also force one to deny, say, that Dora could see after cataract surgery. But why should organic rather than silicon replacements make so great a difference to our plausible beliefs about Dora's phenomenal states?

Re-enter Commander Data. I have finessed the results by giving Dora a different origin and inserting gradualism in the replacements. Moreover, Dora, unlike Commander Data, is largely composed of bone, muscle, sinew, and blood. She is more like the Frankenstein monster with a largely synthetic nervous system. In contrast, Data has been accorded his alleged mental life *de novo*. But the relevance of these distinctions is hard to detect. Unlike the case of Swampman, the only issue here is whether Data has qualia. And with regard only to the working parts of a neural system that matter, the end result for the successors of Dora may be comparable to the difference in the relevant parts of the brain between us and Commander Data. Moral issues aside, if we can create such a creature via a gradual replacement of neurons, what is to prevent us from constructing it along the same lines from factory parts? That Dora came to acquire her silicon parts gradually may be important to show how it is that we acquired strong grounds for a justified belief about her phenomenal properties. But that is the whole of it. Once that is settled, creating a duplicate on site would appear to give us equal justification to accord qualia to it. Cases such as that of Dora, as well as Block's replacement DNA, show that one can't assume that the limits of the *nomologically* possible are the merely familiar.

What about old-school physicalism explains our willingness to extend consciousness to conspecifics? The clearest chauvinist answer has been that we make the tacit assumption that we share a common physical makeup with other humans. Even if that is so, it is at most a sufficient reason for third-person ascriptions of sentience not a necessary condition, much less a necessary and sufficient condition. But there is room for doubt that it is even a leading reason for our effortless belief in the sentience of others. Is it likely that it licenses a very young child's reaction when the child thinks its mother is sad? Does it seem likely that throughout human history this has been the basis for sympathy or pity? I have no specific proposal on offer with which to replace that suggestion, but our reaction to the sentient states of others strikes me more rooted in robust and multi-generational interaction than in the aseptic examples common in philosophical discourses. It is difficult to shake the conviction that the assumption of a similarity of physical makeup seems little more than a speculation about this practice, whether or not there is something better at hand with which to replace it.

These doubts may be reinforced with another equally palpable science-fiction scenario. Suppose that, after interacting in large communities on the same familiar basis for many generations, it is discovered that we were divided into creatures with very different internal structures. Perhaps some were aliens stranded on Earth. Of course, there would be practical complications (e.g., hybrid offspring, remarkable coincidences to avoid our medical discovery of these differences); but if the only thing available was this sort of daily interaction, would we be any less justified than we are now in regarding our fellow interlocutors as sentient beings? Whichever group we belonged to, would we suddenly change our minds about the inner lives of the other group when we discovered their difference? Isn't this more like the less radical difficulty men have in imagining the pain of childbirth, or women have in imagining the pain of a baseball striking a man in his testicles.

This scenario is quite different from what I have been given to understand about the *Star Trek* setup. Commander Data had a number of behavioral giveaways that suggested clichés about robots. His facial expressions were limited, and his movements were more herky-jerky than those of humans. But imagine that none of this were so. Suppose, instead, that "he" had all the human-like reactions that Disney cartoonists give to mice, ducks, and even dinnerware. I am not convinced that after interacting with the race of envisaged aliens over extended periods of time we would be any more skeptical about their sentience than we are about that of our fellow humans. McLaughlin cites "the insight behind John Stuart Mill's argument from analogy" (2003, p. 182). But Mill's argument is based primarily on the evidence of behavior and causation, though shared anatomy is a factor. Why else would children, or anyone, believe that a worm felt pain when it was put on a fish-hook? Again, this is not to offer an explanation of why that is so; it is simply to flesh out reasons for suspicion about the explanation resting on an assumption of a similar anatomy.

Pace certain insinuations (whose seriousness I dare not gauge), this does not open the floodgates to the pathetic fallacy. We are no more in a favorable position than before from which to ascribe consciousness to toasters, ATMs, answering machines, or radios. Consciousness will be ascribed case by case, and only after a number of elements have been factored in, including, but not confined to, overwhelming and persistent behavioral evidence. If we isolate the case of a previously unencountered being from all evidence surrounding it other than its physical makeup, a radical dissimilarity in neural architecture counts against its having conscious states; but this isn't the only evidence, and to the extent that it is evidence it is certainly defeasible. This leaves ample room for indeterminacy in some cases: they may not be resolvable by methods at our disposal or by any foreseeable methods. Conceivably, that is the source of what Block regards as meta-indeterminacy in the case of Commander Data. When at first the creatures come to us full-blown, with no supposition gained from past experience (e.g., aliens or ingenious artifacts), we don't even have a conception of how to go about answering the question whether such creatures are conscious. However, I am as confident about Dora after her operations as I was before she underwent them, and Block expresses confidence about the recipient of a stem-cell replacement for a viral condition, although in both cases we can imagine a material end product not comparably different from the imaginative creatures generating the meta-indeterminacy.

Of course, these reflections have to do with the rationality of ascriptions, not with whether they would be true attributions to its subjects. Owing to our limited past interactions with creations of Commander Data's ilk, we may be less disposed to attribute phenomenal tokens to him than to Dora. But were that reluctance universal, it still wouldn't demonstrate the unreasonableness of ascribing such tokens to Commander Data. No doubt similarity of constitution is a salient and reliable test for our ascribing particular phenomenological tokens to others. The preceding doubt was intended to question only the inadequacy of difference of constitution as a test for the reasonableness of withholding such ascriptions. There are kosher behavioral markers that make up quite nicely for the absence of similarity of constitution. I fail to see why anyone would claim that Commander Data *would not*, even if he in fact *did not*, satisfy these markers fully. Skepticism is always available, but then consistency would dictate that it apply to our conspecifics as well.

My objections are not designed to show that the world is not at bottom physical. But it gives one more hint of a theme I shall harp on in the epilogue: Even if the world is at bottom physical, it is a mistake to suppose that its combinations and products will have to trace a linear path in which we can still discern the lower-level ingredients out of which they arose. The progression from material base to product need not be so transpicuous. Belief to the contrary may be no more than a bit of unexamined lore that has been passed down, rather than a fundamental demand of the physical grounding of all reality.

6.6 Pluralism

Pluralism has the advantage of averting the challenge of multiple realizability while also accommodating type identities. It restricts those identities to species or structures of a single kind. What the chauvinist calls 'pain' the pluralist may call 'pain-for-X' (X being, say, a class structurally similar to humans). And whereas the pluralist also has pain-for-Y in which 'Y' is sufficiently unlike human pain, we have two options. On the first option, the pluralist may maintain that there is no common phenomenality shared in pain-for-X and pain-for-Y. For that outcome, what the chauvinist calls 'pain' the pluralist prefers to call 'pain-for-X'. (Cf. Lewis 1983c, p. 127.) On the second option, the pluralist need not rule out the option of an underlying commonality to account for the homophonic qualia of Xs and Ys. However, this second option abolishes any substantive distinction between chauvinism and pluralism. I will return to the second option later. For the present, let's consider pluralism as if it is a new entrant in the physicalism sweepstakes.

According to an earlier work by Jaegwon Kim (1993b), if there is no single physical kind available for all pain, we have the option of scrapping pain as a unified property. Although there may be no pain property as such, we can devise *local* type identities for structurally similar creatures, including structures that might discriminate within species or cut across them. To simplify the discussion, suppose that pain-for-humans, pain-for-Martians, and pain-for-reptiles are all distinct. If pain is a genuine property, it will be a distinct physical kind. In fact, Kim comes close to demanding this as a condition of being a natural property. (He eventually pulls back from that requirement.) As for the requirement of pain itself—quite apart from physicalism—being a requirement for kindhood, Kim writes:

> . . . either we allow disjunctive kinds and constitute pain and other mental properties as such kinds, or else we must acknowledge that our general mental terms and concepts do not pick out properties and kinds in the world (we may call this "mental property irrealism"). (1993e, pp. 334–335)

Kim maintains that neither outcome suits non-reductive physicalism (the lone alternative to pluralism he took seriously at the time). Let us look more carefully at both alternatives.

6.6.1 Disjunctive Kinds

One view is that a property that is truly disjunctive is likely to be wildly heterogeneous, consisting of a miscellany of disparate items, or that the disjuncts may never close off.[5] Kim doesn't believe that either complaint goes to the heart of the problem. Rather, the real difficulty is that disjunctive kinds aren't projectible. Consider once again the case of jade, which can be either jadeite or nephrite. If we were to devise a law stating

Jade is green

we should be hesitant about accepting a selection of instances as contributions to its confirmation because our sample might have been drawn from only one of its different minerals.[6] Of course, every property can be divided disjunctively; for the sake of argument, I assume that we can distinguish the genuine disjunctions from the concocted ones. Moreover, let's agree with Kim that natural properties should be able to support lawlike generalizations. Consider emeralds, which, Kim notes, can be divided into emeralds in Africa and emeralds outside of Africa. Still, laws regarding the non-relational properties of emeralds, based on an exclusive sample of either disjunct, will contribute to the confirmation of a law that emeralds are green.

5. Glanzberg (2001) explains why infinite disjunctions seem to generate unpalatable consequences for physicalism.

6. This couldn't be the whole story. Green and grue are distinct, incompatible properties, but a single emerald might be evidence that emeralds are green *or* that they're grue. Is neither projectible?

On analogy with jade, Kim argues that 'pain' qua disjunctive predicate is non-projectible. Consider once again pain in humans, pain in reptiles, and pain in Martians—P_h, P_r, and P_m, respectively. A candidate for a psychological law about pain (which, I assume, Kim would agree needn't be exceptionless) such as

Sharp pains cause anxiety reactions (Kim 1993e, p. 324)

cannot be expected to hold for reptiles or for Martians on the basis of a sampling of humans. Ergo, a multiply realized pain property resembles jade rather than emerald.

For argument's sake grant the further assumption that pain, whether or not a property, is disjunctive. This is not enough to establish Kim's claim. He argues for pain's non-projectibility by deploying a feature, extrinsic to the pain itself, causing anxiety reactions. That is understandable: pain figures in very few pure laws, much less in laws that don't rely on its relation to something other than qualia. Obviously, if other creatures do not have the appropriate anatomy and physiology (and the appropriate behavioral tendencies), anxiety and its reactions are not in the offing. That doesn't show that *pain* isn't projectible, any more than it would show that *emerald* is not projectible because an emerald that is not in Africa couldn't be on display in a Cairo museum. Many lawlike generalizations in which pain figures will be behavioral, and behavioral generalizations can be exhibited only by creatures whose physical constitutions enable them to manifest that behavior.

Let's remind ourselves of the importance of supporting counterfactuals for lawlike generalizations. Of course, nothing without a mouth and vocal chords can scream in pain. However, assuming that sharp pain causes anxiety reactions in humans, *ceteris paribus*, we can certainly say that a reptile or a Martian feeling pain, if it had been similarly wired to analogues of the rest of the relevant part of human (neural and non-neural) anatomy, would stand an equal chance of having anxiety reactions to the experience of sharp pain, or of screaming out. Similarly, suppose that emeralds dipped in solution Z turn blue. We then have two sorts of emeralds: those that have been dipped in Z and those that have not been dipped in Z. The former have a feature—turning blue—that the latter lack. But being in Z is an extrinsic feature of emeralds just as having a basically human physiology is extrinsic to pain. We can cancel the difference by saying that emeralds not dipped in

Z, *were* they dipped in Z, *would* turn blue. Or consider philosophers' favorite chemical compound, water. The water in my tub is translucent, that in certain parts of the Aegean is turquoise, that in the mid-Atlantic is green, and that in the Chicago River is muddy brown. But if we were to take any of these samples of H_2O, without their impurities, and transport it to a different location, it would display the same color as the local water.

Once again for argument's sake, let's agree that 'jade is green' isn't projectible and that the fault lies with its lack of proper counterfactual support.[7] Nevertheless, there are crucial differences with pain that do not allow a similar solution for jade. No sense can be made of the hypothesis that *if* nephrite had the molecular structure of jadeite it would be green. That antecedent is impossible: nephrite having that structure would just *be* jadeite. Similar problems don't seem to beset the pain example and the various embodiments of its subjects. And there is no analogous objection to a cross-species counterfactual for pain. Martians need not become humans; they need only supplementation by something allowing them to be anxious. Thus far there is no clear violation of possibility of the sort we encounter in the jade case; that case cannot serve to disqualify a simple pain property.

No doubt, as a science Psychology is primarily interested in the lives of humans. The behavioral patterns and brain states of other species are typically studied in that discipline only for the sake of understanding, predicting, improving, and controlling human mental states and behavior—hence the importance of laws such as that pain tends to cause anxiety reactions. However, anxiety behavior is not internal to the painful feeling. Although we may achieve some scattered cross-species generalizations (e.g., 'pain is distressful', 'it is unusual to seek pain for its own sake', 'upon experiencing pain, those with the capacity to do so will tend to avoid its predictable cause'), they are of limited utility. Useful generalizations will be those that connect pain to its causes and reactions in humans. Virtually no generalizations relating pain to highly specific behavioral patterns or larger psychological syndromes are likely to have much wider application, in large part because other species don't have the limbs, organs, or accompanying

7. For similar reasons, let's also grant a sharply delineated requirement of projectibility. Recall from page 119 what Block (1997) and Shepard (1987) had to say on the subject. Such complications forfeit the sharp distinctions needed for a projectibility requirement's polemical employment here.

character traits of humans. But that concerns the utility of laws, not restrictions on their legitimate scope.

It is even possible to acknowledge that there may be no single very precise 'what it is like' for pain for squids and humans alike. We can thus leave open the possibility that even our rawest sensations are affected by their cognitive surround; an uncontaminated sensational aspect may be incapable of being neatly peeled off. In other words, there may be no common core of pain for sentient creatures beneath the various forms of affective packaging within which it is experienced. Perhaps the best we can hope for is a family of primitively similar sensations. But this leaves us in no worse stead than it does for classifying the variety of pains humans alone suffer under a single heading. (Consider how sensations are responded to in diverse civilizations.) However, sameness of sensation within these limits may also occur across some distinct species having very different physiologies. If there are intelligent extraterrestrials, there is no reason to suppose that their feeling of pain must be unlike our own just because they have evolved very differently. This is bad news even for the second horn of Kim's dilemma, to which I now turn.

6.6.2 Pain as a Real Property

In the passage quoted from "The Myth of Nonreductive Physicalism" (1993d), Kim acknowledges the possibility of species-specific or structure-specific laws for conscious states, although as yet it is not certain that the desired regularities will be found in structurally similar individuals, or even in single individuals at different times. But the former possibility does provide one way to limit the damage done by the MR objection. Although in 2001 Kim seems to have altered his views about such restricted generalizations for pain, let's examine the consequences of his earlier position.

Kim mentions a familiar objection to his view.[8] Species-specific generalizations don't tell us what pain as such is, or why we should use the same constituent 'pain' in the expression 'pain-in-humans' that we use in 'pain-in-reptiles' or in 'pain-in-Martians'. Don't we call them all 'pain' because of a commonality? If there is nothing more to this usage than the proposed species-specific generalizations, the series of letters 'p' 'a' 'i' 'n' makes no more significant a contribution to the hyphenated nouns than

8. See Block 1980a; Pereboom and Kornblith 1991.

the genus *ant* does to the first three letters of 'antecedent'. But it is surely not accidental that the term 'pain' occurs across the board here. We could replace it with a simple predicate for the other Xs, but that abolishes any distinction between pluralism and chauvinism. To remain a pluralist, one would have to agree that this loses something in what the various terms purport to convey. Kim acknowledges this by offering a conceptual gambit explanation for the term's common use, but *qua* explanation it is plainly unsatisfactory; perhaps more important, like a Hegelian "thesis" it bears the seeds of its own destruction. Kim affirms that although there may be no common property, there is a common *concept*, and that it is built largely on our shared criteria for picking out instances.

A first problem with the explanation is that the shared recognitional criteria for the concept *pain* "may well be for the most part functional ones" (Kim 1993e, p. 333). But the functional criteria will be predominantly causal and behavioral, precisely the sources of differences between species Kim cited earlier to show that P_r and P_m are *not* the same properties as P_h. Thus, we can retool the problems Kim cited for finding a single property as an argument against a single concept. If clear anxiety reactions won't work to find a single pain property, what hope is there for finding enough of a common core in other behavioral syndromes to warrant a unified concept? There are many differences between the pain behavior of dogs and that of humans. Dogs don't shout 'ouch', they don't grab the distressed part of their bodies, they have a distinctive yelp (unlike human shrieks), they lick their wounds, and their tails droop. These are just the sorts of external dissimilarities that seem to have led Kim to discount a single pain property across species. On the other hand, dogs do avoid subsequent painful stimuli, they do move away from the stimulus, and they do exhibit apprehensions for similar stimuli, as do humans. If those similarities are enough to frame a single concept, why don't they suffice for a single property?

These remarks don't show that there is no concept *pain* any more than the earlier ones showed that there is no such property. But, given the earlier argument based on a lack of all-encompassing behavioral generalizations, they do bring out that a pluralist is in no position to explain the significance of the single syllable 'pain' in all these distinct X-pain properties by appealing to functional similarities that embrace all its subjects. If a pluralist can now detect a sufficient number of similarities between stimuli and behavior to form a single, functional concept across structurally different subjects, how can he or she claim that the absence of such generalizations prohibits unqualified pain from being a property or having any nomological significance? Just the same connections to behavior would appear to be demanded for the feeling of pain, on the one hand, and pain stimuli, on the other.

Kim justly observes that pain is the sort of thing for which a functional account is unworkable. The phenomenology of pain, its intrinsic nature, is overlooked when it is functionalized. Indeed, more recently he has written that, although we may succeed in functionalizing *intentional* properties, he sides "with those philosophers who believe that phenomenal properties of consciousness are not functional properties" (2001, p. 280). Kim takes the possibility of qualia inversion to show this. But, then, the absence of extrinsic property generalizations, such as those highlighted in his argument against a common pain property, lose their point. If we must seek nomic generalizations to discover the property of pain, or even of P_h, they should not be generalizations such as 'sharp pains cause anxiety reactions', a patently behavioral manifestation. As I explained earlier in this discussion, the relevant nomic generalizations will be relatively rare. But Kim doesn't deny that there are intrinsic features of pains, at least in P_h. If that destroys functionalism, it should be equally fatal to his leading objection to unhyphenated pain.

Even in "The Myth of Nonreductive Physicalism" (1993d), Kim does not wholly ignore the phenomenology of pain. He concedes that the appeal to a common pain found in each of the hyphenated varieties might suit either functionalism or emergentism. But he quickly drops consideration of emergentism because the objection had been raised by functionalists. Functionalists must confront the challenging question "What *functional* similarity do P_h, P_r, P_m and their kind have that cannot be captured in species-specific laws?" Any answer creates a dilemma for them: either more specific pain qualities have something in common or they do not. If the qualities have something in common (call it 'H'), the reductive materialist is as entitled to it as is the functionalist. If they have nothing in common, the most we can hope for are species-specific or structure-specific properties.

This dilemma does not threaten the emergentist. If the pains have nothing more in common than a phenomenology, that is a problem for chauvinism, but it is consistent with emergentism. On the other hand, if the various pains haven't enough in common (in Kim's narrow sense), unhyphenated pain would be a concept rather than a property only if an objection on the order of that to disjunctive properties were sound, and we have yet to encounter an unquestionable objection of that sort.

Let us ask how would one go about devising a unitary concept for a phenomenal property? Kim's account (1999, pp. 10–13; 2005, p. 101; see also Lewis 1980) goes roughly as follows. First, functionalize the property in question—that is, define it in terms of its causal relations and the other (e.g., inferential) nomic relations it bears to others properties. Next, find a realizer, a physical property responsible for its causal relations. Finally, construct a theory that explains how the realizer performs the causal tasks assigned to the phenomenal property. This process is illustrated by the discovery of DNA. Although genes aren't phenomenal, they are abstractly specified. The discoveries of Crick, Watson, Franklin, and Wilkins showed how DNA molecules realize and thereby explain the causal work of genes.

Kim has already identified the difficulty in supplying a purely functional account of sensations. Moreover, a full-blooded functional account ignores any intrinsic properties its explanandum might have, defining its target strictly in terms of the ingredients with which it interacts. The argument of section 1.7 demonstrated why we cannot ignore pain's intrinsic features. But there is more to the story (which will eventually lead us back to section 1.7). Let me explain what I find wanting in a functional account of sensations, even if we think of it as capable of absorbing a sensation's phenomenology.

Humans feel pain; it hurts. Suppose, on the other hand, that intelligent inhabitants of Uranus don't feel pain, but have a highly advanced technology. One of their savants, call him (?) Ür-Dennett, has invented a delicate instrument enabling him to detect in others, via a readout on his device, all the neural activity that is associated with pain in humans, even if that activity comprises a variety of distinct physical states (including those subserving psychosomatic pain). Let us suppose that Ür-Dennett is as competent as our introspective faculties in detecting degrees and types of pain. We may suppose that the readouts on his lightning-fast hand-held i-scanner are as reliable as our own sources. He can also detect, with uncanny accuracy, pain's causes and behavioral consequences. He claims these gadgets give him *a full understanding* of the nature of pain; I, and the vast majority of my conspecifics don't buy it. We persist in declaring that to understand what pain is we cannot omit its experiential disclosure. If, *pace* Kim, Martians felt pain, we would say that Martians could understand human pain, but that Ür-Dennett doesn't.

If pain is an experience, description alone will seem inadequate. This is a not-uncommon awkward predicament. A familiar problem bedevils attempts to capture what is specific to one medium in another one: we cannot taste a sound or see an odor. Unlike ineffable mystical experiences, the former involve no further claims about causes or interpretations that exceed their purely psychological features. Yet the inability to reproduce them adequately in a formula may create difficulties in defending them against the Ür-Dennetts of our own planet. Language is pervasive, leaving an opening for a critic to polemically challenge this phenomenon with the retort "*Tell me* what it is about sensation that I am missing." There is little new to say to dissuade a resolute Uranian. Nevertheless, it seems blatantly unreasonable to defer to this logomachy. How can we honestly suppress intuitions that withstand this objection? And if the objection were correct, wouldn't it have been possible, contrary to the lesson of section 1.7, for the whole race of Uranians to come to understand what pain was without realizing that anyone ever felt it?

Consider intelligible discriminations that an i-scanner seems incapable of capturing. Blindsight occurs when a lesion in one side of the brain's occipital lobe causes a subject to lose normal sight in all or part of a hemifield contralateral to the lesion, but the patient is still able to detect (or guess) significantly above chance gross features of objects in its blind hemifield. Moreover, words appearing there have a robust priming effect when clues are subsequently presented in the unaffected visual field. Blinking and pressing a button yield better response rates than verbal answers (Zihl and Von Cramon 1980), but all have been above chance. For normal perceivers, there is no distinction between seeing and being aware. However, for a blindsight subject "seeing" in that hemifield can amount to no more than an ability to discriminate. Yet there seems to be residual awareness—say, of motion—in a blind hemifield under special conditions. Lawrence Weiskrantz (1997, pp. 53–54) reports an experiment in which a blindsight subject is given two sets of keys to press. The first set is for 'present' and 'not present' for which the subject is asked whether a certain signal has been discriminated; the second set is for 'aware' and 'not aware'. The subject must press one button in each set. Weiskrantz reports that the paradigm "generates lawful results for both sets of keys." This certainly looks like a legitimate distinction, but I do not know how the nifty i-scanner could make it.[9] Of course, a clever Uranian will reject the distinction. 'Aware', when distinguished from 'being able to discriminate', begs the question against him. Nevertheless, the distinction looks intelligible enough even if the Uranian is unable to appreciate it.

Then how does ruling out a functional account bear on pluralism? Recall the original objection. In 'pain-for-X' specifications for each structural type or species, either the 'pain' portion signifies something that justifies our ranking each of them as a single type of property or its occurrence is no more significant to the whole phrase than 'ant' in 'anterior' and 'mendicant'. Neither is a species of ant. Kim's initial response is to throw the ball back into the functionalists' court, giving them two options and threatening them with (gasp!) emergentism if they reject his pluralist solution while insisting on a common feature that can't be functionalized. Kim has in reserve an explanation of the apparent commonality; it leads to a concept of pain rather than its property. But this is effective only if the first response really does result in an inescapable dilemma for the objector, which it fails to do for the emergentist. In fact, Kim's earlier argument against a common property rested on the lack of lawlike generalizations connecting pain sensations to similar behaviors, whereas just such similarities among the behaviors of different Xs are appealed to in devising a common concept.

Note also, depending on how structures are individuated, how pluralism fails to square with mainstream procedures in experimental psychology. Using test animals, including rats, in preliminary trials for human disorders is evidence that researchers regard them as close enough mentally to humans for some purposes, despite what impartial observers should regard as drastically dissimilar physiologies. For example, it was recently reported that mice lack genes for producing two peptides which appear to account for their ability to reduce severe pain. But the pain behavior in mice is certainly radically different from human behavior in many respects, although the absence of distraction may be an important common marker. If researchers did not believe that these experiments bore on the phenomenology of human pain, it is doubtful that they would have undertaken them in the first place, and they would not see a clue to the chemistry of human pain, for which they were searching, in their results. If these differences do not

9. For my reply to Ür-Dennett's Earthling doppelgänger, see Vision 1998.

amount to the sorts of structural ones preventing the projectibility of a simple pain property, what sorts of differences could pluralism cite as significant enough to be a distinct structure?[10] Also, cats and rhesus monkeys have been used as test animals for various experiential deficits, for example hemifield neglect. What would be the point of such tests if the investigators didn't believe that the results were applicable to human visual defects? Of course, researchers may be badly misled in their widespread practice of using lab animals to yield insights into human phenomenal afflictions. But the overwhelming empirical evidence is that such procedures, tentative as their results may be, are not unfounded. I am not suggesting that pluralists are unaware or unappreciative of this work, but only that had they paid careful attention to its implications when developing their own theories it would have been a serious obstacle to determining their 'for-X's in such a way that 'X' didn't become so inclusive as to lack all substance.

We have discovered basic deficiencies in the arguments for both varieties of old-school physicalism. This doesn't demonstrate the falsity of either view, but it undermines their major support. Two other competitors to emergentism remain in our sights: representationalism, and non-reductive physicalism. I turn now to those.

10. A recent issue of *Nature* contained a report on people with severe spinal injuries or palsies who were able to control their limbs by "thoughts"—that is, willfully induced brain activity. The article mentions that the devices were first tested on monkeys.

7 Representationalism

7.1 Prologue

The label 'Representationalism' has been applied to various positions. Here its companion term 'representationism' (which I use because the proponent I discuss most extensively uses that title) means, essentially, the following:

(R) Conscious, particularly phenomenal, properties are features of their intentional contents.

Some add that it also includes the perspective from which the content is experienced,[1] and, because believing, hoping, fearing, etc. differ, other representationists may also include the *type* of conscious state. Yet others may want to factor in functional role alongside content. I begin with some elucidations and ground rules.

First, representationists may discuss states, events, or processes rather than, or in addition to, properties. As before, I often use 'token' as a neutral term when those differences are negligible.

Next, in general I follow the custom of regarding representationality and intentionality as interchangeable ways to characterize the relevant content. But they can come apart, and in at least one instance I shall distinguish them. To give a simple example, in standard (non-Photoshopped) photography, what a photograph represents has no mental determinants; in that sense, it is not intentional. But I ignore such differences at this stage. For present purposes, what matters is that a conscious token represents only if it has intentional content.

---

1. This is more specific than, but otherwise similar to, Tye's (2003) strong representationism: "Phenomenal (viz. subjective) character = representational content (with some further restrictions on the type of representational content)."

Finally, although the view is designed to cover both phenomenal and access consciousness, (R)'s main concern is a certain class of phenomenally conscious tokens. That should not be taken to suggest that representationism is conceded for the rest of the mental, and that only a small class of recalcitrant data remains to be brought in line. As is customary, I take the view here as an unqualified explanation of mentality, or at least its conscious component. A single significant area beyond its reach should be regarded as a counterexample to the general project, reflecting back upon its treatment of less controversial cases.

I shall examine an argument for (R) that comes in two stages. First, one establishes that all conscious properties have intentional contents. Next, it is argued that that those properties are features of their respective contents. Concerning stage one, it goes without saying that belief, desire, and other access-conscious properties have intentional content. Also, some phenomenally conscious tokens—typified by sensory experiences—are certainly contentful. This feature is then extended to mental images and afterimages. The remaining question is whether a certain subclass of phenomenally conscious properties—very roughly, non-epistemic sensations—have intentional content. It is not prima facie evident that phenomenal sensations such as pains, itches, orgasms, tickles, indigestion sensations, and dizzy spells have intentional content. Those are often regarded as having intrinsic properties, qualia, for which representationist theories have no slot. Because they have been the focus of concern, the first stage of the argument may be further divided into two substages. In the first it is argued that the members of this phenomenal subclass have some intentional content. We may label the thesis this argument sets out to establish

(Int)   All phenomenal experiences have representational content.

In other words, there is a (psycho-)semantic (more simply here, semantic) dimension to phenomenal experiences. (Int) is a central theme of much of this chapter. In the second stage of the ancillary argument, that semantic dimension is identified.

Representationists explicitly acknowledge their commitment to (Int). For example, Fred Dretske writes:

Just as a visual experience of a tree is an awareness of a nonconscious object (the tree) pain is an awareness of a nonconscious bodily condition (an injured, strained, or diseased part). . . . When things are working right, pains, tickles, and itches stand to physical states of the body (they are experiences of these physical states) the way olfactory, visual, and auditory experiences stand to physical states of the environment. . . . What we are conscious of when we feel pain (hunger, thirst, etc.) are not the internal representations of bodily states (the pains), but the bodily states that these representations (pains) represent. (1995, pp. 102–103)

Tim Crane concurs:

The consciousness involved in bodily sensations is a result of two things: the intentional content of the sensation, and the intentional mode. (2003, p. 51)

The arguments behind these statements of (Int) are my prime concern in this chapter.

A token's representational, or intentional, content tells us what the token is about, of, or that. This may be called its intentional or representational object or content, terms sometimes occurring interchangeably in the literature. Differences between content and object are important for distinguishing the vehicle by means of which a token refers from its referent; but their differences can be largely ignored for present purposes. The relevant contents are often propositional, as in believes that and desires that. But that isn't always the case. Thus, the content of a perceptual experience, analogous to those for hunting and worshipping, may be expressible by a non-propositional noun clause (Vision 2009).

A central issue dividing philosophers of mind is the standing of semantic externalism. As understood here, externalism is the view that all, or at least many, of the concepts and other ingredients of those contents[2] are determined by environmental and/or socio-linguistic factors. Most of the representationists examined below are externalists, and that feature can come into play. There is a tension between externalism and the Cartesian view that even if one's thoughts fail to correspond to a mind-independent world, an individual is always capable of fully understanding exactly what he or she is thinking. In contrast, an externalist would hold, say, that, because water is a chemical compound, nothing lacking that composition, assumed to be H_2O, would be water. If one thinks of the liquid in one's native environment as superficially similar to water, but it is not H_2O, one's thought is not about water. Externalism therefore implies that what someone's thoughts represent may depend on factors outside the subject's ken. These differences have spawned an extensive literature, which, fortunately, we can avoid. However, because most of the representationists of concern are

2. Terms for the concepts in question are generally sortals designating natural kinds, designations of other physical quantities (e.g., snow, water, gold), and proper names.

externalists, when a choice of wording is needed to avoid baroque formulations I shall describe cases in that idiom. The most important results I reach can be rephrased in a way that internalists shouldn't find objectionable for that reason alone. Indeed, when discussing phenomenally conscious properties, such as pain and other bodily sensations, these differences are mostly negligible. Still, on some occasions the appeal to externalism may be a part of the defense of a position, and will then need to be factored in.

Sadly, we are not yet finished with distinctions among relevant versions. In addition to dustups over differences between representation and intentionality, and between externalism and internalism, some representationists are classical functionalists, others are not; some seem to subscribe to a simple form of naturalized semantics, based only on counterfactual dependence, normalcy of context, or the tracking of genuine cases, others require a teleological sanction. Some of these considerations will loom large shortly, but our initial formulations are concentrated on tenets that a large number of the leading representationists seem to share, enabling us to set aside those differences for the nonce.

Whereas representationists reject identities of conscious properties with strictly neural ones, that doesn't bar them from identifying conscious properties with features of intentional contents. However, identities play a relatively marginal role in these deliberations when compared to sets of necessary and sufficient conditions for phenomenal tokens. Conceivably, when identities are in question, they could be type identities or a series of token identities. But those further elaborations of the position have not been watershed moments for representationists.

I should mention that some of those being criticized in this chapter approach their material in an experimental spirit: their purpose is not to immure themselves in Fortress Representationism, but merely to explore how far one can press an intentionalist account for all mental aspects. However, I treat this view as if its proponents are making sweeping declamations about the mental as such. This is not meant to satisfy a disposition to be censorious, but to see how far it makes sense to push those occasionally tentative suggestions.

7.2 The Setting for Further Discussion

There is a consensus among philosophers of mind that intentionality and consciousness are its two general problem areas. If the latter can be reduced via (R) to the former, issues concerning intentionality would remain, but we will have reduced two basic problem areas to one, and indeed we will have taken off the table what is universally deemed the harder topic. In philosophy that is a good measure of progress. It is the goal—or, ominously, the white whale—of representationism. Its success would be a genuine advance.

Representationism has the advantage of being invulnerable to the multiple-realization objection. In the preceding chapter, an opening salvo of MR undid chauvinism. However, nothing in the current view requires contents with which a type of sensation is identified to be restricted to one or another kind of sentient being. Even if representationists claim that contents yield identities, they could cover a variety of subjects. In addition, representationists, like physicalists, often draw on the advertised difficulties of mental causation. Despite those apparent advantages, the initial case for representationism must be made elsewhere. I turn now to reasons that have been given for adopting the view.

The main argument for (R) has been discursive. Suppose we begin from perceptual or sensory experiences, which do indeed have intentional contents. Appeal is often made to G. E. Moore's (1959) insight that sensory experience is transparent or, as he also puts it, diaphanous. For example, Gilbert Harman writes: "Look at a tree and try to turn your attention to intrinsic features of your visual experience. I predict you will find the only features there to turn your attention to will be features of the presented tree, including relational features of the tree 'from here'." (1990, p. 39) At that point, other phenomenally conscious tokens are assimilated to perceptual experiences, and a comparable transparency is extended to them. I take up this line of argument later, but first I have other fish to fry.

Arguments for the first step—that is, (Int)—have occupied much of representationists' attention. The following strike me as its commonest examples:

(A)   Intentionality is inferred from intensionality.

(B)   A semantics for paradigms of phenomenal tokens, implying their intentionality, may be framed, perhaps based on their operation in optimal or normal conditions.

(C)   (the teleological sanction) Sensations can be understood as having historical functions, which initiate their contents and direct us to them.

I begin with a consideration of arguments (A) and (B), shared by the bulk of representationists. The teleological sanction is taken up in sections 7.5 and 7.6. Each argument begins from visual, auditory, tactile, olfactory, and gustatory experience, thence inferring from a comparison with those cases that other conscious phenomena must also be intentional.

Although it is my intention to examine a broadly corporate view, the exposition basically focuses on two representative examples: the views of Michael Tye and Fred Dretske. In the next section I concentrate on (A); (B) is examined in section 7.4. Despite their separate treatments, (A) and (B) are intertwined and complementary. To explain, (A) is designed to show that every phenomenal token has some intentional content, subjecting those tokens to semantic evaluation. (B) is then introduced to provide the type of semantics capable of supporting conscious token content. The possibility of mistake is a staple in arguments of type (A). "Where there is falsehood there is representation," writes William Lycan (1995, p. 92), though he promptly disclaims being "entirely sure" of it. Nevertheless, it has been generally central to representationist arguments that my thoughts or utterances can misrepresent something, as, say, when I visually mistake a painted mule for a zebra. This has been taken to be a sure sign that something semantic is afoot. The main thrust of my reasons for rejecting both (A) and (B) is that although mistakes with respect to pain and the like are possible, not all mistake is a case of misrepresentation. On the contrary, there is no reason to suppose that mistakes here are more than garden-variety hypotheses about the causes of the sensational property.

Let us now proceed to the arguments for (Int).

7.3   Intensionality and Intentionality

How can it be demonstrated that all phenomenal experiences have intentional content? (A) states that if it can be shown that they bear the marks of intensionality, it follows that they are intentional. Tye (1995b, p. 107) mentions two familiar tests for intensionality[3]: A context (say, Φing) is intensional if (and only if?)

(i)   One can Φ F "even though there are no such things" as Fs.

---

3. A third test—that a propositional clause within the scope of Φ cannot be replaced *salva veritate* by just any other propositional clause with the same truth value—doesn't bear on the current discussion.

(ii)   In cases where F = G, one can Φ an F without Φ-ing a G.

On (i), I can think about, wish for, or hallucinate unicorns, or I can think that unicorns have magical powers, even though there are no unicorns. On (ii), I can think about Voltaire, or think that Voltaire was a deist, without thinking about François-Marie Arouet, or that Arouet was a deist, although Voltaire and Arouet are the same man. Tye (1995a, p. 235) illustrates (ii) as follows: "What it is like to be the subject of this backache is, of course, the same what it is like to be subject of this backache. But what it is like to be subject of this backache is not the same as what it is like to be me, even though I am the subject of this backache."

Setting aside the question whether all phenomenal experiences have content, consider those that do and grant that they have features (i) and (ii). That is not sufficient to guarantee that the phenomenal instances under consideration are intentional only because they are intensional. To ascribe intentionality as it is relevant to the theory under review is to say that whatever has it has at least the following two features: having content and being mental. But whereas content (and therefore representation) may follow from intensionality, it is doubtful that mentality does. Alethic modality provides a well-known counterexample. Necessarily 12 is greater than 10, and the number of Caesars is 12, but it is not true that necessarily the number of Caesars is greater than 10. 'It is necessary that 12 >10' is representational, but is it mental? There have been efforts to bring modality under the jurisdiction of the mental, but they have not been markedly successful. Thus, although the phenomenal is undeniably mental, the question before us should be whether this is explained by its being intensional. If the phenomenal's satisfaction of (ii) could be accounted for on grounds other than its mentality, then this particular reason for supposing that it must have content fails. Thus, let's briefly consider whether there are grounds other than phenomenality for satisfying (ii).

Grant *pro tem* that satisfying (ii) is sufficient for intensionality. Nevertheless, being intensional here could result from a distinctive feature of first-person ascription rather than from mentality. For example, many philosophers regard the idiom 'S sees o', in which 'o' is a non-propositional noun clause, as extensional. Of course, there are cases of seeing spots before one's eyes, or "seeing" pink elephants, but these are often set aside as hardwired idioms. However, even if 'S sees o' is not absolutely extensional, it is broadly open to substitution by co-referential terms. Thus, if we have a truthful utterance of the sentence

(a)   'Mia sees a dolphin'

and a dolphin is a sea mammal, it follows that it is also true that

(b)   'Mia sees a sea mammal'

although Mia doesn't know that dolphins are mammals and may even insist that they are fish. But things change when Mia herself says

(c)   'I see a dolphin'.

Things change not because (ii) is exemplified, but because Mia is in no position to say

(d)   'I see a sea mammal'.

Of course, seeing is a mental state, and, let us concede, a phenomenal state, in (c). But it is no less so in (a), although relevant implications of the two idioms differ. An account of their differences should be chalked up to the differences made by *de se* ascription. The way things seem *to me* is in a similarly distinctive position—perhaps even a stronger one, since our inquiry is just what it seems like to the first person.

In light of the foregoing, consider once again Tye's example of the satisfaction of (ii). I find nothing wrong with saying in the third person that what it is like to be the subject of Michael's backache is what it is like to be Michael. Whatever intensionality we seem to find in this example appears to come from peculiarities of first-person thinking or reporting, not from the sensation of backache. The case doesn't appear to tell us anything about whether that feeling belongs with the representational content or whether it is a quality of the sensation itself. This particular barrier to substituting descriptions—namely, who is doing the reporting—has little to do with its being mental; rather it concerns what one is in a position to state from a first-person perspective. Tye's example fails to establish (Int).

The strength of intuitions about the representationality of phenomenal states varies. At one end of the range are perceptual sensory cases—visual, tactile, auditory, olfactory, gustatory experience—that are clearly intentional. At the other end are conscious states such as pain, itch, and feelings of fatigue. In between are cases such as after-images. J. J. C. Smart (1959) denied that after-images were intentional. As a card-carrying physicalist, Smart did not see how the intentional content of an after-image was capable of being reduced to a brain process in the same way in which the event of sensing an after-image could. Thus, he proposed a neutral translation that reconfigured experiential objects into adjectival qualifiers—e.g., 'being in a state like the state one is when one sees an orange'. From there, it was simpler to identify being in that state with a brain process. This isn't an issue for the representationist, for whom the intentional content is the after-image. Accordingly, Tye (1995b, p. 108) has no difficulty in claiming that "after-images are representational." Moreover, that seems sensible: like seeing, an after-image has a content, and the content is what the after-image is an image of. It is hard to suppress that much when we reflect on the experience of undergoing a particular after-image. It would be difficult to dismiss it merely as a superficial quirk of grammar.[4]

Grant the point. What is to be made of the founding insight that perception is transparent to its object? Certainly when one is seeing something introspection doesn't deliver anything like the jolt one gets from a mild electric shock. Perspective is present, but the representationist takes that as an aspect of the content. However, it is hard to imagine that the only thing in our experience is what is represented. If that were the case, how could one know that one was detecting the qualities of the object by sight rather than, say, by touch or sound? Surely there is a phenomenal difference between seeing and touching a shape, though both yield the same shape information. Some qualities, such as color or the taste of cinnamon, can be detected by only one sense. Even so, to know that I am experiencing a quality is to have unmediated access to my experience of it, and is distinct from what I am experiencing. Thus, even for experiences with representational contents, the variety of the transparency—that is, the mode of the experience—is a quale.

However, the acid test for representationism is for paradigmatic sensations such as pains, itches, twitches, orgasms, anxiety attacks, thirst, or hot flashes. Though it is certainly possible that all these cases yield to the same treatment as perceptual experience, that is not a foregone conclusion. So, we may ask, what other grounds might there be for the intensionality of phenomenal consciousness?

One of Tye's arguments is that intensionality explains why certain initially puzzling inferences are invalid. Block (1983, p. 517) argued that the predicate '___ in ___' systematically changes senses when applied to physical objects and mental particulars. This would account for the failure of an inference from

---

4. But see Lycan 1996, pp. 51–52.

The pain is in my fingertip.

and

My fingertip is in my mouth.

to

The pain is in my mouth.

A different explanation is proffered by Tye (1995b, p. 112): Such inferences fail because "the term 'in' appears in an intensional context." Being
intensional, and using (Int), the pain must have *in my fingertip* as its intentional object.

Intentionality preserves a unitary sense for 'in'. However, there is another
equally good (indeed, I would claim superior) explanation in the offing. If
the 'in' of the first premise expressed only a *hypothesis* about where *the operative cause* of my pain was located (viz., something happening in my fingertip), the argument would still be invalid, but the explanation also would
not need to posit distinct senses of 'in'. (That option is explored more fully
in the next section.) Moreover, in some cases in which basically the same
problems arise, the opportunity for an intentional content is plainly forced.
Consider the following:

The flaw is in the boiler.

The boiler is in Chicago.

The flaw is in Chicago.

On its most natural reading ('in' read roughly as 'with' in the third step),
the argument is equally invalid, but intensionality doesn't explain it. There
is an unnatural way of understanding the first premise on which the argument is valid, but that is offset by an equally unnatural way to read the first
premise of the earlier argument on which that argument is valid.

This does not demonstrate that Tye's interpretation is erroneous, but it
illustrates why his explanation doesn't establish the intentionality of pain
contexts. Because his account leaves at least one alternative in the game,
I believe that account is better suited as a defense against someone who
wants to show that pain cannot be intentional than as a way to show that
sensations are intentional. If we appended to it a semantics for intentional
contexts that comfortably embraced the disputed sensations, that might
strengthen the argument for Tye's case. Thus, let us turn to argument (B).

7.4   Semantics Naturalized

Suppose we have state S of an x. According to Tye (1995b, p. 101; cf. Tye 1998b, p. 472),

(Rep)   S represents that $P =_{df}$ [a] If optimal conditions obtain, S is tokened in x if and only if P and [b] because P.

This is a matter not only of correlation, but also of *tracking* P under optimal conditions (Tye 1995b, pp. 101, 131). In less than optimal conditions, misrepresentation can occur. In standard examples, if x is a tree and S is its rings, then P is the tree's age; if S is the darkness of cloud x, then P is the probability of rain; if S is a sudden outbreak of spots on x's face, then P is measles (or chicken pox). As applied to our topic, if x stubs her toe and undergoes its distinctive pain, then the pain, S, represents a particular, normally disagreeable, something in her toe, which is P.

It is not easy to spell out optimality non-trivially. I return to that issue in section 7.6, but at this juncture, let us assume that that obstacle can be overcome. The present point is only the representationist claim that bodily sensations have semantic contents. That view is a staple of Tye's and Dretske's positions regarding bodily sensations. They compare such tokens to clear cases of representations, focusing primarily on perceptual experiences. Moore's insight into the transparency of perceptual experience plays a central role here. Dretske (1995, p. xiii) claims that his Representational Thesis "helps one understand, for example, why conscious experiences have that peculiar diaphanous quality—the quality of always being present when, but never where, one looks to find them," and Tye (2000, p. 45) writes that the "transparency [of experience] is a very powerful motivation for the representationist view." (Rep)'s best fit is for the authors' prime illustration: perceptual experience. In light of the comparisons and a run through other cases, Tye (1995b, p. 119) writes that he finds it "intuitively very appealing" that (Rep) extends to other conscious tokens. His discussion is rounded off with an account of what it is to introspect those feelings; it is a feature of the representation itself, and the sensation is a state poised for a certain output. Because the content is non-conceptual, it does not follow that the subject need be cognizant of what is represented.

Note some crucial features of the transparency thesis. First, it sets up the case so that the proper venue for discovering the intrinsic nature of experience is the second-order event of introspecting one's first-order experience. Second, not only does this exercise send us forthwith back to the object of the first-order experience, but it drives us to nothing else: the object and its perspectival nature are the only features of the content of the second-order experience. (Recall Harman's remark quoted on page 181.) However, both those phenomenological claims have been contested by authors who argue that the awareness that one is undergoing the experience is an integral part of the original experience, not a separate episode. (See, e.g., Horgan and Kriegel 2007; Chalmers 1996.) The subject doesn't require a second-order episode, and although the first-order experience is transparent in the sense that the object is a component of it, that does not preclude our awareness of our experiencing of the very same episode. I shall not dwell on these differences, but it cannot be overlooked that the representationist employment of transparency isn't self-evident enough to pass unchallenged.

Although the view under consideration delivers a disappointing result to those sometimes labeled "qualia freaks," its intent is not deflationary. It purports to account for phenomenality, not to dismiss it. Before saying more about the way it acknowledges the phenomenal, I want to introduce in stages a competing view that accounts for the features of the situation that the representationist labels intentional content. Any competitive view should countenance the fact emphasized by representationists that pains are locatable in the sufferer's body. But this does not yield a sufficient reason for supposing that pains are embedded as a representational content. If we concentrate the content on a pain's location (which comports with Tye's notion that the array being represented is, for starters, like that of a map), we might offer as an alternative account that the location is a causal hypothesis about the source of the pain's damage. A causal hypothesis can, but needn't be an intentional content. Indeed, it is obvious that many causal hypotheses about our locatable pains (e.g., the pain's recurrence being due to an earlier injury) are not intentional contents. These hypotheses may also be mistaken, just as a representation can misrepresent. Perhaps 'hypothesis' is too exalted a term for so casual and natural a practice. What I have in mind is something that may be satisfied by nothing more than a creature that—say, after stepping on a thorn—raises, licks, or bites its paw. The creature's motion is as compatible with an intuition about, or a purely inherited reaction to, the cause of its distress as with its having content representing its location. This indicates how very broadly 'hypothesis' is intended here.

Choose your favorite example of a non-representing natural object. To get us started let's choose randomly scattered stones on a beach. My term for the view that everything (and I mean everything) represents is pansemanticism. It has a number of intuitive and philosophical burdens, and it is a very real threat under (Rep). Individual stones and their arrangement are sources of information about their causes and origins. If a stone is smooth, it may carry the information that it was corroded by the elements. It might also indicate that it is a fossilized plant or animal. Its current situation, under optimal conditions, permits inference to its causes. It is irrelevant that we may be unable to satisfy the optimal conditions central to information theory. The information is there whether or not we gather it, or whether anyone was ever around to gather it, or whether it requires methods more finely tuned than those of which humans are capable. We might have called the method 'implication' rather than 'inference', thereby removing any hint of a need for a cognizing subject. But implication suggests instead that the information is deductively available, whereas it is abduction that carries the load. (Russell's (1921, p. 159) observation that there is no logical impossibility in supposing that the world was created five minutes ago, with all its traces, including memories of past existence, intact, is enough to show that the information is not strictly deduced from the effect.) Given that the rebarbative 'abduction' reintroduces a hint of inferential agency, I shall use 'causal hypothesis' in my extended sense to indicate the way in which a non-representational token encodes information about its cause. My alternative to representationism is that the location of the pain is a causal hypothesis about a basically qualitative sensation.

The representationist may not see this as a competitor. Tye identifies his semantic element as a kind of "causal variation" and his clause [b]—S is tokened because P—is undoubtedly intended to highlight a causal because. However, if the stone is not representing anything, but supports a hypothesis about its causes and origins, causal hypotheses do not demand intentional content. The causal hypothesis is independent of (Rep) even if (Rep) includes a causal hypothesis.

In lieu of a decisive argument that the causal hypothesis trumps (Rep), here are a few considerations that carry some weight. First, if the two accounts are on a par, the representionalist's semantic argument doesn't make the case for which it is utilized. A point on which both sides can agree, namely that sensations have bodily locations, does not require a semantic dimension for bodily sensations. Second, if we must choose between the accounts, we should favor the causal hypothesis if, as I have claimed, it does not itself imply representational content. Representing X goes beyond causing X, even causing X regularly, in which case the semantic addition demands further reasons. *Ceteris paribus* we should prefer the more exiguous explanation. That second point warrants some elaboration concerning natural starting points.

The issue can be construed as selecting the best of our available starting points. The representationist begins from perceptual experience. Dretske's example is "looking red"; Lycan (1995) begins with a "red patch" (possibly an after-image); Tye (1995b, p. 93) begins by considering "the visual sensations I undergo as I watch a distant plane make its way across a clear sky." And Tye's later (2000, pp. 46–51) ten-step development of the case for representationism confirms that visual-like experience is his paradigm. (See also Hill 2009, chapter 3.) Visual experiences are certainly conscious phenomena with representational contents. In 1995a Tye begins not with perceptual experiences but with afterimages and mental images. They too are counted as representational, but they share with perceptual sensations a feature we may call a perceptual buffer. Mental images draw on iconic memories, and afterimages on aftereffects of visual sensations. In sum, the representationist strategy is to begin with sensations in an imagistic medium. We may contrast these, for the sake of argument, with what I shall label pure bodily sensations. The latter may be introduced via enumeration of some stereotypical members, including the hard cases of pain, fatigue, itch, and the like. We shouldn't assume that pure bodily sensations lack a perceptual buffer; that issue is still on our agenda. My present interest is only in the interaction between these two groups: perceptual plus other imagistic states on the one hand, pure bodily sensations on the other. (There is no need for these to cover the entire spectrum of candidates.)

Even representationists agree that it is not as obvious that pure bodily sensations satisfy (Int) as that perceptual experiences do.[5] Further explanation or argument is wanted, for which the earlier definition of 'S represents

5. Tye (1995a, p. 227) concedes "a *hidden* intensionality in statements of pain location" (emphasis added).

P′ is but a starting point. The most serious reason for extending intentionality from the more explicit cases to pure bodily sensations seems to be the view that pure bodily sensations yield quick and transparent information about bodily location and the state of one's body at that location. Although strictly correct, it does not advance the case for an intentional content. We might have started the comparison from the other end.

Again, take stones scattered on a beach as prototypical of non-representational phenomena. The stones also yield information, this time by causal hypothesis. Of course, the information they yield is not quick or transparent; but then stones on the beach are neither cognizant nor sentient, which accounts for the irrelevance of measuring them by the speed and transparency of their informational transmission. We may then extend this account to pure bodily sensations, and say that they encode information in the same way that the stones do, by causal hypothesis. Mistaken causal hypotheses are as familiar as misrepresentations, so we can account for errors (e.g., phantom limb sensations) on this construal as readily as on the supposition of intentional content. The representationist might reply that on his view the mistake is contained in the content itself, while on the unadorned causal hypothesis the mistake is that of an agent who casts it. True! The mistake cannot be contained in the stones themselves; they possess no norms. However, we can say that the stones, or the pain, embody misleading evidence about their causes. This seems to me to describe the mishap in the evidential situation as effectively as representationism does. Why not proceed on this basis rather than starting from cases on which representationists proceed? If we were to do so, then our first question would not be "Why not classify pure bodily sensations with perceptual buffer sensations?" Rather it would be "What must one add to the yielding of information to get us from 'causal hypothesis' to 'representation'?" And from this second starting point it is clear that something more is needed.

Enter the spectre of pansemanticism. If one responds by accepting any such causal hypothesis as a representation, every effect represents. But think of a forensic pathologist who concludes that a wound must have been caused by a blunt object, or that a victim died around 10 P.M. Do the wounds or the onset of rigor mortis semantically represent those facts? The identity of the cause may be imprecise and not sharply bounded—exactly what Tye (1995b, p. 113) notes for representations of dull aches. And the same is true of the extinction of the dinosaurs, the stratification of layers of rock in a cliff, or the origins of a moon. There are no instances in which no information about a cause can be extracted from features of its effect. Rocks, Brownian movements, snowflakes, meteorites, droughts, salamanders, lima beans, gulf streams, tornadoes, chemical compounds, animal tracks, tectonic plates, viruses, and whatever else one can think of will carry clues to their origins.

Why not just bite the pansemantic bullet? I don't know that anyone has done this outright, but there is at least a hint of it in Tye. In 2000, pp. 139–140, he illustrates his view not with the staple examples of measles spots, mercury columns, or tree rings, but with cats shedding hair. He begins by noting that shedding is causally correlated with the lengthening of days as well as with increasing temperature. But Tye argues that the shedding's correlation to the lengthening of days satisfies his formula for representation in a way that its correlation to increasing temperature does not.[6] If this is a case of representation, how can we refuse it to any event or thing? One way around this might be to treat the various elaborations of (Rep) as no more than "theory sketches." In that vein, Byrne and Tye (2006, p. 253) write: "Theories of psychosemantics . . . are tested by their ability to deal with clear and simple examples, where the relevant differences are comparatively well understood." And earlier (p. 251) Byrne and Tye suggest that "arguably" no account has made only correct predictions. But it seems clear that generalizing from these instances would place every effect in the class of representers. A view that gets its proponents the desired subclass of cases only because it yields false positives for everything else is not what serious theorists regard as a promising sketch. It is akin to a stopped clock that is correct twice each day.

Pace this consequence, those favoring naturalistic semantic theories generally agree that the world is divided into things and features that represent (i.e., metaphorically "reach out" beyond themselves) and things and features that don't. The words on this page exemplify the former phenomenon. But the appearances are that some things just aren't semantic commodities! It would take a much stronger counterargument to dislodge that conviction. Of course, anything can be pressed into service. I can arrange the rocks on the beach into a distress signal, or the peas on a plate to represent

6. Consistently pursuing this line of reasoning leads to disqualifying day lengthening as being represented in favor of any causal mechanism more proximate to the shedding, including chemical changes in the cat. See Vision 1996, pp. 234–235.

a battle or a football play, or, as with the most insignificant gestures, create a prearranged signal with another spy on the Orient Express. But unless natural objects are recruited for a function, the prevailing opinion is that they don't stand for anything. Some, not all, advocates of naturalized semantics hold that certain things which haven't been recruited, such as rings in cross-cuts of deciduous trees or red spots on someone's body, are exceptions. But I assume even adherents of naturalized semantics will agree that there is a division between entities that are semantically evaluable and those that aren't. It is not a question of where the line is drawn but a question of whether one is drawn. I know of no serious suggestion that birds are intentional objects de jure, representing dinosaurs, because we can see from comparing birds' internal characteristics with those of late dinosaurs that they are descended from the latter.[7]

Thus, the earlier definition of 'S represents that P' and others of its ilk leave us with an unattractive set of commitments. First, there appears to be no way to distinguish what we regard as a representation from what is available through causal inference. Second, as a result, there is no principled way of preventing representationism from leading directly to pan-semanticism—everything represents something. Either option renders this notion of representation of little use for the purposes for which the theory under consideration was devised. Conscious properties are now features of intentional content only because everything that has a cause is a feature of intentional content. A further consequence appears to be that the result is not the one the representationist seems to have sought, but rather one that plays into the hands of old-fashioned absolute idealism. Assuming that the very identity of a contentful entity involves its content, we cannot understand an individual without understanding, at the same time, the cause or origin of that individual. If we think of what S represents as an intrinsic property of x, as representationists propose, then every cause (and cause of that cause, and so on) is essential to x's identity. Unless these problems can be resolved, representationism concerning the phenomenal not only courts metaphysical problems but imminently threatens trivialization.

But mightn't this be merely a flaw in the details? Perhaps a better definition would avert those difficulties. We can't vet every possibility, but to

---

7. Fodor (1990a) and Antony and Levine (1991) note that threat for all theories in which bearing information is sufficient for semantic representation. Cf. Burge 2007c.

illustrate the depth of the problem let us consider another candidate. Tye (2000, p. 142, n. 25) regards his proposal as "importantly like" Jerry Fodor's, so let's glance briefly at Fodor's thesis. Altering Fodor's formula for meaning into one for representing, generalizing from his "cow" example, and stipulating that X ≠ Y, we get something like this:

"X" means X and not Y because there being Y-caused "X" tokens depends on there being X-caused "X" tokens, but not the other way around. (I.e., non-X caused "X" tokens are asymmetrically dependent on there being X-caused "X" tokens). (See Fodor 1990a, p. 91.)

Now, many have found reasons to dissent from this (Fodor himself addresses eleven or more objections), but the only issue before us is how it bears on the previous sense of *representation*. So far as I can tell, it provides no support for (Rep). First, although it holds that the symbol 'pain' and the concept-token *pain* themselves represent pain, this does nothing to indicate that either the symbol or the concept *also* has an intentional content. Next, and most important, Fodor's view starts from symbols rather than showing how something becomes a symbol. Not defining a symbol via such asymmetric dependence appears to be part of Fodor's way of avoiding what he has called "type one theories," which threaten circularity. If this is the pattern for naturalized semantics, naturalized semantics as such does nothing to buttress the case for (Rep).

7.5 A Feature of Content

It seems clear that more than content must be taken into account when providing necessary and sufficient conditions for a sensation. For example, consider the following highly abbreviated list of feelings in my right foot:

1. a kneading sensation as my foot is being massaged

2. gentle pressure on my foot from the jet of a whirlpool

3. with my legs crossed, my foot falling asleep (vernacularly, 'pins and needles')

4. a bee sting (or being pricked by a thorn) as I walk barefoot on the grass

5. as I carelessly groom a horse, its stepping on my foot

6. my foot's swelling from a gout attack

7. an excruciating stiffening of a posterior tibial muscle as I stretch my foot awkwardly while lying flat

8. a burning sensation when my foot inadvertently touches a stove

9. the sting of mild frostbite when trekking in the snow

10. stubbing my toe

Each of these might have the content 'something occurring in my right foot', and my right foot is the object to which each is directed. More specifically, at least feelings 4–10, and perhaps feeling 3, could be described as painful and would be covered by 'something distressful in my right foot'. But there are important differences in tone, and distinguishing those requires something more than specifications of their respective contents to distinguish them. Because the content is supposedly non-conceptual, we can ignore a constraint that it be more specifically expressible. But we have yet to see what concept could be available for distinguishing these items that wouldn't smuggle in a distinctive quale. This may supply an opening for a distinguishable quale, but Crane objects:

> . . . in a state of pain (in the ankle, say) there do not seem to be two things going on—the intentional awareness of the ankle, and the awareness of the plain-quale. Rather the awareness of the ankle seems to be ipso facto awareness of its hurting. How the ankle feels . . . does not seem to be an intrinsic property of the intentional awareness of the ankle. (2003, p. 47)

However, the ability to be isolated in a single act of imagining is not the crucial test. An objection of Crane's sort would prevent us from discovering any common aspects between determinates of a single determinable. For example, how could we extract *redness* from patches that were crimson and scarlet? Nothing is simply red without being some more particular shade of that color. And in spite of the notion that determinables are somehow abstract, and thus a level up from the particular, they needn't be any less concrete than their determinates. But a particular red shade of an apple is no less red than, say, the shade red_{31}. Determinables are different from their determinates, but they are not separable even in the imagination. (Compare the contrast with quarks, distinguishable aspects of subatomic particles that do not exist in isolation.)

7.6 Optimal Conditions

Setting aside an earlier assumption, how can we work out what it is for a condition to be optimal? Recall the importance of requiring "optimal conditions" in (Rep) so as to make sense of correct and incorrect representations.

In brief, optimality implies norms. However, the problem exposed in section 7.4 was that the naturalistic semantics endorsed by our representationist led inexorably to pansemanticism. As an alternative, if we could inject teleology into the picture by discovering proper functions for representers, only things that had a function would represent. A natural function would ground the intentional in the non-intentional, and the distinction between representing and misrepresenting (e.g., by an organism, an organ, or a feature) would be enforced as a fulfillment or a flaunting of its proper function. The obvious candidate for a standard with which to judge proper function is evolution. Because only evolved tokens would have proper functions of this sort, anything lacking an evolutionary history would not be subject to its norms. And, of course, if we could distill a notion of proper function from evolution, we would be able to employ it without having to appeal to a conscious agent.

But this comes at a price, as Swampman cases make abundantly clear. Tye (1995b, p. 153) remarks that it is "highly counterintuitive" to hold that "beings who lack an evolutionary history (artificially created beings, for example, or accidental creations of various sorts) cannot be subject to experiences and feelings." Subscribing to a teleological account of optimal conditions, as Dretske does, commits one to holding not only that Swampman lacks phenomenal consciousness but also that any descendants sired with Swampwoman lack it as well, down to however many Swamp generations there may be in my ancestry. The taint of original sin brands the entire Swampcreature lineage. If you happen to be the nth generation from pure Swamp ancestors, you have no phenomenal consciousness. But for the fact that Swampman hypotheses are outlandish to begin with, it would be reckless to let so fundamental a philosophical thesis rest on an empirical conjecture, especially if you have no way of certifying that you yourself aren't a remote descendant of swamp forebears. (See Dretske (manuscript).)

In light of Tye's views on Swampman, it appears that he would avoid appealing to teleology here. However, in a subsequent exchange with Tye, Ned Block (1998) produced cases in which a phenomenal content remained constant through a change in what it represented. Block intended this to show that the phenomenal could not simply be a function of what it represents. In reply, Tye (1998a) appealed to the evolutionary history of an Earthling named Oscar. The details of the reply needn't concern us, nor does it matter that Tye soon abandoned this proposal in favor of one that turned instead on an externalist account of memory.[8] It doesn't even matter that Tye had to divide his original account into two parts in order to leave room for Swampman cases. Though the idiom of optimality is replaced for Swampman by that of flourishing, the pansemanticism that threatened (Rep) earlier is reintroduced unless we can find a more satisfactory account of either optimality or flourishing. And for Oscar we must still spell out what it means to be in an optimal condition under which we can expect him to represent reliably. Tye appeals to what it is for Oscar to function properly, and, as seems inevitable, proper function must be understood in terms of what Oscar is designed to do in a context. As Tye writes, making certain alterations to my visual transducers "prevents [them] from functioning as they were designed to do" (1998b, p. 473). I gather from this that trying to spell out optimal conditions without appealing to proper functions has been abandoned. And well it should be; its prospects are indeed dim. Let us then turn to varieties of teleological support for representationism.

Can teleology do a better job of bringing sensations into the tent of intentional content? That question invites another one: Can proper functioning be spelled out without a personified intelligence imposing that function? Much of the argument for natural teleology in Tye and Dretske has depended on analogies with products of human design. Tye mentions speedometers and tire sizes; Dretske Tercels, columns of mercury, gas gauges, and compasses. Of course, these may only be illustrations of particular points. But Tye doesn't say much more in defense of proper functions, and Dretske uses them to dispatch Swampman's phenomenal life. According to Dretske, it is no more a subject of mental states than Swampy Tercel is a Tercel. However, if we are to believe that mental states of any kind have proper functions without intelligent interference, more than analogies with artifacts are required.

7.7 Teleological Semantic Arguments

Swampman-style cases haven't lost any of their potency, but I put them aside momentarily and tackle two further questions: How do representationist theories work teleology into intentional content? What are the

8. That change is not enough. Levine (2003, pp. 69–70) produces a relevantly equivalent problem in which memory plays no role.

prospects for naturalized teleology (independent of staving off objections to representationism)?

Dretske (1995, p. 4) writes that representation "is here being understood to combine teleological with information-theoretic ideas." Lycan (1995, p. 86) bluntly states "like Ruth Millikan, I think of 'normal cause' not statistically, but teleologically, and I tend to understand teleology in terms of selection history." Dretske's view is succinctly stated as follows (with his schematic letters changed to conform to the present discussion):

The fundamental idea is that a system, S, represents a property, [P], if and only if S has the function of indicating (providing information about) the [P] of a certain domain of objects. (Dretske 1995, p. 2)

Being informational isn't sufficient for being representational. Dretske writes that "there is information without functions, but there is no representation without functions" (1995, p. 4). To illustrate this, Dretske cites the angle of a column of smoke, which may indicate and impart information about wind speed but which does not represent that information. Accordingly, if the rings do nothing for the tree and the darkness does nothing for the impending rain clouds, they do not represent.[9] We might ascend to Dretske's view from Tye's (Rep) by adding to [a] and [b] the condition

[c] x has (or had) the function of tokening P.

Of course, for phenomenally conscious states and properties the function will be evolutionary. It has been useful to the survival of system S (whether S is an individual's system or a type—say, a family, a species, or a genotype) to represent its environment accurately. Because we may set aside conventional functions for our limited purposes, [c] may be refined further as

[c'] P is, or was, of some advantage to x in the course of its evolution or development.

Our norms, then, are grounded in what is and what isn't advantageous to x. But not all working to the disadvantage of evolved creatures is misrepresentation. Volcanic eruptions, tidal waves, lightning fires in forests, and meteors colliding with Earth aren't errors. They are parts of an ongoing natural process, nothing more. Not even a refrigerator, an automobile, or a light bulb is mistaken when it stops working. If such a device is 'defective',

9. On the other hand, Tye (1995b, pp. 100–101) cites tree rings as representing.

it is the producer or the user, not the product, to which a negative assessment attaches. On the other hand, the possibility of mistake imposes the authority of norms somewhere. Dretske's task is to show how teleology belongs to a scheme in which brute nature without a directing intelligence makes such norms appropriate.

Much that Dretske has to say on the topic in 1995 isn't in dispute. We may grant that a state's representational content is an inherent (defining, conceptually related) feature of it. We may also grant that the determinants of content can be environmental or social. We can even accept that painful sensations flourish in species as a result of their original evolutionary advantages and the transparency of this information. Still, the combination of those points doesn't lead inexorably to the conclusion that representational features are to be understood in terms of their current evolutionary advantages to species susceptible to them, or even that phenomenally conscious properties should be understood in terms of the causes of their onset or their persistence.

Importing teleology into our understanding of mental content is a major theme of Dretske 1995. According to that line of reasoning it must be something on the order of [c'], evolutionary advantage, that makes beliefs and other mental states intentional. However, as was noted earlier, in arguing that [c'] is involved in our understanding of intentionality, Dretske presents a long list of analogies with artifacts. So not much progress can be detected on this front. Moreover, little serious attention is given to phenomenally conscious properties such as painfulness or itchiness, whose intentionality is the central concern here. However, Dretske's approach isn't to argue first for sensations' intentionality and then for grounding it by definition in teleology. Rather, he seems to be contending that a property's being contentful, and having the specific content it does have, follows from its being teleological. So let us ask, "How does teleology enter the strictly natural world?"

Dretske's most serious effort at extracting the teleological from unvarnished nature, without a direct invocation of evolution, occurs in his 2002 essay. We need nothing more than a minimal notion of need: "[All] that is here meant by a need (for system of type S) is some condition or result without which the system could (or would) not exist as a system of type S." (Dretske 2002, p. 499, n.12). Summing up,

x is a *need* for S $=_{df}$ x is a necessary condition for the existence or persistence of S.

Necessary conditions are indeed stalwart features of the natural world. The notion of need, however, is double-edged. On the one hand, it can be deflated and thereby brought in line with what is austerely natural; on the other, it can be inflated to support normativity. But no single interpretation of need can do both. Immediately after the remark I quoted earlier, Dretske writes that "[needs], in this minimal sense, are merely necessary conditions for existence." This is a deflationary reading, although Dretske takes it as allowing the introduction of a function. However, it is only the normative sense, going beyond strict necessary conditions, that can support the idea of its having a function. I explain.

Earlier Dretske seemed to limit the reach of the semantic by requiring that [c] be added to an account of intentionality. However, everything has necessary conditions for its existence and/or continuation. To transform a necessary condition into a semantic norm, Dretske adds (i) a detector to indicate when the condition, say, F, is present and (ii) an effector mechanism harnessed to the detector to enable S to respond, say by doing A, when it detects F. Those additions allow a dimension of evaluability and thus the relevant notion of teleology. But it was the previously defined, deflationary, notion of need that was supposed to introduce teleology, and that didn't require either the detector or the effector mechanism. A deflationary reading should not exclude the needs of earthquakes, pandemics, cancers, blindness, gravity, big bangs, and anything else we can summarize as an S (= a system) with necessary conditions for its existence or continuation. In that sense of need, either teleology is unsupported or it runs rampant. Deflationary needs have roughly the explanatory value for content that the existence of space has for the explanation of live organisms.

What then of the view that a natural teleology, supporting a theory of content, is an inherent feature of evolution?

There is a robust sense in which anyone who denies that the heart's function is to pump blood, that a kidney's function is to filter urine, or that senses function to enable creatures to detect features in the world will have got his facts wrong. However, these are not non-perspectival facts. They presuppose the adoption of a certain point of view, one that is so universal that it's practically invisible.[10] That the heart pumps blood, that the kidneys

10. The views here closely mirror those expressed in chapter 1 of Searle 1995.

filter urine, and that the senses record aspects of reality are facts belonging to a less encumbered reality.[11] But they deliver salient necessary conditions only for the production and continuation of their respective systems, and disasters of every sort are also systems with necessary conditions. This is not to claim that investigators are interested only in the production and endurance of things with we value. We are also interested in the conditions for the flourishing of all sorts of microbes. But we are nonetheless selective in what counts, which is yet another observer-relative norm. These decisions are so deeply entrenched that their pedigrees go unnoticed. However, once challenged, they become manifest. For example, why not make the goal of evolution something at which it is equally effective—extinction? Or, what about an unimpeachable (?) definition of "life" as "a sexually transmitted disease that is always fatal"? Does life on that definition have a proper function? Does AIDS?

Ardent Darwinism can survive the discovery that proper functions are imposed on the raw material studied rather than picked like a specimen from it. In his lifetime, Darwin's only serious traffic with teleology was to drive its theological variety out of the study of organic development. No doubt part of a natural point of view adopted in studying this material is functioning effectively in an environment. Once imposed, it provides standards for judging the beliefs and other attitudes creatures may have about nature. Given the predilection for evolution favoring fitness, it is indisputable that natural selection preserves features favorable to something's survival and reproduction and weeds out those that hamper it. That does not mean that the facts of proper function are a part of nature independent of an observational stance; rather, it means that given the adoption of this prevalent slant we all have reason to adopt some choices as right and others as flatly wrong. It amounts to the conditional, "if value V, then F is the proper function of S." It is exceptionally unreasonable to dispute V.

One occasionally comes across the claim that this is a technical notion of function; attempts to undermine it through our customary folk

11. The description is at the level of ordinary objects, but it makes intentionality a project rather than a part of the original description. This seems to be a starting point that all sides must accept. It does not aspire to provide a fundamental ontology of the physical world.

understanding miss the point. But should anyone be tempted by that move, it would merely turn a vulnerable position into an enigmatic one. The functions of current interest must have a grounding in our familiar understanding, even if the notion being proposed proceeds to precisify it in further ways. That grounding alone makes it susceptible to questions about its introduction in this setting.

8 Non-Reductive Physicalism and Pure Token Identity

8.1 Introducing Pure Token Identity

Thus far little has been said about token or non-reductive physicalism, probably the most popular version of materialism on offer. It is now time to look more closely at that view.

The token physicalists and emergentists under consideration agree that mental aspects are supervenient on ("or realized by" hereafter understood) physical ones. Token physicalists will maintain this for each instance of a phenomenal property, but not for the supervenience of its types on physical types. Emergentists are not required by their view to agree, but they often will. More important, token physicalists reject mental-physical identities at typal levels. Of course, emergentists reject the identities of emergent and physical properties at any level. For the token physicalist to distinguish that position from emergentism, she must subscribe to one of two views about the relation between tokens of conscious aspects and their physical bases:

(a) Particular mental tokens are identical with their physical bases.

(b) There is a materialistically kosher explanation of why the mental supervenes on that base; put otherwise, the mental is *superdupervenient* on the physical.

A token physicalist might also hold a combination of views (a) and (b)— say, one for functional tokens, another for those resisting functionalization.

View (b) is occasionally phrased in terms of the base's necessitating, rather than explaining, its conscious tokens. That terminology muddies an important distinction. Suppose it amounts only to the claim that the physical supplies necessary and sufficient conditions for its mental counterpart. If that falls short of being an additional explanation of its base, (b) remains unsatisfied. It is unproductive to quibble over titles, but, as I am confident the bulk of physicalists will agree, merely supplying such conditions is too anemic for the leading school of current physicalism. Thus, in this discussion (with the exception of a view, taken up in section 8.6, which maintains that superdupervenience can be achieved independent of explanation), (a), (b), or their combination, are taken as the options for non-reductive physicalism.

Generally, physicalists hold that if a property or a state is mental, there is a physical property or state with which it is identical. There are some notable exceptions among token physicalists. Pereboom and Kornblith clearly opt for (b) alone, Horgan (1993) and Antony more indirectly so. That option is discussed in section 8.6. But first I want to explore the more popular version, (a)—that conscious property tokens are *identical with* their physical base tokens.

The typical form taken by token-identity statements and thoughts involves different names, descriptions, or concepts referring to a single particular. Affirming or entertaining such statements and thoughts is commonplace. Past philosophical favorites have included 'Hesperus = Phosphorus', 'Mark Twain = Samuel Clemens', and even 'Clark Kent = Superman'. In a different setting, general philosophical differences over the nature of identity itself might be aired. But those particular claims are straightforward, and stand in no need of an elaborate philosophically charged defense. The evidence for or against each identity begins and ends with the spatiotempoal coincidence of the individuals involved in the each case. They are cases of what I am calling *pure token identity*. (Their purity will become clearer when we contrast them with their impure counterparts.) It is frequently mentioned that, for these cases, it is crucial that the individuals involved share times and spatial locations. In section 8.4 we shall see that there are all sorts of subtleties surrounding questions of spatiotemporal coincidence. But taking into account the qualifications that those may dictate, it is still hard to see how continued, albeit flexible, spatiotemporal coincidence can be displaced as a requirement of material identity. What else is there to latch on to for anyone making an identity claim in this neighborhood?

A lesson of chapter 3 is that spatiotemporal coincidence is not sufficient for identity. Statues and their matter may be different though not discrete. But the basis for their identity commenced from mereological considerations, a constituter-constituted relation. Because identities of conscious and material aspects do not invoke mereological relations as their base, complications involving overlapping entities and different levels of description don't arise. Thus, we may consider spatiotemporal convergence as good enough for our purposes. Let us say it is a *central* condition. Where the overlap is for the whole existence of the token(s) in question, it may even be nearly sufficient. Moreover, the identities between certain classes of things that have some claim to be non-physical (e.g., the smallest prime number and the number 2), or to be not archetypally physical (e.g., The Great C Major Symphony and Schubert's Ninth), converge in respects that are not, or need not be (depending on one's analysis), spatiotemporal.[1] Nevertheless, doubts that those are legitimate instances of identities seem frivolous, and treatments of such cases normally aim at clarifying this result without raising doubts about the legitimacy of the phenomenon.[2] However, the thesis that individual phenomenal and physical tokens are identical raises issues that go beyond the sorts of convergences just alluded to. Accordingly, the defense of such cases seems to require supplementation by serious conceptual resources whose influence is no part of the earlier examples. I want to explore the prospects for pure token identity, and to apply it to cases of current interest in which there is no opportunity for an appeal to the impure defenses on which philosophers almost invariably rely.

The foregoing seems to me consonant with the position in which token physicalists find themselves in light of the combination of their own prior commitments and the results of chapter 4. To see this clearly, we must first say something about *impure* token identity. It is a method of arguing for token identities in which considerations of a different provenance move its claims along. To the best of my knowledge, its leading arguments can be divided into three broad types, each of which has been effectively undermined in previous chapters. They enter the topic of token identity either in a top-down fashion or at an oblique angle. They are as follows.

1. Are (often imperfect) performances of a symphony tokens of its type? Whatever one's answer, the only point here is that, *qua* abstract, their convergence is not wholly spatiotemporal.

2. I exempt those *rara aves* who are skeptical about any identity claims going beyond those of the form 'A = A'. Even someone who acknowledged only the strictest identity requirement, which no longer preserved the same A when something lost a single atom, could allow that a *this* could be identical with a *that* demonstrated simultaneously of a single individual.

(i) Old-school physicalism, which identifies types of phenomenal tokens with types of physical ones. The identity of each instantiation of a type-phenomenal token with an instantiation of its relevant type of physical token then falls out directly from their type identity.

(ii) Coherence and simplicity, as rationales for an inference to the best explanation. Because phenomenal and some physical tokens (perhaps not always neural ones) are correlated without exception, simplicity and explanatory coherence dictate that it is reasonable to believe that they are the same thing rather than merely correlated.

(iii) Problems with mental causation. How can mental, and in particular phenomenal, tokens be causes of anything, physical or mental? The Redundancy and Causal Exclusion arguments purport to show that independent mental causes are trumped by physical causes.

Token physicalists themselves reject the typal identities of (i). Multiple realization, cited in chapter 6, is given as a leading reason for dissenting from old-school physicalism.[3] However, in line with their type counterparts, token physicalists sometimes appeal to considerations of type (iii) to sustain their view that the only sensible option is to identify each mental cause with its physical base, and on occasion they also invoke the simplicity and coherence in (ii) to fortify that result. Serious problems with (ii) and (iii) were exposed in chapters 4–6.

In chapter 6 it was argued that appeals to simplicity and coherence, questions of ontological relevance aside, don't support their desired identities. The illustrations with which explanatory coherence was introduced made it difficult to see how that device is deployable for the task assigned to it (viz., promoting the rationality of identity over causal correlation), and the appeals to simplicity conflated its natural target for the case at hand (the elegance of laws) with the promotion of ontological parsimony.

In chapter 4 it was argued that the problems cited for mental causation dissipate upon close examination. In addition, it has been shown that the realizer-realized relation is not tantamount to identity. Not only are plausible reasons to go from realization to identity far from evident; differences in persistence conditions are obstacles to doing so. There is no need to repeat those arguments here. What remains are the sorts of pure identity claims illustrated a few pages back. We have yet to deal with those.

3. Davidson is a notorious exception among non-reductive physicalists.

(i)–(iii) are top-down approaches: they import themes extraneous to the evidence in the individual case for use in evaluating the token identities of current interest. I brand them *impure* here not to impugn them once more, but to contrast them with the cases that remain to be considered. What is being called *pure token identity* starts from our understanding of the clearest cases; it is a bottom-up approach. This does not preclude extracting general lessons about identity from a closer scrutiny of those tokens. However, the resulting general lessons come out of considerations dictated by the instances, rather than being imposed by theory-driven prescriptions framed for more general metaphysical purposes and not directly related to pure token identities. I am not claiming that regarding these identities as pure is a superior approach to this subject; I am, however, claiming that, once we are deprived of appeals to (i)–(iii), that appears to be the only path still open to token physicalists' claims of phenomenal-physical identities.

This limitation needn't seriously hamper token physicalism. The commonplace character of a multitude of cases of pure token identities indicates that it is a rich resource on which such identities may draw. Beyond the several cases mentioned earlier, we are swamped with unmistakably good instances: Harry Houdini = Erik Weisz, Performance α of Beethoven's Third Symphony = Performance β of the Eroica, Edmund Dantes = the Count of Monte Cristo, the English Civil War = the Great Rebellion, Bombay = Mumbai, Cassius Clay = Muhammad Ali, the Falklands Conflict = la Guerra de las Malvinas, Anthony Eden = Lord Avon, Lewis Carroll = Charles Lutwidge Dodgson, the Republican Party = the GOP, $\sqrt{225} = 15$, and so on *ad nauseam*. No one would be tempted to concoct background considerations or generalizations from which these drop out as instances or as by-products of a generic philosophical commitment of a different provenance.

Let us then proceed to inquire into what happens to the thesis of token identity when it is regarded as pure. As before, I confine attention to a proper subset of conscious mental phenomena embracing both phenomenal consciousness (pain being a time-tested example) and a number of access-conscious states (including typical instances of belief and desire). Next, although this exposition is conducted in terms of instantiated properties (tropes), I shall once again make frequent use of neutral terms such as 'token' and 'aspect'; differences among properties, states, events, processes, facts, and substances (= individual propertied things) seldom matter to the issues I want to raise. Finally, for simplicity, although the discussion is in terms of neurological properties, no stand is taken here on the dispute between internalists and externalists. If the contention that mental tokens cannot be identical with neurological ones is true, that will also hold for the mental's inability to be identical, say, with neurological-*cum*-environmental tokens.

In what follows, m is an arbitrarily selected mental token and p is an arbitrarily selected physical token. M and P are their respective types.

8.2   A Most Curious Conundrum

Suppose one were to ask "What content does saying that $m = p$ add to saying that m and p occur together, or perhaps even to saying that the former depends on the latter?" That question certainly sounds naïve. After all, it is obvious what saying that Emily Brontë and Ellis Bell are the same person comes to, and it certainly states more than that they are correlated with each other. It is not that they just happened to live in the same house, share a wardrobe, and the like. There is only one of them! However, for conscious and neural tokens, in contrast with the case of Emily Brontë and Ellis Bell, the strictly empirical evidence runs out with co-occurrence. Two features distinguish the case of concern from the familiar examples recently listed.

First, although we believe it possible to trace the continual spatial whereabouts of Ellis Bell (although no one, except perhaps Brontë herself, has ever done so) and see whether they coincide with those of Emily Brontë, not only is the correlation of m with p supposed to be evidence for their identity; it is also the only source for our very understanding of what it is for m to have determinate spatial whereabouts and thereby to trace it for the same or different paths.

Second, in our paradigmatic samples, neither of the named tokens is asymmetrically dependent, either constitutionally or causally, on the token otherwise named—they are simply one and the same. No doubt a minimal sense of dependence intrudes even here; supposing that names designate rigidly, we can't have Bell without Brontë and vice versa. But supervenience and realization come apart for pure token identity. Neither *realizes* the other, which rules out the varieties of unidirectional dependence that realization (that is, embodiment) conveys. In the case of m and p, in addition to their identity there is a decided hint of m's hanging around only because it is identical with p. The dependence of m on p may be a holdover from past enterprises in which the identity is justified either via a type-identity thesis or as a solution to causal problems. But, whatever the explanation, along with the previous point, these points certainly provide grounds for raising the question of just what $m = p$ contributes beyond the fact that m and p happen to occur at the same time. And that fact alone is all we have, or can have, in the way of strict empirical evidence. We might also concede, from their co-occurrence and everything else we know about the neural subserving the mental, that m's occurrence depends causally on p's occurrence. But if they are the terms in a causal relation, that wouldn't be an argument in favor of their identity; indeed, on a strict account of causation it would be incompatible with their identity.

So we might venture that if there are no empirical facts beyond the co-occurrence of p with m, it is puzzling what further fact is stated in saying or thinking that they are identical. Bear in mind that this is *pure* token identity; appeals to the methodological virtues of theoretical reduction, to the problems of mental causation, and to reductive type identities are not relevant. Thus, once co-occurrence has been established, there is not even a further fact to seek, as there would be in the case of Lewis Carroll and Charles Dodgson.

The point I am raising may be easily misunderstood, so kindly allow me a brief exculpation. The claim is not that the conundrum shows that $m = p$ cannot be true. Nor is it claimed that such an identity fails to make sense. It may be thought that these claims were put to rest long ago. Suppose we accept Fodor's objection to the so-called Law of Transferable Epithets: "[I]f x is identical with y, and if Fx makes sense (is linguistically possible), then Fy must also make sense (be linguistically possible)." (1968, p. 100) That law should not be confused with, or sanctioned by, the similar sounding indiscernibility of identicals (see section 3.2). Thus, the impure identity of tokens following from the identities of their types—that is, from M = P—might bring off the identity, overcoming any intuitive objection that the terms belong to different and incongruent semantic categories. My point is that *if we forgo that sort of extraneous support*, as current token physicalism is committed to doing, we seem at a loss to discover further evidence to get us moving from 'm and p are correlated' to '$m = p$'. I offer this consideration only as a tantalizing hint of the way that the situation for m and p should strike any judiciously minded sleuth when considering token identities shorn of interference or help from commitments forged with other concerns in mind. But I hope it spurs readers, as it has me, to seek a further explanation of the identity claim, or at least a moral, from less controversial instances. The worry is that the identity claim, adopted only because it seemed the least objectionable of various options, should leave us with an uneasiness that it may be no more than a bit of empty verbiage. If substantive reasons driving the unease can be fleshed out, that would convert this hunch into a serious obstacle to the pure token identity of conscious and physical aspects.

8.3   Background Conditions for Identity Claims

Coinciding goes beyond co-occurring. Of course, as chapter 3 affirmed, coinciding isn't sufficient for identity, but it is its most important necessary condition. So let us look into the circumstances that make coincidence so central a factor in identity determinations.

Coincidence requires background conditions for two reasons.

First, background conditions enable us to distinguish what counts as evidence for coincidence from what does not count. I am not dismissing as senseless every claim for which we have no idea about how to test it; perhaps that is just a by-product of the widely accepted hypothesis of theory underdetermination. But underdetermination of that sort occurs at the level of high-pitched theories, not in the evidential trenches. When we consider particular matters, we can always imagine some evidence that can be cited as relevant. (The present availability of such evidence is a different matter.) And if we do have some notion of the standards for testing a hypothesis, it will be in light of the background conditions governing tokens of those sorts.

Second, background conditions make coincidence *intelligible*; they provide it with substance beyond simultaneous occurrence, and they distinguish it from a "mere" causal relationship. For brevity, let us call such background conditions *props*. In the most favorable case—where, say, a relation of mere *constitution* is ruled out at the level at which the inquiry occurs—they may supply decisive evidence (in some circles, "criteria") for the claim. Even if Jack the Ripper wasn't Prince Albert Victor, the hypothesis that he was can't be dismissed on conceptual grounds alone; the two were contemporaries abiding in the precincts of London. That similarity—contemporary humanity plus proximity—supplies a prop under which one can proceed to gather further evidence. The evidence may be weak, as in this case, and there are other, more specific props which I am ignoring; here I emphasize only the capacity for an identity claim that opens the door for continued gathering and discussion of details. Nor is there a sharp distinction between props and ordinary evidence. A prop is simply what is taken as a standing condition under which further investigation may be conducted, and may shift with an investigation's point. On the other hand, the identity of Julius Caesar with the proposition *that woolly mammoths are extinct* makes no sense. And David Cameron may be a prime minister; but that he is a prime number has no conceptual license. However, at this stage I am as interested in props as *enablers* for legitimate token-identity concerns as I am in their role as *inhibitors* to close off possibility for some claims.

Other sorts of props may make the identity of 15 and $\sqrt{225}$ a legitimate (indeed true) claim, since both belong to a common system of calculation, whereas "7 is identical to the number of days of the week" passes inspection because each is a number, even if one of its terms requires a *numbering*. And although a symphony's performance cannot be on display at a hardware store, performance α (of Beethoven's Third) and performance β (of the *Eroica*) may be the same performance if they coincide spatiotemporally.[4] Moreover, the same is true even for the reduction of a law in one theory to that in another, the prop being a general background of both having as their exclusive functions explanation, prediction, and/or control within a limited (although not well-defined) target area. Of course even familiar concepts such as heat, lightning, and salt may be identified with molecular motion, electrical discharge, and NaCl, respectively. However, these are once again cases of typal identities, for which there is a more generous background of props modulo global concerns.

Two disclaimers are in order. First, my observations do nothing to favor verificationism; second, no official theory of categories is needed to acknowledge the limits drawn by props. Each warrants elaboration.

First, what is being claimed is not that without the right common props *we* have no capacity to verify an identity claim. That is a mere corollary, not the issue around which the need for props revolves. The point is rather that nothing could count as a verification by *any* cognizer of *any* capacity

---

4. For an actual case of this sort of event identity, I once discussed with someone the antics of Professor X at a conference. He told me that he too had seen Professor X behaving erratically at a conference. Only later did I realize that we had been talking about the same incident.

given *any* placement. Even God couldn't identify Caesar with the proposition that woolly mammoths are extinct, but presumably God would know whether Jack the Ripper was Prince Albert Victor. The lack is not a comment on the human condition but a comment on the nature of a perfectly cognition-independent reality. The limits of what is sensible invoked here are not the limits *per se* of what we may be in a position to confirm, disconfirm, or even gather evidence for or against.

Next, claims such as this may suggest to many a need to be backed by a general principle for flagging cases of radical semantic failure. However, history has been unkind to attempts to frame a principled theory of categories useful for weeding out vacuity or nonsense. Notoriously, philosophers have defended limitations on comprehensibility that were later overtaken by the march of science. But those achievements have concerned typal identities and explanations, and the restriction to purity disqualifies their role in supporting token identities. This should help us to overcome prohibitions based solely on those past failures. Of course we should welcome any plausible theory of semantic categories if one could be found, but I don't believe we need a theory of semantic categories in order to see that Julius Caesar isn't a proposition and David Cameron isn't a number. We would be in sorrier shape, and our attempts at understanding would be seriously hampered, if we had to abandon such firm, indeed unshakeable, judgments for lack of a general theory from which they could be derived as instances.[5] The track record of failures advises caution, but not the abandonment of all efforts to eliminate semantically vacuous or senseless claims.[6] In

5. Conceivably, that is why Frege (1960, p. 50)—if we assume that by 'has a sense' he meant something like what we mean—suggested that substituting 'Julius Caesar' for 'the concept square of 4' in a sentence in which the latter is the subject term yields a falsehood rather than nonsense. Of course, there is no general semantic theory of *sense* (beyond the syntactic test for wffs) in first-order logic. Could this have been factored into his conclusion that the substituted sentence would express nothing more than a *false* thought?

6. Some—e.g., Wimsatt (2007)—conclude from the record of shipwrecked schemes that no such judgments should be made. However, I doubt that they would support the following analogous inference: Because of a long history of abandoned theories in the sciences, we shouldn't rely on our current ones (while perhaps always on the lookout for improvements). In both cases, specific reasons for rejecting particular judgments, either via a theory or via a counterexample, are in order; such cosmic misgivings are not.

the absence of a large theory from which one's judgments fall out, battles should be waged at the level of particular cases. Indeed, any general theory would be deeply flawed if it yielded a different evaluation for all but the rare exception among these compelling specimens of non-starters.

Let us then turn to paradigms of token identities, those involving a (purported) single material thing denoted by more than one name or description.

8.4   Undisputed Cases and Complications

For concrete tokens, the relevant identifiers are spatiotemporal phenomena; neural property, state, and process tokens are uncontroversial members of that class. To get a good fix on our subject, let's begin with clear cases, such as that of Samuel Clemens' alter ego, Mark Twain. A prominent, indeed indispensable, piece of evidence on which one can base an identity claim is that the differently named objects *trace the same path through time and space*. This warrants two qualifications. First, such tracings are, with very rare exceptions,[7] very sporadic and selective: monitoring doubly named, independently indexed entities throughout the whole of their existence exceeds human capacities. Second, this isn't the only evidence for identity. We may have noticed, say, that Twain and Clemens have indistinguishable handwriting, smoke the same brand of cigar, owe money to the same creditors, and so on. But at the end of the day, that they can be located in the same cities or counties over the same stretch of time is not only a criterial piece of evidence; it delivers what constitutes there being only one twice-named individual. Spatiotemporal coincidence is akin to spotting a book on the library shelf rather than seeing it listed in a catalogue.

However, the notion *spatiotemporal identity* raises further issues, especially on the spatial side. Following the same spatiotemporal path is not *sufficient* for token identity, *pace* Neil Wilson (1955). Recalling our trusty specimen, a certain lump of clay may constitute a statue without being identical to the statue. Nor is following the same spatiotemporal path strictly necessary: if we identify a spatial location as a collection of points, a volume, or even a chunk of bounded space, there will be few if any continuants. The loss of a crumb from a piece of toast, or even the loss of an atom,

7. The rare exceptions are briefly existing particles detected, say, at CERN.

could count as a discontinuity in the object. When speaking of continuants, rather than momentary existents, we do not cleave to this degree of specificity. As individuation is commonly employed, such rarefied considerations have not led us simply to discard co-location as a central test for the individuation and identification of a concrete particular. Rather, we settle on a more relaxed notion of 'same place'. Whatever the degree of precision demanded for our quotidian practices, a willingness to accord a companion level of spatiotemporal continuity is both central to and necessary for the identity of persisting physical things. Relatively gradual and/or smooth changes in both place and constituents are tolerated. Anyone claiming that the Smithers of yesterday is the same Smithers we see today after he has been changed by having a haircut is implying that if we had traced a path from the former to the latter there would have been the amount of continuity that should satisfy us. Of course, pains and their subservient neurological activity do not generally continue over very long stretches. But the latter are paradigms of spatial events or properties, and so the co-location of a particular pain and a particular neural occurrence would seem to be a non-negotiable requirement for their identity. If we didn't require it, it is difficult to see what plausible test we might substitute in making sense of judgments of identity and difference for these pure token cases. Some such liberal macroscopic level of spatiotemporal locatability, whose boundaries may vary with a token's relevant type, is presupposed in identifications of spatial particulars.

It would be a mistake to claim that when x and y are identical they must be identical throughout the whole of their history. Fusion and fission complicate plausible schemes of the identity of individuals. Two drops of water may fuse into one larger drop, or a cell may divide into two. And this leads to a yet further question of how to distinguish fusion and fission from a temporary overlap of two nonetheless different individuals. An indicator of mere overlap (nonidentity) may be the conceivability of x and y beginning existence separately, coalescing for a time, and then separating once again into individuals similar to the distinct ones with which we began.[8] But I imagine that even some of those cases could be regarded as fusion plus

8. Wiggins (1968) and Sanford (1970) each hold that two distinct material things may intersect completely at a single time. And while neither of them appears committed to holding that this might be so for the whole of their existence, Wiggins seems to encourage us to ponder this possibility.

fission. However, complexities in a scheme of this order, just as those of the preceding paragraph, do not prevent spatiotemporal continuity from being a centrally necessary condition for the identity of material individuals.

I have been proceeding on the assumption that persons are material. That is because the only identity between m and p envisaged by the token physicalist is a material one, making it of prime importance for eliciting the requirements of material identity. However, although substance dualism has been ruled out, it has not been my intention to favor a bodily-continuity notion of identity over a quasi-Lockean view emphasizing a form of continuity of consciousness in which memory (or its ancestral relation) is the vital link. On that view, even if disembodied existence is not an option, it may make sense to talk about changing bodies, or about replacing a body over time with wholly synthetic parts. Or, for all that I am claiming, it is optional to take on board Derek Parfit's deconstructivist position of regarding a focal interest in identity as misguided, to be replaced by one of psychological continuity. There is no commitment here on any of those issues. If the Neo-Lockean view is correct, principles for identity over time are more complex, but in ways that do not directly affect our current concerns. None of the variations mentioned here supplies a lesson to help us understand the token physicalist's identity proposals.

Nor are spatiotemporal requirements the same for every type of material entity. Watches and engines can be taken apart for cleaning, and when re-assembled they are without exception regarded as the same watches and engines that they were before. But notice that even here the parts retain their identity, and their fates can be traced. Without the restoration of a certain proportion, it would be difficult to see what basis there was for our intuition that the reconstructed entity was the same. Interesting cases arise from transformations in fabulous fiction; they bear a resemblance to a prospect left open by Neo-Lockeanism of instantaneous changes of body. Homer describes Proteus as turning into a panther, and even into a flame, Kafka writes of the transformation of Gregor Samsa into an insect, and there is a vast store of tales in which enchanted heroes and heroines are turned into frogs and other creatures. Two points about the intelligibility of these tales are worth noticing. First, they do not violate spatiotemporal continuity, despite the radical nature of the changes. In this they are unlike the superficially doubtful case of the Star Trek teletransporter discussed earlier. Second, in the various fabulous scenarios that may not violate the boundaries of the intelligible, notice that the potential for recovery to one's original state looms large.[9] It may be worth considering whether these "life-lines" are left intact just to ensure that one's tales do not drift enough from palpability to confuse rather than bring along one's audience.

The issues just raised about spatiotemporal continuity don't bear only or primarily on the identity statements or thoughts of differently referenced individuals. Problems of imprecision for spatiotemporal continuants can be raised even if we are using the very same name. What makes Smithers (or Emily Brontë, or Italy, or a piece of toast, or anything else) the same over time despite a loss or gain of matter? This issue could be raised even if there were no prospect of a thing's being referenced by more than one name, description, or indexical. What is important for us is that no matter how loose our spatiotemporal requirements for persistence may be, both Emily Brontë and Ellis Bell must satisfy those requirements in exactly same way, point for point, in order for them to be identical. That is, fission aside, there can be no point in time at which Bell satisfies the spatiotemporal conditions for existence while Brontë does not.

8.5 Token Physicalism Revisited

The *evidential* force of indistinguishable spatiotemporal worms scarcely needs belaboring. However, spatiotemporal coincidence is even a more basic condition of *intelligibility* for pure token identities of material things. The relation of interest is not that in which Emily Brontë stands to her body, a constitutive mereological relation, but that in which she stands to *Homo sapiens* Ellis Bell. On that basis, the very intelligibility of the claim that they are one and the same person relies on their occupying the same locations every moment of their (?) existence. Only a currently unimaginable conceptual revolution could dislodge that requirement. This assumption, generalized, underlies the practice of identity ascriptions for spatiotemporal entities, although not for property instances.

9. Well, perhaps not in Gregor Samsa's case. There intelligibility is sought through psychic continuity. But notice that in Samsa's case, unlike that of the teletrans-porter, we are given no reason to suppose that a substantial degree of dislocation occurs. If the insect began its run in Bogota rather than Prague, further questions of intelligibility should arise for Kafka's readers.

What moral might this have for the identity of *m* with *p*? The problem isn't that *m* can't have a spatial location. That complaint would beg the question against token physicalism, and it would be a juicy target for an attack on the Law of Transferable Epithets (see page 209). If *m* = *p*, then, *a fortiori*, *m* has the same location as *p*. However, the comparison with typical physical pure token identities shows not only that it is important for a referent to have spatial location, but that it is equally important that this location be determinable in a particular way—namely, independent of the truth of the identity in question. Whereas *m* certainly takes place at a time and has a temporal stretch, how can we identify it *independent of the episode with which it is alleged to be identical* in order to maintain that it coincides spatially with *p*? An implication of paradigm cases of concrete pure identities seems to be not only that coincidence is a central requirement, but also that, in the order of logic (not historically), anterior to the coincidence the locatability of each referenced term must be capable of being independently established. That condition appears to be the *ratio essendi* of such identities. Of course, if the identity is genuine, locating the one *is* locating the other. But the locatability cannot depend on that fact. The referent-*cum*-name must have an independent status under the relevant prop. We could make this a principle for pure token identities:

It is necessary that any candidates for a pure token identity have their locations secured under their governing prop independent of the assumption of their identity.

For the case of spatiotemporal individuals, the more specific maxim would be the following:

It is necessary that any candidates for a pure token identity of spatiotemporal tokens have their spatiotemporal location secured independent of the assumption of their identity.

There may be a temptation to reply that such requirements are merely artifacts of selectively chosen cases. Why impose them as a requirement on *m*? A leading reason is at hand. If they were not in force it would nullify any attempts to distinguish legitimate candidates from flagrant misfires. Whereas Julius Caesar was a material object, on its face the proposition (considered as the content of a used sentence) that woolly mammoths are extinct is not. But if Julius Caesar is identical with that proposition, then the proposition is *eo ipso* a material object. Thus, we ought to be able to say in all seriousness that a semantic content crossed the Rubicon, was stabbed in the Senate on the Ides of March, and was Cleopatra's lover. Similarly, we could say that a certain prime number is a prime minister, a member of the Conservative Party, and British. Of course, none of these would be true, but not because they are false: they are not good enough to deserve that epithet. Without this crucial condition on pure token identity, what absurd identity claims could be dismissed from consideration?

Whereas m has a temporal beginning and end, how can its location in space be determined independent of the physical token with which it is alleged to be identical? Without that, we seem unable to confirm that it coincides spatially with p, and it is hard to see what fact there could be that would constitute its coincidence with p. This is not meant to suggest that m isn't spatial, much less that it can't be spatial. It is only to note that we have yet to detect a way to gather evidence for its spatiality at the level of pure tokens other than through its alleged identity with p. That does not prohibit us from agreeing with David Lewis (1983b, p. 100) that there is "no reason to believe that the principle that experiences are unlocated enjoys any analytic, or other, necessity." The point is not that we have discovered a conceptual link between experiences and the absence of a location. Rather, it is the impossibility of discovering a way to introduce determinative facts for specifying any spatial location other than by appealing to that identity. Whereas pure identity for material tokens rests on spatiotemporal coincidence, the spatiotemporal coincidence of m and p has been made to rest on their pure token identity. A paradoxical upshot of this line of argument is that if we did find a way to determine m's spatiality independent of p, its identity with p would be superfluous in the context: we would have shown m to be physical, which was the point of identifying it with p in the first place.

Returning to the conundrum of section 8.2, the underlying problem is not just that of knowing where to get further evidence for token identity; rather, it is the difficulty of making coherent a hypothesis of a pure token identity between m and p. If the pure token identity $m = p$ were intelligible, we might have a handle on the kind of evidence that is relevant to its truth or falsehood. As was noted earlier, we must make room for intelligible hypotheses for which we may be at a loss as to how we are to gather evidence. However, finding a hypothesis intelligible is nearly sufficient for delivering the kind of evidence that would be relevant, and it is always necessary.

The situation is radically different for claims of type identities. Background conditions, props, would then be much more flexible. In view of the premium often put on explanation for types, that function could overcome doubts arising at the token level. But that is not the predicament in which the non-reductive physicalist finds herself. Even if typal identities in this area also fail, they do not fail for the same reason. Whereas forms of M = P make sense, and thereby (impurely) endow identities such as $m = p$ with sense, pure forms of generating $m = p$ have yet to be given any clear sense.

These aren't particularly subtle considerations. No doubt a major reason they have not gained more traction in the literature is that typical arguments for token identity are not pure, or at least that they vacillate between pure and impure groundings. Typical reasons cited for token physicalism have been the difficulties attending mental causation. Donald Davidson has a distinctive slant on those difficulties. Supposing that m causes p, "then under some description m and p instantiate a strict law" (1980, p. 224). However, Davidson rejects such type identities (psychophysical laws) "because of the disparate commitments of the mental and physical schemes" (p. 222). Nevertheless, "if m falls under a physical law, it has a physical description; which is to say it is a physical event" (p. 224). Hence token identity. But the inference is impure in the present sense, proceeding top-down from general commitments on another philosophical issue (viz., strict laws for causation to supply alternative designations for m and p) to a conclusion about token identities.[10]

Pure identity solutions for token physicalism have been sought here because impure ones were dealt with in earlier chapters. Problems concerning

10. It may be instructive to compare Davidson's view with Samuel Alexander's emergentism. Revising his term 'process' to conform to Davidson's 'event', Alexander agrees with Davidson when he declares that "the mental [event] and its neural [event] are one and the same existence, not two existences" (Alexander 1920, volume II, p. 9). Alexander diverges from Davidson when he goes on to claim that "out of certain physiological conditions nature has framed a new quality of mind, which is therefore not physiological though it lives and moves and has its being in physiological conditions" (volume II, p. 8). Translation: Mental and physical *events* are identical, mental and physical *properties* are not. Davidson stops with events. Although Alexander's emergentism concedes more than I have conceded to the physicalist—because part II seems to show that problems Alexander raises for property identity can also be raised for event identity—his point of departure from Davidson is revealing.

mental causation were addressed in chapter 4. I cannot vouchsafe that all the misgivings about mental causes have been ferreted out. but the concrete ones I have surveyed haven't survived close scrutiny. Nor did purely methodological considerations, such as those falling under the generous heading of "inference to the best explanation," fare better in chapter 6. This leaves the token physicalist in the position of having to defend identities on grounds similar to those illustrated by my list of pedestrian samples. Innumerable cases of that kind have shown this practice to be unimpeachable. But strict adherence to the mundane grounds that determine those token identities exposes token physicalism as lacking the tools needed to bring off the claims to which it aspires.

8.6   Materially Kosher Explanation

Option (b), *superdupervenience*, remains on the table. Terry Horgan (1993) used the term to designate a method for salvaging physicalism through supplying a materialistically kosher explanation of *why* it is that the mental property supervenes on its base. Everyone seems to agree that if one's token physicalism relies on explaining the mental's relation to the physical, something more than the bare fact of the mental supervening on the physical is needed. Not everyone agrees about what the "something more" should be. Let's have a closer look at the prospect of superdupervening by way of these additional explanations.

Distinctions between type and token physical physicalism are not as sharp when (b) is the crucial issue. In all strictness, to merit the qualifier 'token' a physicalist's explanations would have to be a large and diverse collection for each M explained. Although multiple realizability would still prevent old-school physicalists from explaining M by a single physical type, perhaps they can find some further unity in the motley collection of subvenient *p*s that explain the Ms. This dampens any reductionist aspirations they may have, but it may satisfy them in other respects, thereby blunting their differences with token physicalism. However, because 'token' and 'non-reductive' are generally taken as interchangeable ways to describe the view now under consideration, I take that situation to fulfill (b) for token physicalism.

Nomenclature aside, wherein are such explanations to be found? A first place to look might be functionalism, but functionalism neglects the something it is like of the phenomenally conscious. Even for the access conscious, functionalism's strongest claim is that it can deflect questions about the causal power of the mental. However, in chapter 4 it was argued that the most clearly articulated worries about mental causation evaporate upon scrutiny and that problems for those objections to mental causation show up for questions of property individuation. Moreover, chapter 5 unearthed further difficulties for the effort to get along without mental causation for certain types of behavior.

It is hard to know where to begin to look once deprived of functional explanations. The requirement that the explanations be materialistically kosher rules out ungrounded psychophysical principles. Those would mention the connection between physical and psychological properties, and requiring reference to unreduced psychological properties would be fatal to any project of explaining properties of that type in strict physical terms. But how can such laws be avoided, either explicitly or as implicitly underwriting the resulting explanation? (Bear in mind that even token identities are no longer available as support.) While it would be unwise to foreclose on yet-to-be-discovered concrete proposals, it is not easy to see how any attempt to establish (b) could avoid psycho-physical generalizations.

Jessica Wilson (1999, 2002) proposes a method for securing superdupervenience without additional explanations. She holds that we can achieve it by paying closer attention to the way causal powers of a mental property, M, are bestowed by its physical base, P. We need not explain a "relation of intelligibility . . . between characteristic features of the properties"; we need "merely establish . . . that no new fundamental forces are in operation in either the instantiation of or causal transactions involving the property" (Wilson 2002, p. 75). The test is not designed to favor either emergentism or physicalism, but to sharpen the difference between them. Also, Wilson's treatment is confined to cases in which the base and the supervenient properties belong to the same subject: that squares, agreeably, with my earlier restriction to cases in which supervenience and realization overlap. To manage this, Wilson emphasizes causal profiles. Whereas those apply in the first instance to property *types*, they can be retrofitted for tropes by taking in the range of counterfactual circumstances they *might* support. (See section 4.4) At the token level, one can still expose a full panoply of m's or p's causal powers. Suppose we can identify a group of fundamental forces; call them F. For illustrative purposes, Wilson imagines F to comprise electromagnetic, gravitational, and strong and weak nuclear forces. Now suppose that P's causal profile is *grounded in* F and that supervenient M derives its causal powers from its base P. The second conjunct may violate conclusions reached in chapter 4 (depending on the interpretation of 'derives . . . from'), but let's overlook that for our limited concerns. We may then ask whether M's causal profile consists of powers it gets from P that are not similarly grounded in F. If it does, we have emergentism; if it doesn't, physicalism has succeeded. A simplified version of the principle backing Wilson's test might go as follows:

(W)   Where M is supervenient on (or realized by) P, M is emergent on P if and only if M has causal powers not derived from those causal powers of P grounded in F.

The application of (W) that Wilson highlights (2002, p. 76) is the experimental result of an anomaly in a measured transfer of energy, which led physicists to expand F to include weak nuclear forces. I will return to the example later, but first let me lay out the position in greater detail.

Wilson is in broad agreement with others that the bone of contention between physicalism and emergentism is the status of mental causation. Indeed, she recommends locating their difference in the causal profiles themselves rather than in the properties possessing them. Other than that, her way of bringing out emergentism's distinctive feature seems close to a formulations of my condition (2): that the relation to an emergent's base must be brute. Does this show that superdupervenience gets around the need for a further explanation? I don't think so. Explanation is rejected in this setting because Wilson (1999) takes it to be an epistemological notion, unsuitable for ensuring an ontological distinction. But as explained in chapter 2, and as I believe coincides with the natural interpretation of her target, Terry Horgan's view that "no explanation" states no more than that the information needed for a further understanding of *why* the supervenience holds does not exist. This is a statement about the world, not about anyone's current understanding of it. Any further information, such as (W), could count as that further explanation.

A more urgent question is whether (W), whatever it amounts to, supplies the desired superdupervenience. As I mentioned, Wilson locates superdupervenience in the causal powers themselves rather than in the properties or states possessing them. This departs from the emphasis on mereological constitution in most past discussions. It strikes me as an improvement, but not much else seems changed. Whereas it may make it look as if the properties that own the focal powers are otiose, locating the difference in the properties possessing causation comes out of this account quite naturally: a superdupervenient property is one in which all of its causal powers are grounded in the same F that its base powers are grounded in; for an emergent property at least one of its causal powers is not so grounded. Indeed, the statement of (W) closely resembles this last gloss.

The crucial question remains "Does this account of superdupervenience deliver the missing ingredient?" By adopting the notion of a grounding, Wilson has chosen something flexible enough to sidestep concerns over fundamental-level causation and causal drainage. If all else is in place, a grounding would hold for each of what emergentists call *resultant* properties, including discoveries about chemical compounds and life that led to the demise of earlier emergentisms. However, it is difficult to see how the distinction in (W) can apply to the present case, and the central reliance on the "forces" and "powers" that are in operation reinforces doubts about its relevance.

For a property's causal power to lack a grounding in F, does it require a substitute, an energy of a different sort? If so, what sort of energy could M introduce? Certainly emergentists needn't be committed to mental causes introducing a new form of energy transferable from cause to effect, much less a non-physical variety. In fact, some authors have proposed that mental causes do no more than redistribute physical energy without violating its conservation. That would be a grounding-neutral form of novel causation. The notion of grounding doesn't explicitly require that we are conjuring solely with types of energy. But if it doesn't require something we could call a power or force, then what it amounts to deserves a more detailed explanation. (W) virtually ensures the gross implausibility of emergent mental properties.

Certain causes, taken as paradigms in some discourses, involve energy transfer. But when running across the whole spectrum of causal ascriptions it can be seen that cause and force come apart in some cases. For example, how does the notion of force figure in causal ascriptions of a particular abstraction, such as a center of gravity ('the lamp's low center of gravity caused it to remain stable during the quake'), or the aforementioned cases of causation by omission (e.g., 'The recession was caused by the SEC's

failure to oversee the banks', 'His relapse resulted from not taking his medi-
cation')? Perhaps talk of causal ability or capacity fits these cases better than
talk of power or force, but even causal ability and capacity are not natural
ways to describe omissions. Wilson's test seems to overlook such cases. She
is entitled to reject them, but not simply by introducing a notion of causation that ignores them. And the omission idiom in particular, whatever
one's verdict, is commonplace, occurs frequently, and is readily incorpo-
rated into more than one popular general account of causation. If we are to
search for a relation that does not comport with previously admissible cases
of causation, as Wilson's test for emergentism recommends, it would be
wise to start from a full slate of the generally accepted causal data, including
those just mentioned. From there, someone preferring the transference-of-
energy model can provide grounds for winnowing the original collection
of data as reason dictates. But that approach is quite different from the one
now under review. Because the spade work has not been thorough, the
prospect of finding a place for superdupervenience is as cloudy as it was
when our search began. Without that preliminary, the quest for a materialistically kosher explanation of the supervenience of emergent properties is
at a standstill. The last best hope of materialism, token physicalism, doesn't
appear to have satisfied either option (a) or (b). Emergentism *invictus*!

Epilogue

Fitting together the pieces of this extended argument, the first part consists of an explanation of the relevant emergentism for conscious properties and a *prima facie* case for its plausibility. The upshot is that whatever evidence there is regarding the difference between conscious properties and their physical bases (that is, their subvenients or realizers), the so-called hard problem, isn't solved by the relationship between them. There are limits to what supervenience and realization can demonstrate: it cannot show that conscious properties and their physical bases are identical (section 3.2). Some hold that these shortcomings can be overcome, say, by citing problems for mental causation that are resolvable only through the identities of mental properties with their bases (sections 4.1 and 4.2). Against that view, I argued in chapter 4 that the objections to mental causation fail, and that there are powerful alternative reasons supporting the indispensability of mental causation (chapters 4 and 5).

But the matter doesn't end there. Others attempt to comprehend the mental within a more restrictive physicalist framework. Perhaps one of those schemes is plausible enough to suppress any credible motive to find a separate status for conscious properties. The second stage of my argument consists in examining leading versions of those theories. In various ways they are attempts to integrate conscious properties into what is considered more natural, either by identifying the conscious with something non-mental or by providing a further explanation of its relation to their physical bases. In each case, I find that the view in question is basically flawed. This rounds off the tentative case for emergentism made in part I. It is not a strict demonstration, but it is a powerful result. I contend that it makes emergentism plainly the most reasonable option among the various realist theories of conscious aspects.

In spite of the grave difficulties for each of the alternatives I have reviewed, it is very doubtful that internal inconsistencies will be found in them. The problems covered here have to do with the ways in which those views are defended, not with logical or conceptual flaws in their conclusions.[1] Moreover, each has The Conceptual Gambit as a handy panacea with which to debunk recalcitrant data. I know no way to show that those views *cannot* be true. But their chief support has been undermined.

It is naïve to imagine that this will start a stampede to emergentism. But I am fascinated by the fact that in my experience those who earlier opposed property dualism, if pushed by objections to their realist versions, tend to gravitate toward eliminativism rather than emergentism. To accept the latter is to admit that we are so culturally conditioned as to be deluded about the most intimate aspects of experience. The reasons behind a willingness to scrap this tenacious belief must be very potent indeed. Comparisons with how we are easily misled elsewhere by appearances—say, of the Sun circling the Earth—just don't wash. There are clear explanations in those cases for which there are no successful counterparts in the present case once the defenses of realist physicalism have failed. Thus, before closing up shop I shall briefly mention a few of what I take to be the motives behind this resistance. Such remarks must be highly speculative. I offer them only with the greatest trepidation, because in general I find conjectures about opponents' motives an unworthy mode of argument. But here I am more interested in understanding this motivation than in criticizing it; and, as I have stated, the willingness to discard this evidence even in light of the failure of physicalist explanations has been puzzling to me. So I proceed, albeit sheepishly.

One obvious candidate is that many regard emergentism as outside the pale of naturalism, although not everyone agrees. Emergentism's earliest leading lights offered it as a naturalist rejoinder to a non-natural view of life—vitalism—and Jaegwon Kim, among others, regards universal physical supervenience as a minimal form of physicalism. But of course the boundaries of the natural have been steadily shifting toward the physical. In addition, not all of emergentism's prominent advocates have been fiercely naturalistic. In 1925, C. D. Broad famously wrote: "I shall no doubt be blamed by certain scientists, and, I am afraid, by some philosophers, for

1. With the exception of a suspicion of vacuity in the identity form of non-reductive physicalism.

having taken serious account of the alleged facts which are investigated by Psychical Researchers. I am wholly impenitent about this. The scientists in question seem to me to confuse the Author of Nature with the Editor of *Nature.* . . ." Psychic phenomena go well beyond even the most generous notion of the natural. And although the bulk of emergentist-leaning theorists I'm familiar with regard it as hokum, there may still be the stigma of its historical association (through Broad) with the extra-sensory. Nor is there anything in the emergentism of conscious properties that has a whiff of the supernatural about it. Emergentism in these pages is simply the view that physicalist and reductionist efforts fail, and for principled reasons, to rein in stubbornly irresistible views of mental aspects. All those on the realist side of these debates will insist on the existence of phenomenal and access-conscious properties. And if those aspects cannot be further domesticated by physicalist or reductionist methods, the natural lesson to draw would appear to be that conscious phenomena are, in Chalmers' terms (1996, p. 214), "part of the basic furniture of nature." That may be naturalism enough for some.

As I have noted, mental causation has been a big stumbling block in these deliberations. The causal exclusion and the redundancy arguments are popular ways of giving voice to those troubles. But it is not uncommon to find critics maintaining that separate mental properties affecting the physical world are "mysterious" or "enigmatic," even when that complaint is not fleshed out by such clearly formulated arguments. Of course the charge must be explained further if there is to be any hope of sensibly evaluating it. But the feeling that there is something beyond respectable comprehension in the view may be hard to shake even when unaccompanied by further articulations.

However, I wrap up these musings with a few words on a rather different sort of impulse for digging in one's heels, though it may also serve as a motive behind the misgivings already mentioned. Setting aside possibilities such as causal drainage, I have in mind the assumption that *if* reality is at bottom physical, everything that comes out of it must be related to the physical in a certain narrow and unvarnished way, a way that makes the relationship to the fundamental transparent or at least palpable from a mechanistic perspective. In the best case, it allows us to trace back from the product to the elements giving rise to it. Our knowledge is very partial. But it is supposed that ideal investigators would see that our world worked in a way almost as good as that of John Conway's game of life, in which a simple starting point plus a tiny set of rules would allow one to arrive at any possible destination. And the point at which we arrived would always retain the delineation of its building blocks. Moreover, retracing should be able to recover those simple ingredients. This combines physicalism with reductionism's basic creed.

Let us re-enact the steps of this overview. First let us assume the following:

(A)   At bottom the world is physical.

Some things in this world are constituted by other things, while the former are constituted by more basic things down to a level at which we arrive at what is not constituted by anything else. Call the ingredients at the fundamental level of the physical world 'Ω', and call those aspects of reality that are determined by it 'χ'. χ consists not only of particulars and their collections, but also of properties, events, and processes, including many things constructed from other χs. Among the χs are what might appear at first glance to be non-physical particulars, properties, events, states, facts, and processes. Then let's also grant the following:

(B)   All of χ is determined by materials and interactions at the level of Ω.

Thus far, nothing conflicts with the emergentism of tenets (1)–(3), whose differences aren't with (A) and (B), but with what many believe to follow from them. Here are two further assumptions that often accompany (A) and (B):

(i) The intrinsic character of an χ property is detectable in the individual ingredients of its base, or at least in the individual ingredients of earlier stages in the base (say, in those of fundamental particles).

(ii) We should be able to retrace, step by step, a linear progression from that base to any tokens to which it gives rise, and be able to delineate clearly in those states the specific contribution of each of its constituents and their relations to the final product.

These conditions are downward tracking to Ω and upward tracking from Ω, respectively. We might summarize them by saying that all construction from the physical base must be arithmetical.[2] (The apt metaphors may differ

---

2. An ironclad formulation of these intuitions is elusive. (i) and (ii) are not rigorous, but I hope that they point clearly enough to familiar working assumptions of many participants in these controversies.

for different supporters, but they point to a close-knit family of outlooks.) These would be what earlier emergentists called 'resultants'; roughly, they would behave in the manner of products that could be understood mereologically, or by the individual contributions of the still operative separate components. That will include not only individuals constructed from the material base, but also features of those things. That is, what is believed to follow from (A) and (B) is the following:

(C)   Every χ must be related to Ω so that χ contains nothing whose character does not explicitly display more than the Ω elements that entered into its composition.

This does not demand that each of the features of χ be a feature of Ω: mountains are not typically composed of mountains, chairs do not consist of other chairs. Nor is stating that the display must be explicitly intended to suggest that finding the Ω elements in χ will not require serious study. It may even exceed human competence. But in the end, if there is an element of χ that is not evident in something about Ω, on a view driven by (C) it would be a mistake to suppose that if χ does not come from Ω it could be an objective feature of reality.

Notice, however, that nothing in (A) and (B) mandates (C). Rather, (C) is inspired by the notion that whatever is determined by a physical base must be related to that base in a certain transparent way. This mindset could have played a role in animating the Unity of Science movement. It is further encouraged by the fact that in the modern scientific era many prime instances of χ constructions have been discovered to follow this pattern. But the confident expectation that this will continue without exception is justified, if at all, by a loose ampliative inference that emergentism threatens to undermine. The view aired in this work is neutral with respect to (A) and (B). It can accept, but is not committed to, either or both. Of course emergentism rejects (C).

Other than to indicate that (C) doesn't follow from (A) and (B), I have no dramatic, overwhelming argument that I believe should force those committed to (C) to abandon it. At any rate, it has not been my intention in this place to show that (C) is false. Its reach is too visionary, and an adequate statement of it too elusive, to provide neutral ground rules for a debate about it that all sides can willingly enter. It is more a mindset than a thesis. For example, some have held that it forces us to await a conceptual revolution, others that it shows only that some explanations lie outside human competence. Each is a backhanded defense of (C). Whereas we may never achieve its completion, they provide excuses for holding on to it in the face of an open-ended string of failed efforts. However, I hope that bringing (C) out into the open will encourage further careful reflection on its *bona fides*. All too often its influence in these disputes has been surreptitious or at least not fully recognized even among those motivated by it.

References

Alexander, Samuel. 1920. *Space, Time, and Deity*. Macmillan.

Anscombe, G. E. M. 1957. *Intention*. Blackwell.

Anscombe, G. E. M. 1971. *Causality and Determination*. Cambridge University Press.

Antony, Louise. 2007. Everybody Has Got It: A Defense of Non-Reductive Materialism. In *Contemporary Debates in the Philosophy of Mind*, ed. B. McLaughlin and J. Cohen. Blackwell.

Antony, Louise, and Joseph Levine. 1991. The Nomic and the Robust. In *Meaning in Mind*, ed. B. Loewer and G. Rey. Blackwell.

Aristotle. 1941. *The Basic Works of Aristotle*, ed. R. McKeon. Random House.

Bain, Alexander. 1887. *Logic*, new and revised edition. Appleton.

Baker, Alan. 2004. Simplicity. In *Stanford Encyclopedia of Philosophy*. http://plato.standford.edu/entries/simplicity/.

Beckermann, Angsar. 1992. Supervenience, Emergence and Reduction. In *Emergence or Reduction*, ed. A. Beckermann, H. Flohr, and J. Kim. Walter de Gruyter.

Beckermann, Angsar, Hans Flohr, and Jaegwon Kim, eds. 1992. *Emergence or Reduction*. Walter de Gruyter.

Bedau, Mark A. 1997. Weak Emergence. In *Philosophical Perspectives 11: Mind, Causation, and World*, ed. J. Tomberlin. Blackwell.

Bennett, Karen, and Brian McLaughlin. (2005). Supervenience. http: //plato.stanford.edu/entries/supervenience

Berkeley, George. 1710 [1970]. *A Treatise concerning the Principles of Human Knowledge*. Bobbs-Merrill.

Block, Ned. 1983. Mental Pictures and Cognitive Science. *Philosophical Review* 92: 499–541.

Block, Ned. 1995. On A Confusion about a Function of Consciousness. *Behavioral and Brain Sciences* 18: 227–287.

Block, Ned. 1996. Biology versus Computation in the Study of Consciousness. *Behavioral and Brain Sciences* 19: 259–265.

Block, Ned. 1997. Anti-Reductionism Slaps Back. In *Philosophical Perspectives 11: Mind, Causation, and World*, ed. J. Tomberlin. Blackwell.

Block, Ned. 1998. Is Experiencing Just Representing? *Philosophy and Phenomenological Research* 58: 663–670.

Block, Ned. 2003a. Do Causal Powers Drain Away? *Philosophy and Phenomenological Research* 67: 133–150.

Block, Ned. 2003b. The Harder Problem of Consciousness. www.nyu.edu/gsas/dept/philo/faculty/block/papers/harder.htm.

Block, Ned, and Robert Stalnaker. 1999. Conceptual Analysis. Dualism, and the Explanatory Gap. *Philosophical Review* 108: 1–46.

Broad, C. D. 1925. *The Mind and Its Place in Nature*. Routledge & Kegan Paul.

Brooks, D. H. M. 1994. How to Perform a Reduction. *Philosophy and Phenomenological Research* 54: 803–814.

Burge, Tyler. 1979. Individualism and the Mental. *Midwest Studies in Philosophy* 4: 73–121.

Burge, Tyler. 2007a. *Foundations of Mind*. Oxford University Press.

Burge, Tyler. 2007b. Two Kinds of Consciousness. In *Foundations of Mind*. Oxford University Press.

Burge, Tyler. 2007c. Reflections on Two Kinds of Consciousness. In *Foundations of Mind*. Oxford University Press.

Byrne, Alex, and Michael Tye. 2006. Qualia Ain't in the Head. *Noûs* 40: 241–255.

Chalmers, David J. 1996. *The Conscious Mind*. Oxford University Press.

Chalmers, David J., ed. 2002a. *Philosophy of Mind*. Oxford University Press.

Chalmers, David J. 2002b. Consciousness and Its Place in Nature. In *Blackwell Guide to the Philosophy of Mind*, ed. S. Stich and T. Warfield. Blackwell.

Chalmers, David J. 2006. Strong and Weak Emergence. In *The Re-emergence of Emergence*, ed. P. Clayton and P. Davies. Oxford University Press.

Chalmers, David J., and Frank Jackson. 2001. Conceptual Analysis and Reductive Explanation. *Philosophical Review* 110: 315–361.

Chomsky, Noam. 1972. *Language and Mind*, enlarged edition. Harcourt Brace Jovanovich.

Collins, John, Ned Hall, and L. A. Paul, eds. 2004. *Causation and Counterfactuals*. MIT Press.

Crane, Tim. 2001. The Significance of Emergence. In *Physicalism and Its Discontents*, ed. C. Gillett and B. Loewer. Cambridge University Press.

Crane, Tim. 2003. The Intentional Structure of Consciousness. In *Consciousness: New Philosophical Perspectives*, ed. Q. Smith and A. Jokic. Oxford University Press.

Craver, Carl F., and William Bechtel. 2007. Top-Down Causation without Top-Down Causes. *Biology and Philosophy* 22: 547–563.

Davidson, Donald. 1980. Mental Events. In *Essays on Actions and Events*. Oxford University Press.

Descartes, Rene. 1641/1984. *Meditations on First Philosophy*. In *The Philosophical Writings of Descartes*, volume II. Cambridge University Press.

Descartes, Rene. 1951. *Correspondance,* volume V. Presses Universitaires de France.

Dretske, Fred. 1981. *Knowledge and the Flow of Information*. MIT Press.

Dretske, Fred. 1993. Conscious Experience. *Mind* 102: 263–283.

Dretske, Fred. 1995. *Naturalizing the Mind*. MIT Press.

Dretske, Fred. 2002. A Recipe for Thought. In *Philosophy of Mind*, ed. D. Chalmers. Oxford University Press.

Dretske, Fred. How Do You Know You Are Not a Zombie? Manuscript.

Endicott, Ronald. 1989. On Physical Multiple Realization. *Pacific Philosophical Quarterly* 70: 212–224.

Feigl, Herbert. 1958. The 'Mental' and the 'Physical'. In *Minnesota Studies in the Philosphy of Science*, volume II, ed. H. Feigl, M. Scriven, and G. Maxwell. University of Minnesota Press.

Field, Hartry. 2003. Causation in a Physical World. In *Oxford Handbook of Metaphysics*, ed. M. Loux and D. Zimmerman. Oxford University Press.

Fine, Kit. 2008. I—Coincidence and Form. *Aristotelian Society Supplementary Volume* 82: 101–118.

Fodor, Jerry. 1968. *Psychological Explanation*. Random House.

Fodor, Jerry. 1990. A Theory of Content I and A Theory of Content II. In *A Theory of Content and Other Essays*. MIT Press.

Frege, Gottlob. 1960. *Translations from the Philosophical Writings of Gottlob Frege*, ed. P. Geach and M. Black. Blackwell.

Geach, P. T. 1967. Identity. *Review of Metaphysics* 21: 3–12.

Gibbons, John. 2006. Mental Causation without Downward Causation. *Philosophical Review* 115: 79–103.

Gillett, Carl. 2002. The Varieties of Emergence: Their Purposes. Obligations and Importance. *Grazer Philosophische Studien* 65: 95–121.

Gillett, Carl, and Barry Loewer, eds. 2001. *Physicalism and Its Discontents*. Cambridge University Press.

Glanzberg, Michael. 2001. Supervenience and Infinitary Logic. *Noûs* 35 (3): 419–439.

Goldman, Alvin. 1970. *A Theory of Human Action*. Prentice-Hall.

Grimes, Thomas R. 1988. The Myth of Supervenience. *Pacific Philosophical Quarterly* 69: 152–160.

Hall, Ned. 2004. Two Concepts of Causation. In *Causation and Counterfactuals*, ed. J. Collins, N. Hall, and L. Paul. MIT Press.

Harman, Gilbert. 1990. The Intrinsic Quality of Experience. In *Philosophical Perspectives 4: Action Theory and Philosophy of Mind*, ed. J. Tomberlin. Ridgeview.

Hawthorne, John. 2001. Causal Structuralism. *Philosophical Perspectives* 15: 361–378.

Heil, John, and Alfred Mele, eds. 1993. *Mental Causation*. Oxford University Press.

Heller, Mark. 1990. *The Ontology of Physical Objects*. Cambridge University Press.

Hempel, Carl G., and Paul Oppenheim. 1948. Studies in the Logic of Explanation. *Philosophy of Science* 15: 135–175. Reprinted in Hempel, *Aspects of Scientific Explanation and Other Essays in the Philosophy of Science* (Free Press, 1965).

Hill, Christopher S. 1991. *Sensations: A Defense of Type Materialism*. Cambridge University Press.

Hill, Christopher S. 1997. Imaginability, Conceivability, Possibility and the Mind-Body Problem. *Philosophical Studies* 87: 61–85.

Hill, Christopher S. 2009. *Consciousness*. Cambridge University Press.

Hill, Christopher S., and Brian McLaughlin. 1999. There Are Fewer Things in Reality Than Are Dreamt of in Chalmers's Philosophy. *Philosophy and Phenomenological Research* 59: 445–454.

Hitchcock, Christopher. 2007. What Russell Got Right. In *Causation, Physics, and the Constitution of Reality: Russell's Republic Revisited*, ed. H. Price and R. Corry. Oxford University Press.

Horgan, Terence. 1989. Mental Causation. *Philosophical Perspectives* 3: 47–76.

Horgan, Terence. 1993. From Supervenience to Superdupervenience: Meeting the Demands of the Material World. *Mind* 102 (408): 555–586.

Horgan, Terry, and Uriah Kriegel. 2007. Phenomenal Epistemology: What Is Consciousness That We May Know It So Well? *Philosophical Issues* 17: 123–144.

Hume, David. 1739 [1978]. *A Treatise of Human Nature*, ed. L. Selby-Bigge. Oxford University Press.

Humphreys, Paul. 1997. How Properties Emerge. *Philosophy of Science* 64: 1–17.

Jackson, Frank. 1993. Armchair Metaphysics. In *Philosophy in Mind*, ed. J. O'Leary-Hawthorne and M. Michael. Kluwer.

Jackson, Frank. 1998. *From Metaphysics to Ethics*. Oxford University Press.

Jackson, Frank. 2007. A Priori Physicalism. In *Contemporary Debates in the Philosophy of Mind,* ed. B. McLaughlin and J. Cohen. Blackwell.

Jackson, Frank, and Philip Pettit. 1990a. Causation in the Philosophy of Mind. *Philosophy and Phenomenological Research* 50: 195–214.

Jackson, Frank, and Philip Pettit. 1990b. Program Explanation: A General Perspective. *Analysis* 50 (2): 107–117.

Kim, Jaegwon. 1992. Downward Causation: Emergentism and Nonreductive Physicalism. In *Emergence or Reduction*, ed. A. Beckermann, H. Flohr, and J. Kim. Walter de Gruyter.

Kim, Jaegwon. 1993a. *Supervenience and Mind*. Cambridge University Press.

Kim, Jaegwon. 1993b. Supervenience as a Philosophical Concept. In *Supervenience and Mind*. Cambridge University Press.

Kim, Jaegwon. 1993c. Mechanism, Purpose, and Explanatory Exclusion. In *Supervenience and Mind*. Cambridge University Press.

Kim, Jaegwon. 1993d. The Myth of Nonreductive Physicalism. In *Supervenience and Mind*. Cambridge University Press.

Kim, Jaegwon. 1993e. Multiple Realization and the Metaphysics of Reduction. In *Supervenience and Mind*. Cambridge University Press.

Kim, Jaegwon. 1997. Does the Problem of Mental Causation Generalize? *Proceedings of the Aristotelian Society* 97: 281–297.

Kim, Jaegwon. 1999. Making Sense of Emergence. *Philosophical Studies* 95: 3–36.

Kim, Jaegwon. 2000a. *Mind in a Physical World*. MIT Press.

Kim, Jaegwon. 2000b. Making Sense of Downward Causation. In *Downward Causation*, ed. P. Andersen, C. Emmeche, N. Finnemann, and P. Chistiansen. Aarhus University Press.

Kim, Jaegwon. 2001. Mental Causation and Consciousness: The Two Mind-Body Problems for the Physicalist. In *Physicalism and Its Discontents*, ed. C. Gillett and B. Loewer. Cambridge University Press.

Kim, Jaegwon. 2003. Blocking Causal Drainage and Other Maintenance Chores with Mental Causation. *Philosophy and Phenomenological Research* 67: 151–175.

Kim, Jaegwon. 2005. *Physicalism or Something Near Enough*. Princeton University Press.

Kim, Jaegwon. 2006. *Philosophy of Mind*, second edition. Westview.

Kim, Jaegwon. 2007. Causation and Mental Causation. In *Contemporary Debates in the Philosophy of Mind*, ed. B. McLaughlin and J. Cohen. Blackwell.

Kitcher, Philip. 1984. 1953 and All That: A Tale of Two Sciences. *Philosophical Review* 93: 335–373.

Kripke, Saul A. 1980. *Naming and Necessity*. Harvard University Press.

Lamme, Victor A. F. 2006. Toward a True Neural Stance on Consciousness. *Trends in Cognitive Sciences* 10, no.11: 494–501.

Laughlin, Robert B., and David Pines. 2000. The Theory of Everything. *Proceedings of the National Academy of Sciences* 97: 28–31.

Levine, Joseph. 2003. Experience and Representation. In *Consciousness: New Philosophical Perspectives*, ed. Q. Smith and A. Jokic. Oxford University Press.

Lewes, George Henry. 1875. *The Problems of Life and Mind*, volume 2. Trübner.

Lewis, David. 1980. Psychophysical and Theoretical Identifications. In *Readings in Philosophical Psychology*, volume I, ed. N. Block. Harvard University Press.

Lewis, David. 1983a. *Philosophical Papers*, volume I. Oxford University Press.

Lewis, David. 1983b. An Argument for the Identity Theory. In *Philosophical Papers*, volume I. Oxford University Press.

Lewis, David. 1983c. Mad Pain and Martian Pain. In *Philosophical Papers*, volume I. Oxford University Press.

Lewis, David. 1986a. *Philosophical Papers*, volume II. Oxford University Press.

Lewis, David. 1986b. Causation. In *Philosophical Papers*, volume II. Oxford University Press.

Lewis, David. 1986c. Postscripts to 'Causation'. In *Philosophical Papers*, volume II. Oxford University Press.

Lewis, David. 1986e. *On the Plurality of Worlds*. Blackwell.

Lewis, David. 1999. Reduction of Mind. In Lewis, *Papers in Metaphysics and Epistemology*. Cambridge University Press.

Lewis, David. 2004. Causation as Influence. In *Causation and Counterfactuals*, ed. J. Collins, N. Hall, and L. Paul. MIT Press.

Loar, Brian. 1997. Phenomenal States. In *The Nature of Consciousness*, ed. N. Block, O. Flanagan, and G. Guzeldere. MIT Press. [Pages cited in version reprinted in *Philosophy of Mind: Classical and Contemporary Readings*, ed. D. Chalmers (Oxford University Press, 2002).]

Locke, John. [1700] 1973. *An Essay concerning Human Understanding*, ed. P. Nidditch. Oxford University Press.

Loewer, Barry. 1997. A Guide to Naturalizing Semantics. In *A Companion to the Philosophy of Language*, ed. B. Hale and C. Wright. Blackwell.

Loewer, Barry. 2007. Mental Causation, or Something Near Enough. In *Contemporary Debates in the Philosophy of Mind,* ed. B. McLaughlin and J. Cohen. Blackwell.

Lovejoy, Arthur O. 1927. The Meanings of 'Emergence' and Its Modes. In Proceedings of the Sixth Internal Congress of Philosophy, ed. E. Brightman. Longmans, Green.

Lowe, E. J. 2000b. Causal Closure Principles and Emergence. *Philosophy* 75: 571–585.

Lycan, William G. 1995. Layered Perceptual Representation. *Philosophical Issues* 7: 81–100.

Lycan, William G. 1996. *Consciousness and Experience*. MIT Press.

Maslen, Cei. 2004. Causes, Contrasts, and the Nontransitivity of Causation. In *Causation and Counterfactuals*, ed. J. Collins, N. Hall, and L. Paul. MIT Press.

Maslen, Cei, Terry Horgan, and Helen Daly. 2009. Mental Causation. In *The Oxford Handbook of Causation*, ed. H. Beebee, C. Hitchcock, and P. Menzies. Oxford University Press.

McGinn, Colin. 2001. How Not to Solve the Mind-Body Problem. In *Physicalism and Its Discontents*, ed. C. Gillett and B. Loewer. Cambridge University Press.

McLaughlin, Brian. 1992. The Rise and Fall of British Emergentism. In *Emergence or Reduction*, ed. A. Beckermann, H. Flohr, and J. Kim. Walter de Gruyter.

McLaughlin, Brian. 1993. On Davidson's Response to the Charge of Epiphenomenalism. In *Mental Causes*, ed. J. Heil and A. Mele. Oxford University Press.

McLaughlin, Brian. 1995. Varieties of Supervenience. In *Supervenience: New Essays*, ed. E. Savellos and U. Yalçin. Cambridge University Press.

McLaughlin, Brian. 1997. Emergence and Supervenience. *Intellectica* 25: 25–43.

McLaughlin, Brian. 2001. In Defense of New Wave Materialism: A Response to Horgan and Tienson. In *Physicalism and Its Discontents*, ed. C. Gillett and B. Loewer. Cambridge University Press.

McLaughlin, Brian. 2003. A Naturalist-Phenomenal Realist Response to Block's Harder Problem. *Philosophical Issues* 13: 163–204.

McLaughlin, Brian, and Jonathan Cohen, eds. 2007. *Contemporary Debates in the Philosophy of Mind*. Blackwell.

Mellor, D. H. 2004. For Facts as Causes and Effects. In *Causation and Counterfactuals*, ed. J. Collins, N. Hall, and L. Paul. MIT Press.

Menzies, Peter. 2003. The Causal Efficacy of Mental States. In *The Metaphysics of Mind and Action*, ed. S. Walter and H.-D. Heckmann. Imprint Academic.

Menzies, Peter. 2004. Difference Making in Context. In *Causation and Counterfactuals*, ed. J. Collins, N. Hall, and L. Paul. MIT Press.

Mill, John Stuart. 1851. *A System of Logic*, third edition. J. W. Parker.

Moore, G. E. 1903. *Principia Ethica*. Cambridge University Press.

Moore, G. E. 1959. The Refutation of Idealism. In Moore, *Philosophical Studies*. Littlefield, Adams.

Morgan, C. Lloyd. 1923. *Emergent Evolution*. Williams & Norgate.

Nagel, Ernest. 1961. *The Structure of Science*. Harcourt, Brace & World.

Nagel, Thomas. 1965. Physicalism. *Philosophical Review* 74: 339–356.

Nagel, Thomas. 1974. *What Is It Like to Be a Bat? Philosophical Review* 83: 435–450.

Nida-Rümelin, Martine. 2007a. Dualist Emergentism. In *Contemporary Debates in the Philosophy of Mind,* ed. B. McLaughlin and J. Cohen. Blackwell.

Nida-Rümelin, Martine. 2007b. Doings and Subject Causation. *Erkenntnis* 67: 255–272.

Nida-Rümelin, Martine. 2008. Phenomenal Character and the Tansparency of Experience. In *The Case for Qualia*, ed. E. Wright. MIT Press.

Norton, John D. 2007. Causation as Folk Science. In *Causation, Physics, and the Constitution of Reality: Russell's Republic Revisited*, ed. H. Price and R. Corry. Oxford University Press.

O'Connor, Timothy. 1994. Emergent Properties. *American Philosophical Quarterly* 31: 91–104.

Parfit, Derek. 1984. *Reasons and Persons*. Oxford University Press.

Pascual-Leone, Alvaro, and Vincent Walsh. 2001. Fast Backprojections from the Motion to the Primary visual Area Necessary for Visual Awareness. *Science* 292: 510–512.

Paul, L. A. 1998. Problems with Late Preemption. *Analysis* 58: 48–53.

Pereboom, Derk. 2002. Robust Nonreductive Materialism. *Journal of Philosophy* 99: 499–531.

Pereboom, Derk, and Hilary Kornblith. 1991. The Metaphysics of Irreducibility. *Philosophical Studies* 63: 125–145.

Perry, John. 1970. The Same F. *Philosophical Review* 79: 181–200.

Peters, R. S. 1958. *The Concept of Motivation*. Routledge & Kegan Paul.

Price, Huw, and Richard Corry, eds. 2007. *Causation, Physics, and the Constitution of Reality: Russell's Republic Revisited*. Oxford University Press.

Putnam, Hilary. 1973 [2002]. The Nature of Mental States. In *Philosophy of Mind*, ed. D. Chalmers. Oxford University Press.

Quine, W. V. 1966. Variables Explained Away. In *Selected Logic Papers*. Random House.

Rea, Michael. 1998. In Defense of Mereological Universalism. *Philosophy and Phenomenological Research* 58 (2): 347–360.

Reid, Robert G. B. 2007. *Biological Emergences*. MIT Press.

Rizzolatti, Giacomo, et al. 2001. Neurophysiological Mechanisms Underlying the Understanding and Imitation of Action. *Neuroscience* 2: 661–670.

Rosen, Gideon, and Cian Dorr. 2002. Composition as a Fiction. In *The Blackwell Guide to Metaphysics*, ed. R. Gale. Blackwell.

Russell, Bertrand. 1912–13. On the Notion of Cause. *Proceedings of the Aristotelian Society* 13: 1–26.

Russell, Bertrand. 1921. *The Analysis of Mind*. Macmillan.

Sanford, David. 1970. Locke, Leibniz, and Wiggins on Being in the Same Place at the Same Time. *Philosophical Review* 79: 75–82.

Schaffer, Jonathan. 2000. Causation by Disconnection. *Philosophy of Science* 67: 285–300.

Schaffer, Jonathan. 2003. Is There a Fundamental Level? *Noûs* 37: 498–517.

Schaffer, Jonathan. 2005. Contrastive Causation. *Philosophical Review* 114: 327–358.

Schaffer, Jonathan. 2010. Monism: The Priority of the Whole. *Philosophical Review* 119: 31–76.

Schiffer, Stephen. 1987. *Remnants of Meaning*. MIT Press.

Schneider, Susan. Forthcoming. Why Property Dualists Must Reject Physicalism about Substance.

Schröder, Jürgen. 1998. Emergence: Non-Deducibility or Downwards Causation. *Philosophical Quarterly* 48: 433–451.

Scriven, Michael. 1962. Explanations, Predictions, and Laws. In *Minnesota Studies in the Philosophy of Science*, volume III, ed. H. Feigl and G. Maxwell. University of Minnesota Press.

Searle, John R. 1992. *The Rediscovery of the Mind*. MIT Press.

Searle, John R. 1995. *The Construction of Social Reality*. Free Press.

Shapiro, Lawrence. 2000. Multiple Realization. *Journal of Philosophy* 97 (12): 635–654.

Shepard, Roger N. 1987. Toward a Universal Law of Generalization for Psychological Science. *Science* 237 (4819): 1317–1323.

Shoemaker, Sydney. 2002. Kim on Emergence. *Philosophical Studies* 108: 53–63.

Shoemaker, Sydney. 2003. Identity, Properties, and Causality. In Shoemaker, *Identity, Cause, and Mind*, expanded edition. Oxford University Press.

Shoemaker, Sydney. 2007. *Physical Realization*. Oxford University Press.

Sider, Theodore. 2003. What's So Bad about Overdetermination? *Philosophy and Phenomenological Research* 62: 719–726.

Smart, J. J. C. 1959. Sensations and Brain Processes. *Philosophical Review* 68: 141–156.

Smith, Quentin, and Alexander Jokic, eds. *Consciousness: New Philosophical Perspectives*. Oxford University Press.

Smocovitis, V. B. 1996. *The Evolutionary Synthesis and Evolutionary Biology*. Princeton University Press.

Sober, Eliot. 1999. The Multiple Realizability Argument against Reductionism. *Philosophy of Science* 66: 542–564.

Sosa, Ernest. 1984. Mind-Body Interaction and Supervenient Causation. *Midwest Studies in Philosophy* 9: 271–281.

Sperry, R. W. 1969. A Modified Concept of Consciousness. *Psychological Review* 76 (6): 532–536.

Sperry, R. W. 1976. Mental Phenomena as Causal Determinants. In *Consciousness and the Brain: A Scientific and Philosophical Inquiry*, ed. G. Globus, G. Maxwell, and I. Savodnik. Plenum.

Sperry, R. W. 1980. Mind-Brain Interaction: Mentalism, Yes; Dualism, No. *Neuroscience* 5: 195–206.

Stephan, Achim. 2002. Emergentism, Irreducibility, and Downward Causation. *Grazer Philosophische Studien* 65: 77–93.

Stoljar, Daniel. 2001. Two Conceptions of the Physical. *Philosophy and Phenomenological Research* 62: 253–281.

Strevens, Michael. 2008. *Depth*. Harvard University Press.

Sturgeon, Scott. 1998. Physicalism and Overdetermination. *Mind* 107: 411–432.

Sturgeon, Scott. 2001. The Roots of Reductionism. In *Physicalism and Its Discontents*, ed. C. Gillett and B. Loewer. Cambridge University Press.

Thomson, Judith. 1998. The Statue and the Clay. *Noûs* 32: 149–173.

Tye, Michael. 1995a. A Representationalist Theory of Pains and Their Phenomenal Character. In *Philosophical Perspectives*, volume 9, ed. J. Tomberlin. Ridgeview.

Tye, Michael. 1995b. *Ten Problems of Consciousness*. MIT Press.

Tye, Michael. 1998a. Response to Discussants. *Philosophy and Phenomenological Research* 58: 679–687.

Tye, Michael. 1998b. Inverted Earth, Swampman, and Representationism. *Philosophical Perspectives* 12: 459–477.

Tye, Michael. 2000. *Consciousness, Color, and Content*. MIT Press.

Tye, Michael. 2003. Blurry Images, Double Vision, and Other Oddities. In *Problems for Representationalism?* ed. Q. Smith and A. Jokic. Oxford University Press.

Tye, Michael. 2007. New Troubles for the Qualia Freak. In *Contemporary Debates in the Philosophy of Mind*, ed. B. McLaughlin and J. Cohen. Blackwell.

Urmson, J. O. 1959. On Grading. In *Logic and Language*, second series, ed. A. Flew. Oxford University Press.

Van Cleve, James. 1990. Mind Dust or Magic? Panpsychism Versus Emergence. In *Philosophical Perspectives*, volume 4, ed. J. Tomberlin. Ridgeview.

Van Gulick, Robert. 1993. Who's in Charge Here? And Who's Doing All the Work? In *Mental Causation*, ed. J. Heil and A. Mele. Oxford University Press.

van Inwagen, Peter. 1990. *Material Beings*. Cornell University Press.

Vision, Gerald. 1970. Essentialism and the Sense of Proper Names. *American Philosophical Quarterly* 7: 321–330.

Vision, Gerald. 1974. Essentialism vis-à-vis Identifying Procedures. *Philosophical Studies* 26: 23–37.

Vision, Gerald. 1996. *Problems of Vision*. Oxford University Press.

Vision, Gerald. 2005. Truly Justified Belief. *Synthese* 146: 403–440.

Vision, Gerald. 1998. Blindisght and Philosophy. *Philosophical Psychology* 11: 137–159.

Vision, Gerald. 2009. Fixing Perceptual Belief. *Philosophical Quarterly* 59: 292–314.

Weinberg, Steven. 1974. Unified Theories of Elementary-Particle Interaction. *Scientific American* 231: 50–59.

Weiskrantz, Lawrence. 1997. *Consciousness Lost and Found: A Neurpsychological Exploration*. Oxford University Press.

Wiggins, David. 1968. On Being in the Same Place at the Same Time. *Philosophical Review* 77: 90–95.

Wiggins, David. 1980. *Sameness and Substance*. Oxford University Press.

Wilson, Jessica. 1999. How Superduper does a Physicalist Supervenience Need to Be? *Philosophical Quarterly* 49: 33–52.

Wilson, Jessica. 2002. Causal Powers, Forces, and Superdupervenience. *Grazer Philosophische Studien* 63: 53–78.

Wilson, N. L. 1955. Space, Time, and Individuals. *Journal of Philosophy* 52: 589–598.

Wimsatt, William C. 2007. *Re-Engineering Philosophy for Limited Beings*. Harvard University Press.

Wittgenstein, Ludwig. 1953. *Philosophical Investigations*. Macmillan.

Woodward, James. 2007. Causation with a Human face. In *Causation, Physics, and the Constitution of Reality: Russell's Republic Revisited*, ed. H. Price and R. Corry. Oxford University Press.

Yablo, Stephen. 1992a. Mental Causation. *Philosophical Review* 101: 245–281.

Yablo, Stephen. 1992b. Cause and Essence. *Synthese* 93: 403–449.

Yablo, Stephen. 2002. De Facto Dependence. *Journal of Philosophy* 99: 130–148.

Zihl, J., and D. Von Cramon. 1980. Registration of Light Stimuli in the Cortically Blind Hemifield and Its Effect on Localization. *Behavioural Brain Research* 1: 287–298.

Zimmerman, Dean. 1995. Theories of Masses and Problems of Constitution. *Philosophical Review* 104 (1): 53–110.

Index